Cultural Grammars of Nation, Diaspora, and Indigeneity in Canada

TransCanada Series

The study of Canadian literature can no longer take place in isolation from larger external forces. Pressures of multiculturalism put emphasis upon discourses of citizenship and security, while market-driven factors increasingly shape the publication, dissemination, and reception of Canadian writing. The persistent questioning of the Humanities has invited a rethinking of the disciplinary and curricular structures within which the literature is taught, while the development of area and diaspora studies has raised important questions about the tradition. The goal of the TransCanada series is to publish forward-thinking critical interventions that investigate these paradigm shifts in interdisciplinary ways.

Series editor:

Smaro Kamboureli, Canada Research Chair in Critical Studies in Canadian Literature, School of English and Theatre Studies and Director, TransCanada Institute, University of Guelph

For more information, please contact:

Smaro Kamboureli
Professor, Canada Research Chair in Critical Studies in Canadian Literature
School of English and Theatre Studies
Director, TransCanada Institute
University of Guelph
50 Stone Road East
Guelph, ON N1G 2W1
Canada
Phone: 519-824-4120 ext. 53251
Email: smaro@uoguelph.ca

Lisa Quinn
Acquisitions Editor
Wilfrid Laurier University Press
75 University Avenue West
Waterloo, ON N2L 3C5
Canada
Phone: 519-884-0710 ext. 2843
Fax: 519-725-1399
Email: quinn@press.wlu.ca

Cultural Grammars of Nation, Diaspora, and Indigeneity in Canada

Christine Kim, Sophie McCall, and Melina Baum Singer, editors

**WILFRID LAURIER
UNIVERSITY PRESS**

This book has been published with the help of a grant from the Canadian Federation for the Humanities and Social Sciences, through the Aid to Scholarly Publications Programme, using funds provided by the Social Sciences and Humanities Research Council of Canada. We acknowledge the financial support of the Government of Canada through the Canada Book Fund for our publishing activities.

Library and Archives Canada Cataloguing in Publication

    Cultural grammars of nation, diaspora, and indigeneity in Canada / Christine Kim, Sophie McCall, and Melina Baum Singer, editors.

(TransCanada series)
Includes bibliographical references and index.
Also issued in electronic format.
ISBN 978-1-55458-336-2

    1. Canadian literature (English)—Minority authors—History and criticism. 2. Canadian literature (English)—Indian authors—History and criticism. 3. Minorities—Canada—Social conditions. 4. Native peoples—Canada—Social conditions. 5. Canada—Social conditions. 1 Kim, Christine, [date] 11. McCall, Sophie, [date] 111. Baum Singer, Melina, [date] 1v. Series: TransCanada series

PS8089.5.M55C84 2012   C810.9'8   C2011-904879-5

Type of computer file: Electronic monograph.
Also issued in print format.
ISBN 978-1-55458-417-8 (PDF)

    1. Canadian literature (English)—Minority authors—History and criticism. 2. Canadian literature (English)—Indian authors—History and criticism. 3. Minorities—Canada—Social conditions. 4. Native peoples—Canada—Social conditions. 5. Canada—Social conditions. 1. Kim, Christine, [date] 11. McCall, Sophie, [date] 111. Baum Singer, Melina, [date] 1v. Series: TransCanada series (Online)

PS8089.5.M55C84 2012a   C810.9'8   C2011-904880-9

© 2012 Wilfrid Laurier University Press
Waterloo, Ontario, Canada
www.wlupress.wlu.ca

Cover design by Martyn Schmoll. Front-cover image by istockphoto. Text design by Angela Booth Malleau.

This book is printed on FSC recycled paper and is certified Ecologo. It is made from 100% post-consumer fibre, processed chlorine free, and manufactured using biogas energy.

Printed in Canada

Contents

Acknowledgements

CULTURAL GRAMMARS **WAS**, from its very beginnings, conceived at the edge of acceptable grammar. As we struggled for the words that would articulate the present moment in Canadian literary studies, with its conflicted critical conversations about nation, diaspora, and indigeneity, we often found ourselves trailing off into ellipses … or expletives. But the outstanding papers we received in response to our call for papers amply demonstrated to us that we were taking part in a larger conversation, a conversation that was more comprehensive than we first realized, and more comprehensible when shared among many voices. We are convinced that *Cultural Grammars*, with its inspired and inspiring analyses, will set Canadian cultural criticism on new pathways.

We are deeply grateful, first and foremost, to our contributors, who so thoughtfully engaged with the collection's main questions. Through the din of their wise, insurgent, collaborative voices, the contributors demonstrated so powerfully that the constraints of cultural grammars can become possibilities. We are also thankful to Smaro Kamboureli, Canada Research Chair in Critical Studies in Canadian Literature and director of the TransCanada Institute, for encouraging us to pursue this project with rigour and for supporting it as part of her TransCanada series, and to Lisa Quinn, our editor at Wilfrid Laurier University Press, who was in equal parts supportive and exacting in her efforts to help us produce the best possible book. Thanks are also due to the two anonymous readers of the manuscript for their excellent suggestions for revision; to the entire editorial and publicity team at WLUP, including Rob Kohlmeier and Heather Blain-Yanke; to copy editor Valerie Ahwee; to Dave Gaertner, the indexer; to the Canadian Federation for the Humanities and Social Sciences, through the Aid to Scholarly Publications Program, using funds provided by the Social Sciences and Humanities Research Council of Canada; and to Simon Fraser University, for funding through a Publications Grant. The idea for *Cultural Grammars* began as a panel discussion as part of the annual meeting of the Canadian Association of Commonwealth Literatures and Languages Studies (CACLALS) at the University of British Columbia in 2008, and we are grateful to the organizers for facilitating our initial discussions.

Throughout the process of putting together this book, all three of us were taking care of very small children. We are forever in the debt of our partners, close friends, and extended families, as they helped out with pickups and drop-offs and supported us warmly with their love and encouragement. In many ways our children are our inspiration and we thank them for their patience as we took time away from them to work on this book. *Cultural Grammars* is dedicated to our children whose collective ancestries underwrite a larger story of Canada: Zahra, Zidan, Maya, Skye, and Zev.

—Christine Kim, Sophie McCall, and Melina Baum Singer, co-editors

PERMISSIONS

Kristina Fagan, Daniel Heath Justice, Keavy Martin, Sam McKegney, Deanna Reder, and Niigaanwewidam James Sinclair wish to acknowledge that an earlier version of Chapter 2 was published in the *Canadian Journal of Native Studies* 29.1 and 2 (2009).

Sophie McCall gratefully acknowledges permission to quote from Gregory Scofield's poetry. The sources are: *I Knew Two Métis Women* (Gabriel Dumont Institute, 2010), reprinted with the permission of Gregory Scofield and the Gabriel Dumont Institute; *Native Canadiana: Songs from the Urban Rez* (Polestar, 1996); and *Singing Home the Bones* (Raincoast, 2005), reprinted with the permission of Gregory Scofield.

Alessandra Capperdoni gratefully acknowledges permission to quote from Trish Salah's poetry. The source is *Wanting in Arabic* (TSAR 2002), reprinted with permission of TSAR Publications.

Julia Emberley acknowledges permission to reproduce Andy Clark's photograph, dated May 2, 2002. Permission granted by Thomson Reuters.

Melina Baum Singer acknowledges the University of Toronto Press for permission to reprint excerpts from the following poems by A.M. Klein, from *The Complete Poems, Volumes 1 and 2*, © University of Toronto Press, 1990: "Ave Atque Vale," "Indian Reservation: Caughnawaga," "Childe Harold's Pilgrimage," and "Portrait of the Poet as Landscape." Reprinted with permission of the publisher.

Introduction

Christine Kim and Sophie McCall

THE IMPETUS FOR THIS VOLUME comes from a sense that over the past couple of decades, both the tenor of Canadian cultural and literary studies and its terms of critical debate—such as race, nation, difference, and culture—have shifted in significant ways. The chapters in this collection focus on literary and cultural treatments of a wide range of topics pertaining to Canadian history and politics spanning one hundred years. Our contributors explore, for example, the Asian race riots in Vancouver in 1907 (Lee), the cultural memory of the internment and dispersal of Japanese Canadians in the 1940s (Kim), the politics of migrant labour and the "domestic labour scheme" in the 1960s (Mason), the role of foster care in fracturing Aboriginal families and communities in the 1960s and 1970s (Eigenbrod), the politics of the transgendered and transsexual body in queer studies in the late 1980s and 1990s (Capperdoni), and the trial of Robert Pickton in Vancouver in 2007 (Emberley). Our particular interest lies in how diaspora and indigeneity have and continue to contribute to this critical reconfiguration, as well as how conversations about diaspora and indigeneity within the Canadian context have themselves been transformed. *Cultural Grammars* is an attempt to address both the interconnections and the schisms between these multiply fractured critical terms, as well as the larger conceptual shifts that have occurred in response to national and post-national arguments.

The objective of the volume is to examine tensions within and between concepts of indigeneity and diaspora, and to analyze the ways those tensions transform concepts of nation. *Cultural Grammars* is shaped by a number of timely and provocative questions: Whose imagined community is the nation?

What are the limits of "Indigenous literary nationalism" and how can the movement acknowledge the complexities of its own terminology? What does it mean for subjects to be precariously positioned in relation to one or more nation-states? To what degree are diasporas comparable? On what grounds might Indigenous and diasporic critics converse? *Cultural Grammars* does not offer an overarching narrative or single line in response to any of these questions; rather the volume places side by side chapters that analyze very different discourses and practices. In this sense, the book generates an open field for further research and reading.

POSTCOLONIAL NATION

In attempting to address the tensions between indigeneity and diaspora, we noted that the term "nation" often impinged upon our discussions. Indeed, we found that theories of diaspora and of indigeneity, while often critical of the discourses associated with modern, industrialized nation-states, silently relied on nation-based imaginings of collectivities. We came to realize that diaspora and nation are interdependent and mutually constituting, just as indigeneity and nation are reciprocally contingent and responsive. This insight echoes critics such as Benedict Anderson (1983), Himani Bannerji (2000), and Sneja Gunew (2004), who draw attention to the persistence of the nation in an age of globalization and of Aboriginal sovereigntist social movements. While the death of the nation has so often been prophesied, with varying degrees of optimism, fear, and ambivalence, it nevertheless continues to shape the language of Canadian cultural and literary studies. How do we understand the mixed feelings that arise in response to the prediction that the nation will disappear, especially when paired with its refusal to do so? This situation compels us to consider the endurance of national discourse and question why the nation is a site we continue to return to in our deliberations of literature, culture, and politics. Such an investigation demands that we consider the historical stakes of conversations about the nation and literature in Canada and how have they been reconfigured in the contemporary moment.

At the same time, such a project reminds us that the study of Canadian literature is a relatively recent phenomenon. In her introduction to *Home-Work*, Cynthia Sugars traces the emergence of Canadian literature as a subject of scholarly study from 1952 with the inclusion of a panel at ACUTE, and dates the teaching of the subject as beginning in the 1960s (1–4). The surprise that A.S.P. Woodhouse voiced at the high degree of interest generated by this panel on Canadian literature indicates how lingering colonial attitudes toward education, culture, and emerging literatures have shaped the development of the study of Canadian literature. In this way, it can be seen that the push toward a national literature in the Canadian context, particularly in the 1960s and 1970s, was tied to a particular kind of decolonization that addressed issues of value (national and aesthetic), tradition, and canonicity. Denis Salter's "The Idea of a National Theatre" speaks to these pressures as they manifested themselves specifically within the sphere of Canadian drama. He describes the process of developing a national theatre as a tense struggle that took place during the nineteenth and twentieth centuries, and points out that it continued to be waged because of the belief that the production of "*the* classic Canadian play" would help alleviate the persistent colonial cringe within Canadian theatre (90). A similar debate unfolded in the perpetual search for the great Canadian novel, which was to be both "quintessentially Canadian" and unmarked by particularities that might detract from its acclaim as a "universal" story.

The institutionalization of Canadian literature as part of a growing wave of nationalism and an effort to decolonize Canada is perhaps not surprising given that similar links were being made around the world as various decolonization movements between the end of the Second World War and the 1960s resulted in declarations of independence.[1] The official end of European colonial rule in numerous countries had significant and far-reaching symbolic and material effects, and tied together nationalism and decolonization in complex ways. 1961 also marked the publication of Frantz Fanon's *Les damnés de la terre* (translated into English as *The Wretched of the Earth* in 1963), which in turn inaugurated the rise of postcolonial theory within the academy. Postcolonial theory has been immensely important to critics grappling with matters of power, representation, and empire in Canada, both because it provides a language to discuss these kinds of issues and because the entry of postcolonial concerns politicized the academy in particular ways.[2] As the liberation movements around the world and the growing body of writings about them demonstrated, the project of decolonization needed to address the material realities of colonialism as well as the representation of these political and economic conditions.

As a settler colony, Canada was postcolonial, but it clearly presented a very different postcolonial condition from those countries that had physically struggled to liberate themselves from European rule. The challenge of holding onto the potential that postcolonial discourse offered for Canadian conversations while working through the imperfect fit of this discourse is two-fold: firstly, the settler colonies and "actual colonies" had different relationships with the colonial empire and, secondly, because Canada as a nation was and continues to be marked by unequal power relations. In other words, part of the problem lies with the fact that in the Canadian context the imperial centre is not singular. While nationalist movements during the 1960s and 1970s equated the emergence of nationalism and decolonization to a certain degree, subsequent critics and groups demanded an interrogation of whose imagined community the nation is. Of the Canadian context, Himani Bannerji critiques notions of national identity as "ideologically homogenous" and exclusive, arguing that a certain

> core community is synthesized into a national we, and it decides on the terms of multiculturalism and the degree to which multicultural others should be tolerated or accommodated. This "we" is an essentialized version of a colonial European turned into Canadian and the subject or the agent of Canadian nationalism. It is this essence, extended to the notion of a community, that provides the point of departure for the ideological deployment of diversity. (*The Dark Side* 42)

The dominant vision of the nation is itself a colonizing representation, and multiple constituencies have and continue to express their dissatisfaction with the material and ideological limits of Canada as a nation. Elsewhere in *The Dark Side of the Nation*, Bannerji further examines the ideological basis of the Canadian nation and claims that Canada has long been imagined—in terms of race, history, language, and culture—as a "white" community (64). Interestingly, however, many marginalized groups have chosen to use the language of decolonization as a way to express their frustrations. Rather than abandoning the framework of the nation, there has tended to be a recuperation of it.

Critical race politics in the 1980s, for instance, was deeply invested in creating a place for minorities within the nation. The Writing thru Race conference (1994) is one example of how these sentiments would generate effects into the next decade. While other anti-racist events designed to build coalitions between visible minorities and larger communities such as Telling It (1988), In Visible Colours (1989), About Face, About Frame (1992), ANNPAC conference (1992), and The Appropriate Voice (1992)[3] held during the late 1980s and early 1990s brought together First Nations and people of colour, none received the explosive attention that Writing thru Race did. Much of the public outcry focused on the use of federal funds to hold a conference whose participation was limited to racialized and Aboriginal writers, and the desire to explore the experiences of racialized writers outside of the centre/margin model that Bannerji critiques above was denounced by many as exclusionary. And while the conference was certainly a moment of community building—indeed, the funds withdrawn by the Department of Canadian Heritage were replaced and exceeded by fundraising efforts—tensions between and within First Nations and visible minority communities and individuals did exist (Lai, "Community Action" 123). Monika Kin Gagnon notes that this dialogue between writers of colour and First Nations writers made evident the "radically different ideological positions" they occupy and emphasized the need to continue to struggle with these issues and for existing cultural politics to "give way to different, if more dramatically effective, crises of representation" (*Other Conundrums* 71).

The difficulty of sustaining these affiliative politics to some extent reflected the radically different arguments the groups had with the Canadian nation-state: while community activists from a range of ethnic minority groups were demanding greater space *within* the nation, Aboriginal social movements were pushing *against* government's efforts to ever more closely incorporate their nations within institutional structures of citizenship and national belonging. Following Prime Minister Pierre Elliott Trudeau's proposed White Paper of 1969, which sought the rapid assimilation of Aboriginal groups into mainstream Canadian society, a new era of First Nations activism began, shaped by the goals of self-determination and self-government. First Nations groups across Canada formed political organizations, such as the Indian Brotherhood, the Native Women's Association of Canada, and the Inuit Tapirisat of Canada, and launched friendship centres, newspapers, and magazines. Thus, the period of the 1970s and 1980s, key moments in the emergence of postcolonial and nationalist discourse in Canada, was also critically important for the development of Indigenous politics.[4] Feminists, queer and trans communities, Quebec, and regionalists also challenged the exclusivity of the Canadian nation during this time. As the grievances of these multiple communities suggest, the Canadian nation has never been a homogeneous entity, but instead has always been comprised of multiple threads, concerns, and groups, and the locus of much contention precisely because so much is at stake in being represented as part of this imagined community.

INDIGENOUS AND DIASPORIC INTERVENTIONS

Our interest here is in the ways in which diaspora and indigeneity put pressure on discourses of nation and the potential transformations they make possible. Along with paradigms of globalization and transnationalism, diaspora and indigeneity have supplemented, and in some cases even replaced, discourses of postcoloniality, perhaps suggesting that the broader project of decolonization requires multiple kinds of tools and strategies, including reimagining nation and community. At the same time, it is necessary to recognize that each of these theoretical frameworks has undergone a series of transformations and that tensions exist between the postcolonial, diasporic, and Indigenous. For example, Daniel Heath Justice points out that while Aboriginal peoples might sympathize with the challenges immigrants face, they must still remember that "the opportunities for non-Natives in Canada come as a consequence of the land loss, resource expropriation, social upheaval, and political repression of Aboriginal peoples" ("The Necessity" 145). Furthermore, as Sophie McCall argues in her contribution to this volume, First Nations studies has long had a troubled relationship with postcolonial studies, the most well-known airing of this tension perhaps being Thomas King's article, "Godzilla vs. the Post-colonial." That colonialism is far from over is evident in contemporary legal struggles over matters such as land claims and residential schools.

Diasporic and Indigenous scholarship is often critical of Canadian national discourses and the practices of the state, yet both critical streams maintain certain investments in the language of nations. For instance, the discourses of sovereignty and nation-to-nation relations have become key words in Indigenous literary studies. This is a crucial shift for, as critics have argued, nationalism is problematic not just because it excludes certain constituencies, but also because of the colonial assumptions that are inherent in nation as a discourse itself. It is particularly significant then that the language of nation continues to be taken up by Aboriginal critics and activists interested in matters of sovereignty. First Nations critics' discussions of literary sovereignty rework the language of nationalism in order to promote a linking together of politics and literature and advocate historicizing and politicizing Indigenous writing to avoid the reduction of literature to ethnography (Womack, "A Single Decade" 78).[5] Such an approach locates Aboriginal literature within specific tribal contexts as well as within the broader category of indigeneity as a way to guide interpretive practices (Justice, "The Necessity" 151). At the same time, it must be noted that Indigenous literary nationalism is also undeniably "a political act" as it effectively denies "the power of the State to claim either historical or moral inheritance of the land or its memories" (Justice, "The Necessity" 146).

Different but related pressures are placed upon the language of nation by diaspora in the Canadian context as it provides a vocabulary for working through national displacement and the condition of (un)belonging. In Canada, diaspora studies has largely moved away from its initial affiliation with Jews and Jewish experiences and increasingly has drawn upon the language of critical race theory, as Melina Baum Singer argues in this volume. The displacement and migration that are part of diaspora, as well as visible in the history of diaspora studies, open up new ways of thinking about identification, nation, and community. Paul Gilroy, for instance, moves away from national identities in order to consider the "processes of cultural mutation and restless (dis)continuity that exceed racial discourse and avoid capture by its agents" (*The Black Atlantic* 2). In so doing, Gilroy recognizes that structures of domination and cultural practices and identities, among other things, exceed national borders (7). Gayatri Gopinath interrogates the connection between diaspora and nation through queer diasporas, arguing that it asks us to "reimagine and reconstitute their particular, fraught relation to multiple national sites, and demands a rethinking of the very notions of 'home' and nostalgia.... a queer diasporic subject prompts a different understanding of the mechanisms by which national belonging is internalized in the constitution of 'modern' national subjects" ("Nostalgia, Desire, Diaspora" 264). While neither Gilroy nor Gopinath argue for an abandonment of the nation, both throw it into question by focusing on diaspora as a source of culture and identity. That said, while diaspora is a useful tool for exposing the limitations of national identity and interrogating the notion of national belonging, we recognize that a potential pitfall of the term lies precisely in its seemingly infinite applicability. As the editors of *Theorizing Diaspora* note in their introduction, diaspora "is often used as a catch-all phrase to speak of and for all movements, however privileged, and for all dislocations, even symbolic ones" (Braziel and Mannur 3). Diana Brydon voices similar concerns about current deployments of diaspora while also noting that it has much in common with globalization as both promote an emphasis on mobility rather than on a state or society and operate as "totalizing explanation[s] for contemporary experience" ("Postcolonialism" 700). While it is not our intention to limit conversations about diaspora, we hope that future debates might maintain sight of the political spirit in which the term has tended to be used in earlier discussions.

The current scholarship on indigeneity and diaspora in Canada asks us to think about the kind of work discourses of the nation perform, and what leverage the nation provides at this moment. Taking a cue from Katherine Verdery, who argues that the homogenizing work of the nation must be seen as not an end in itself but as "serv[ing] various ends, such as creating a common foundation of skills for a workforce or a space amenable to managing the state" (231), we ask what function the nation performs and how diaspora and indigeneity might transform that work. More recently, the nation has been repositioned in relation to transnationalism and globalization. This shift, far from propelling us away from the challenges of the nation, has proven to be, according to Roy Miki, "a mode of translation in which previous hierarchies undergo reconstruction in their 'interaction with transnational cultural referents'" ("Globalization" 95). Belén Martín-Lucas, in this volume, illustrates this reinstatement of cultural hierarchies and of Orientalist imaginings in national discourses in an analysis of the global book market, an industry dominated by one very large fish (Random House) with mind-boggling economic reach. Also palpable in this age of transnationalism, coupled with an ongoing security crisis in a post-9/11 world, is a retrenchment of the nation's powers to assert a sharp distinction between those citizens protected by law and those subject to a dramatic curtailing of their rights. Another point of contention are current struggles by Aboriginal land claims negotiators to effectively distinguish corporate rights from Aboriginal rights in ongoing disputes over land, resources, and energy development in Canada.[6] What these and other examples illustrate is that the nation continues to play a constitutive role in how we conceptualize transnational formations, and that the language we employ to track these permutations continues to shift.

While there have been coalitions between Indigenous and visible minority scholars, artists, and activists in the past that have produced multiple useful discussions and interventions, there have been fewer conversations between Indigenous and diasporic critics of late. This is not to say that such discussions are not taking place at all. A panel at The 1907 Race Riots and Beyond conference (2007) on women and community activism, which involved Dorothy Christian, Joanne Lee, Xiaoping Li, and Rita Wong, is just one example, as are discussions about reconciliation and the history of redress and apology movements in Canada.[7] Yet as many of the chapters in this volume demonstrate, there are more ways in which debates about indigeneity and diaspora in Canada connect with each other. The deployment of common terms or concerns in different ways produces valuable tensions and debates that we believe might be generative for ongoing and future work. The potential movement of these critical ideas and terms suggests new directions for scholarship in and about Canada, as well as productively furthers ongoing conversations about literature, culture, and politics.

CHANGING CULTURAL GRAMMARS

The goal of this collection is to take stock of ongoing conversations about the cultural politics of contemporary Canadian literature and to consider the "cultural grammars" for speaking about race and ethnicity in the current moment. A grammar is engaged with relations between different parts of speech, with their inflections and their integration in the sentence. It outlines the roles, functions, and relations of words according to established usage. A cultural grammar inquires into the relations among different discourses. Thus, *Cultural Grammars* raises three significant questions: What does the framework of the postcolonial allow us to ask? What do the frameworks of diaspora and indigeneity allow us to ask? And, finally, what are the implications of this shift in terminology for thinking through questions of citizenship, human rights, and the politics of representation? In this collection we investigate a larger shift in the field of Canadian criticism and the literatures of colonialism, postcolonialism, and neo-colonialism. This transformation is important because diasporic and First Nations texts are often read with many of the tools of postcolonial theory and in relation to texts that have more traditionally been located within the academy as "postcolonial." Thinking through how diasporic and Indigenous criticism has competing and often conflicting interests from postcolonial theory, but still possesses certain links to this initial overarching project, is an important turning point for these literatures and theories.

The title of our collection, *Cultural Grammars*, is an attempt to make discernible the language rules governing our critical choices and the conceptual frameworks we mobilize, consciously or not. Cultural imperatives in language evidence assumptions about difference and identity, of self and other, and inevitably produce unstated hierarchies. The grammar of time and chronology regulates a host of principles that guide our sense of, for example, the relationship between cause and effect, the syntactical connections we make as writers and thinkers, and the moral verdicts we tacitly activate through the logic of the "sentence." Thus, our book is divided into three sections, each evoking a temporal mode, beginning with "Present Tense," or the urgency of "now," moving through the manifold legacies of the past in "Past Participles," and opening up horizons of expectation in "Future Imperfect." Rather than suggesting a progression from the past, through the present, and into the future, our intention is to suggest the interpenetration of these chronological clusters; we aim, in other words, to go back to the future, to dwell in the "presents" of the past, and to witness the remains of today.

Our contributors took up the challenge of thinking through grammar, offering some provocative interpretations of how we learn and unlearn the cultural scripts embedded in language. While Belén Martín-Lucas's title "Grammars of Exchange" (borrowed from Edward Said) is meant to underline the seemingly endless substitutions of images of ethnic difference in an era of globalization that in the end reassert a homogenizing sameness in the international publishing industry, Alessandra Capperdoni's reference to "the grammar of the nation" points to the possibility of writing through and against the hegemony of the state by engaging with its logic in order to subvert it. Deena Rymhs goes further than Capperdoni in suggesting that bending language rules may provide a way to overcome social inequities and stereotypes; she proposes a "grammar of recovery" to describe Aboriginal men in prison who, through developing a sense of belonging to a pan-Native collectivity, "invent new 'cultural grammars' of their own." Julia Emberley provides a symptomatic reading of a "grammatological 'error'" in a letter by convicted serial killer, Robert Pickton, suggesting that his mistake in using "there" instead of "their" is "only one among many in his narrative prose that *dispossess* Indigenous women of *their subjecthood*." And Christine Kim, engaging with critical debates about diaspora, suggests that a "particular form of diasporic grammar" has developed, leading to the installation of a "model of trauma and pain that is paradigmatic."

Kim's argument that the establishment of a paradigmatic, "diasporic grammar" has led to the privileging of certain kinds of diasporic experience to the exclusion of others is also explored in Sophie McCall's "Diaspora and Nation in Métis Writing," a chapter that lays out many of the central theoretical queries of this volume. McCall's chapter points to some schisms between diasporic and Indigenous literary studies, while at the same time arguing persuasively in favour of bridging these two critical approaches. Through readings of the poetry and prose of Métis writer Gregory Scofield, McCall crafts a hinge between diasporic and Indigenous-sovereigntist viewpoints, arguing that such a perspective recognizes the internal displacement of Aboriginal nations within the borders of what is now Canada, redrawing the articulation between the maps of the settler nation-states and the maps of the First

Nations in North America. McCall argues that Scofield's poetry demands an interfusional critical paradigm, especially when Scofield connects an Aboriginal history of forced relocation to a Jewish history of diaspora and genocide, as he does in his latest collection of poetry, *Singing Home the Bones*.

In their collaboratively written chapter, Kristina Fagan, Daniel Heath Justice, Keavy Martin, Sam McKegney, Deanna Reder, and Niigaanwewidam James Sinclair continue the debate over the potential uses and pitfalls of the language of nationalism for conversations about indigeneity, specifically for those taking place in the Canadian context. "Canadian Indigenous Literary Nationalism?" highlights a series of challenges that currently confront Indigenous literary nationalism in Canada, a critical movement that locates Indigenous writing within specific historical, political, cultural, and aesthetic contexts and traditions. The main aim of their chapter is both to articulate enabling approaches to Indigenous literary nationalism and to challenge homogenizing approaches to the concept. While Sinclair questions the American bias that sometimes surfaces in these theories, Martin focuses on the uneasy fit between Inuit literature and Indigenous literary studies. McKegney speaks of the dangers of privileging texts that respond in more obvious ways to ongoing political goals while overlooking other emerging literary voices, and Reder's contribution suggests that Indigenous literary nationalism offers a way of framing texts within the classroom. Both Justice and Fagan highlight the question of community in relation to institutional definitions of Indigenous groups in order to foreground the complexity of Indigenous experience and literature and, in the words of Fagan, to "move towards a truly inclusive and expanding form of Indigenous literary nationalism."

The *lack* of complexity in dominant media representations of Indigenous communities in Canada preoccupies Julia Emberley in "Breaking the Framework of Representational Violence: Testimonial Publics, Memorial Arts, and a Critique of Postcolonial Violence (the Pickton Trial)." Like McCall, Emberley makes a connection between Jewish and Aboriginal histories of genocide by comparing the marking of Jewish bodies with a yellow star to the "public secret" of marking Indigenous women's bodies with sexualized violence, and "rendering them as signs of social debris by news media." Emberley's chapter addresses the painful legacy of the murdered and missing women in Vancouver and the ensuing trial of Robert Pickton by focusing on the violence of media representations of the women, the murders, the trial, and Pickton himself. Yet Emberley's point is not simply to critique these representations; indeed, she is interested in a wide range of "testimonial practices" that emerged from the trial in a number of paradoxically aligned sites that include the websites of Canadian newspapers such as *The Globe and Mail* and *The Vancouver Sun*, and community memorials for missing Indigenous women. One of Emberley's key goals is to illuminate how testimonial practices potentially "break the frame of violence associated with Indigenous women's bodies through a symbolic enactment of violence."

Belén Martín-Lucas is also concerned with the power and potential violence of representation in her analysis of the "Orientalist marketing tactics" that package texts by "ethnic" writers from Canada for international book markets in ways that "raise their economic value while devaluing their political ones." Martín-Lucas is unambiguous in her assessment that Random House's publishing monopoly has severely curtailed the available selection of "ethnic" writing distributed internationally. The exploitative practices of multinational publishing houses, which regulate the distribution of ethnic writers overseas as well as the relations between small and large publishers, suggest that colonial inheritances continue to shape the conditions of post-colonial cultural production in the current moment. That said, she is also careful to show that many of the creative works that she surveys—mostly Asian Canadian women's writing—"present imaginative strategies of resistance to commodification and co-optation." In spite of marketing strategies that capitalize on images of ethnic difference, Martín-Lucas argues that "alternative readings" of international bestsellers like Anita Rau Badami's *Tamarind Mem* and Shauna Singh Baldwin's *What the Body Remembers* "are not only possible, but also invited by the texts themselves."

Melina Baum Singer's "Unhomely Moves: A.M. Klein, Jewish Diasporic Difference, Racialization, and Coercive Whiteness" opens the next section of *Cultural Grammars*, entitled "Past Participles," and investigates how to bring "Jewish difference into the contemporary critical grammar of diaspora." While on the surface Jewish history has a privileged historical relation to discourses of diaspora, Baum Singer argues that recent critical commentaries have narrowed diaspora's terms of reference. The result is that dynamic and contemporary formations of Jewish diasporic subjectivity to some extent have become invisible in recent critical debates on diaspora, which, she argues, shape identity formations in key ways. Reading A.M. Klein's poetry, as well as the critical reception of his work by modernist critics, enables Baum Singer to craft a critical approach, which she calls "unhomely moves": "a way of reading the contemporary cultural grammar of Jewish diasporic difference that accounts for absence." Her purpose is "not to reinsert the centrality of Jewish experience, but rather to point out possible trajectories from which Jewish diasporic difference can extend the conversations taking place in postcolonial diaspora, Jewish, and modernist studies."

Christopher Lee's "Asian Canadian Critical Practice as Commemoration" looks both backwards and forwards in time in order to disrupt common historiographical assumptions about the aftershocks and the presentiments of the past. Lee proposes an idea of commemoration as "engendering an ethical practice between the present and the past that exceeds, even as it animates, concrete actions." Lee explores the 2007 Anniversaries of Change coalition, which marked various significant moments in Asian Canadian history, and the 1988 settlement for the internment and incarceration of Japanese Canadians during the Second World War. His chapter asks scholars and cultural workers to "understand the responsibility to commemorate and how [that] temporality [is] reconfigured through such a call." Using Roy Miki's reading of the redress movement as "a possible loss of an entire way of *being in time*," Lee calls for an understanding of commemoration as "one that interrupts our experience of temporality, arresting its movement as it were in order to grasp the circuits of exchange that constitute it as well as what lies outside them."

In "Diasporic Longings: (Re)Figurations of Home and Homelessness in Richard Wagamese's Work," Renate Eigenbrod argues that diaspora is best suited to understand the multiple displacements Indigenous peoples face as a result of colonialism. She aligns her project with Cree scholar Neal McLeod, who "outlines two aspects of diaspora: spatial and ideological." Illuminating the interconnection of diasporic cultural formations through a reading of Wagamese's work, she explores the problematics inherent in thinking about home for First Peoples, as the reserve and residential school systems each in its own way created transgenerational forms of violence. Eigenbrod notes that Wagamese's writing positions storytelling as a type of homecoming, but is careful to point out that Wagamese's narrative does not bracket the importance of resolving land claims.

Jody Mason's work draws attention to the important and often overlooked role class and labour play in restricting citizenship for racialized communities in Canada. Articulating another way of thinking of the unhomeliness of home, Mason's "Afro-Caribbean Writing in Canada and the Politics of Migrant Labour Mobility" argues that Canada is unwilling to recognize itself as a major player in the market of a transnational migrant labour force, even as it has historically relied on this force since the postwar period. She critiques theories of diaspora and globalization that mobilize "untethered" tropes of de-territorization, as "these tropes are implicated in the reterritorializing politics of ... the Canadian state, which in the late twentieth century has refined and strengthened its ability to police the mobility of migrant workers." Mason's analyses of the work of Austin Clarke and Cecil Foster, Beijan-born Canadian writers who explore the institutionalization of migrant worker programs in Canada, demonstrate the imbrications of social processes through which space and place are given meaning. Her readings ask that diasporic formations be considered in relation to materialist studies on the politics of migrant labour mobility, a phrase influenced by Doreen Massey's "politics of mobility" to refer to "systems of power that divide and distribute mobility."

In the final section, "Future Imperfect," each contributor theorizes iden-tification—both its possibilities and pitfalls—in different ways, approaching the problem, for example, in terms of "interdiasporic post-memory" (Kim); the specific and the collective (Cho); the location of bodies within systems of gender, sexuality, and nation (Capperdoni); and Indigenous political activism within prisons and as part of the communities beyond (Rymhs). These chap-ters encourage us to examine the negotiations of broader patterns, histories, collectives, and communities that individuals might or might not be read as part of or against. How, these contributions collectively ask, might we think about relationality differently? What kind of a cultural grammar is necessary to express non-linear and non-reductive relations, allowing us to think and speak simultaneously, alongside, and even diagonally to and from each other? These contemplations about future directions for discussions of nation, diaspora, and indigeneity propose that we envision new speaking positions, terms of debate, and modes of engaging with each other. Our hope is that the shared interest in history, memory, bodies, community politics, and social institutions explored by the whole of this volume will become the basis of critical conversations to come.

Christine Kim's "Racialized Diasporas, Entangled Postmemories, and Kyo Maclear's *The Letter Opener*" introduces the question of "diasporic relational-ity" by asking us to reflect upon what is at stake in particular relationships and how we might understand the desire to forge particular relationships instead of others. Kim's chapter reads *The Letter Opener* through the lens of post-memory and witnessing, taking Marianne Hirsch's idea of post-memory and turning it on its side. What then spills out is "interdiasporic post-memory," a set of relations between a single generation that extends over multiple geographic locations and historical affiliations, and that enables a thinking through of the desires and difficulties of social intimacy. Kim's chapter asks, "What causes us to be moved by certain narratives of diaspora and not others? How might we understand psychic and social investments in another's pain? How are various diasporic populations affectively bound together?" In posing these kinds of questions, her work complicates the language of coalitions and recognizes the often-contradictory psychic and social investments in collectivities.

Yet if "diasporic relationality" in Kim's chapter is an enabling critical tool to imagine new kinds of identifications, in Lily Cho's "Underwater Signposts: Richard Fung's *Islands* and Enabling Nostalgia," relationality becomes the temptation to substitute the specific for the collective and one diaspora for another. Cho asks us to consider how we might speak of the specific without fetishizing difference and while still holding onto what is "exceptional" about particular groups and experiences. At the same time, she stresses the need to discuss the collective without falling into the trap of universalizing and overlooking difference. Her chapter uses Richard Fung's *Islands* to think through the relations between Black Atlantic and Asian diasporic cultures. Fung's video provides a way of understanding Stuart Hall's ideas about identity and difference as it "calls for a way of living *with* specificity *through* relation" (Cho), but Cho modifies this insight to suggest that in the case of *Islands*, the "call for specificity ... emerges *through* relation and is routed through nostalgia." Using Gayatri Gopinath's work on nostalgia, Cho reads *Islands* as seeing doubly, by viewing spaces as constructed through memory and as fantasy, and consequently demonstrating that home is rife with contradictions.

Alessandra Capperdoni's work on gender, transsexuality, nation, and diaspora extends these conversations about relationality by analyzing "trans" as a signifier that suggests different forms of connection and disconnections. In "Phoenicia ≠ Lebanon: Transsexual Poetics as Poetics of the Body within and across the Nation," she considers the erasure of transsexuality and transgenderism in conversations about the nation. At the same time, she notes that while much critical interest has been generated in gender performativity and gender-crossing, very little attention has been paid to the material realities of trans people. The elision of the transsexual body is explored through Capperdoni's reading of Trish Salah's poetry, *Wanting in Arabic*, as she examines the diasporic as part of the speaker's ancestry, and as a movement that shapes the poetic, propelling the speaker away from practices of identification. This emphasis on becoming asks us to rethink identificatory practices in a range of spaces—national, gendered, ethnic, literary, and political—and addresses the degrees of invisibility and marginalization experienced by trans subjects. The challenge that trans sex workers pose to "notions of global migrancy, citizenship, and, indeed, the imagined community of the nation" is useful to think about alongside Julia Emberley's reading of the forms of discursive and physical violence directed toward female Indigenous sex workers in Canada.

The final chapter in this section, Deena Rymhs's "Word Warriors: Indigenous Political Consciousness in Prison," contemplates future relations by connecting traditional practices to political activism. Rymhs introduces the question of social transformation by examining the possibilities of changing institutional structures and the representation of Indigenous peoples. Traditions of civil rights are yoked together with spiritual and cultural traditions in order to invoke change within colonial institutions, and Indigenous prison writing and activism are analyzed as forms of political engagement that shape the nation well beyond the walls of its correctional institutions. Rymhs argues that prison is a key site of political change for many Indigenous prisoners who view their new social consciousness as "born of a place where state-sanctioned violence and colonization persist in our so-called 'postcolonial' moment." While she describes the transformation of prisons from colonial spaces to sites of political activism and cultural regeneration, Rymhs also recognizes that prison is nonetheless still a form of traumatic displacement and a way of understanding Indigenous diasporas. One particularly salient aspect of "Word Warriors" is its discussion of how the structures of the prison themselves are being transformed through the incorporation of Aboriginal spirituality into workshops and counselling practices, thereby broadening how healing is understood and put into practice. In this way, Rymhs's work sketches out the possibility of reinventing impossible conditions and ways of negotiating the relations between indigeneity, nation(s), and states, which give us hope and act as models for social transformations to come.

Through its focus on diaspora, indigeneity, and the nation, this volume gives us new ways of speaking about symbolic and material violence, local and global movements, citizenship rights and responsibilities, and emerging and established communities. We suggest new directions for future conversations about diaspora, indigeneity, and the nation as they intersect with and are influenced by discourses of transnationalism, globalization, class, gender, and sexuality. Clearly, the nation itself is a concept that is constantly being transformed through engagements with Indigenous, diasporic, transnational, postcolonial, and neo-colonial forces, pressures, and communities. It is our hope that the questions posed by *Cultural Grammars* will be taken up in future dialogue in order to generate new critical frameworks for examining the overlaps, as well as the dissonances between Indigenous and diasporic literary studies.

NOTES

1   A very short list of such countries includes the partitioning of India and Pakistan in
    1947 and the end of British colonial rule, both Burma and Ceylon declaring indepen-
    dence in 1948 from Britain, Israel forming in 1948, Nigeria declaring independence
    from Britain in 1960, Algerian independence from France in 1962, and Kenya achiev-
    ing independence from the British in 1963.

2   The shift in terminology from "Commonwealth" to "postcolonial" literature, brought
    about to a large extent with the publication of Ashcroft, Griffiths, and Tiffin's *The
    Empire Writes Back* (1989), illustrates this move to politicize literary studies, though
    critics such as Aijaz Ahmed (1992) and Arun Mukherjee (1998) have questioned
    whether this amendment in vocabulary has led to more significant change. It should
    also be noted that the postcolonial was not the only lens of political consciousness
    available during this period. Feminism and socialism, for example, pushed for social and
    political transformations by addressing problems of power and representation from dif-
    ferent angles within and outside the university during this time; Norman Feltes (1986)
    and Barbara Godard (2008) are two such critics who developed feminist, Marxist, and
    historical materialist conceptual frameworks in their literary analyses.

3   For further reading about these and other related events, please see Monika Kin
    Gagnon's *Other Conundrums*, especially "Building Blocks," and her 13 *Conversations
    about Cultural Race Politics*, co-edited with Richard Fung, as well as essays by Dionne
    Brand ("Notes for Writing thru Race"), Larissa Lai ("Community Action"), Lee Mara-
    cle ("Ramparts Hanging in the Air"), Scott Toguri McFarlane, and M. Nourbese Philip.

4   Craig Womack notes a comparable trajectory in the American Indian context ("A
    Single Decade" 12). The Indigenous political presence also translated into the estab-
    lishment of Indigenous courses and programs at universities and the publication of
    anthologies by Indigenous authors in the 1970s and 1980s (13).

5   The resistance to ethnographic readings has also been a major preoccupation for visible
    minority writers who have grappled with biographical and sociological interpretations
    of their literary work and struggled to assert the aesthetic merit of their writing. For
    further reading about resistance to ethnographic readings by Asian Canadian writers,
    please see Rocio Davis's *Transcultural Reinventions: Asian American and Asian Canadian
    Short-Story Cycles*, *Asian Canadian Writing beyond Autoethnography*, ed. Eleanor Ty and
    Christl Verduyn, and Fred Wah's "A Poetics of Ethnicity." This issue also has sparked
    much debate in the context of African literary studies, with well-known critiques of the
    ethnographication of contemporary African artistic production by Paulin Hountondji
    in *African Philosophy: Myth and Reality* (1996) and Kwame Anthony Appiah in *In My
    Father's House: Africa in the Philosophy of Culture* (1993). In the Canadian context,
    Rinaldo Walcott's *Black Like Who?* and Himani Bannerji's *Thinking Through: Essays on
    Feminism, Marxism, and Anti-racism* explore the legacy of ethnographic approaches to
    cultural difference in current politics of identity.

6   For more on how legal definitions of Aboriginal rights are becoming increasingly entan-
    gled with corporate rights to land and resources, see Kent McNeil, *Defining Aboriginal
    Title in the 90s: Has the Supreme Court Finally Got It Right?*

7   The first plenary session at the Japanese Canadian Redress Anniversary conference
    (2008) was moderated by Art Miki, former NAJC president, and featured Albert Lo,

Chief Robert Joseph, Avvy Go, Andrew Hladshevsky, David Divine, and Harbhajan Gill as speakers and respondents. As each of the speakers discussed the history of reconciliation movements with respect to the particular communities they are involved in, this panel can be seen as a conversation between Indigenous and diasporic critics.

1 Present Tense

Diaspora and Nation in Métis Writing

Sophie McCall

FOR THE PAST SEVERAL YEARS, a growing split has become increasingly evident in critical studies of diasporic and Aboriginal literatures in North America: while most critics of diasporic literatures engage with questions of migrancy in an era of transnational corporatization, the majority of critics of Aboriginal literatures have turned to the language of sovereignty and nation-hood in an era of land claims, self-government agreements, and modern-day treaties. On the surface, this gap may seem appropriate. Theories of diaspora may be best suited to address immigrant experiences of displacement, while sovereignty, nationhood, and cultural autonomy are key terms to address cur-rent trends in Native politics. Many Aboriginal literary critics, such as Lee Maracle (1996), Craig Womack (1999), and Lisa Brooks (2006), directly link their arguments for "intellectual sovereignty" to current political negotiations over land and governance. Meanwhile, in the work of critics engaged with studies of diaspora—such as James Clifford (1997), Diana Brydon (2000), and Lily Cho (2006)—the language of nation is an unresolved tension, as these critics attempt to grapple with complex transnational formations of identity, labour, technology, and security. It is possible, as Brydon has argued, that "con-cepts of diaspora reach their limits in the claims to indigeneity" (23), especially in light of current decolonization movements in Aboriginal communities.

However, in this chapter I argue that a diasporic-Indigenous-sovereigntist critical approach may be best suited to address Métis writing, which paradoxi-cally enacts national (i.e., the Métis nation) and diasporic (i.e., Métis-sage) identifications.[1] The work of Gregory Scofield, a Métis poet and writer whose ancestry can be traced back five generations to the Red River Settlement, and

whose father he recently discovered was Polish-Jewish and German, underlines the necessity to articulate a flexible critical framework that explores
both diasporic and national imaginings. Reading the poetry collections *Native
Canadiana: Songs from the Urban Rez* (1996), *I Knew Two Métis Women* (1999),
and *Singing Home the Bones* (2005), as well as his memoir *Thunder through My
Veins: Memories of a Métis Childhood* (1999), I argue that nation and diaspora
cannot be understood as binary opposites, but rather should be viewed as interdependent and mutually constitutive. More pressingly, I argue in favour of
bringing in conversation discussions of diaspora, Aboriginal literary nationalism, and Métis subjectivity for the following reasons. Theories of diaspora may
offer some vital insights into the history of displacement of Aboriginal peoples
in Canada (i.e., the creation of reserves, the forced relocation of Aboriginal communities, and the scattering of Aboriginal communities and families
through residential schools and foster care). By countering the tendency to
look at specific diasporas separately, and to hierarchize them according to
unspecified criteria, as Lily Cho warns against, we have an opportunity to
build coalitions between disparate minority histories and to produce a model
for relational history writing (Cho 13). Diaspora may also help address experiences of mixed-race, urban, or off-reserve Native peoples, who may or may
not maintain strong ties to a sovereigntist nation based on a defined territory. We might garner a better understanding of sovereignties-in-motion, or
confederacies, and develop new ways of conceptualizing Native nationalisms
that address the wide range of relationships that Aboriginal peoples have to
their ancestral territories.[2] By the same token, theories of Aboriginal nationhood have much to contribute to conversations about diaspora. Indigenous
sovereigntist perspectives may help articulate community-based processes of
participatory citizenship. Diasporic and Indigenous-sovereigntist standpoints
share the desire to challenge settler nationalisms and expose the exclusions
that have produced Canadian citizenship, even as they grapple with the often
devastating effects of a highly mobile, neo-liberal, global capitalism. And
theories of diaspora, in conjunction with theories of Indigenous sovereignties,
potently acknowledge the underlying maps of Native North America and how
First Nations territories traverse the 49th parallel.

It is my hope that the very awkwardness of a cobbled-together diasporic-
Indigenous-sovereigntist critical perspective will produce a critical jostling
that will question both Nativist and neo-colonial leanings that sometimes surface in these critical debates. In *Scandalous Bodies: Diasporic Literatures in Canada* (2000), Smaro Kamboureli states that her efforts to "trace the possibilities

of diaspora" is reflective of her "desire to release [herself] from the hold that Nativism has on Canadian literature" (8). What she means by Nativism here is a false claim to belonging in settler-nationalist discourses, based on a manufactured one-to-one relationship between land, language, literature, and community.[3] Nativism produces a fairly high degree of anxiety in the work of other theorists of diaspora, most notably in the work of Paul Gilroy, who argues that diaspora furnishes an alternative to "primordial kinship and rooted belonging," as well as a principled critique of "the disabling assumptions of automatic solidarity based on either blood or land" (Gilroy 123, 133, qtd. in Chariandy, "Postcolonial" par. 4). Similarly, in *Nations without Nationalism* (1993), Julia Kristeva speaks forcefully against Romantic-nationalist constructions, arguing that the "cult of origins" creates "a weird primal paradise—family, ethnicity, nation, race"—which, combined with "the soil, the blood, and the genius of the language," are the roots of a xenophobic national idea (Kristeva, qtd. in Hoy 127). Yet as much as I support these critiques of Nativism, the question must be asked: What are the ramifications of the portrayals of claims to Indigenous belonging in light of Native peoples' current struggles over land, resources, and development in Canada? Though none of these critics is talking about Indigenous populations in their hopes that diaspora as a critical tool may critique "a positivistic image of the ethnic imaginary" (Kamboureli xii), or offer a way to think "against race" (Gilroy), or imagine "nations without nationalism" (Kristeva), this silent space between Indigenous and diasporic theories demonstrates that bringing into conversation theories of diaspora, Aboriginal sovereignty, and Métis subjectivity is highly contentious; I need to proceed with caution in moving within and between these overlapping yet explosive discourses.

There is no doubt that Aboriginal people's experience in Canada has been and continues to be diasporic—forced relocations of communities (Canada, "Relocation" 251ff), as well as the seizure of children from families for enrolment in residential schools or in the foster care system (Fournier and Crey), are some clear examples. The reserve system, in which tiny postage-stamp-sized allotments of land were carved out of vast First Nations' territories, is also part of a violent history of uprooting and relocation (C. Harris). Gregory Scofield's work, much of it drawing on his own autobiography, relates his multiple dislocations as he, sometimes alone but usually with his mother, moved back and forth between British Columbia, Saskatchewan, the Yukon, and Washington state, in urban, rural, and reserve settings, in apartments, shacks, trailers, and houses, as well as in two foster homes and a treatment centre. In his memoir, *Thunder through My Veins*, Scofield describes the painful memories he carries in relation to these multiple dislocations: "The houses, hotels, shacks, and apartments where I grew up are too numerous to count though many of them loom in my memory like misshapen rocks jagged with the indecipherable ghosts of my childhood" (xiii). A sense of displacement and ambivalence shapes Scofield's process of learning about his Métis roots. Scofield first identifies as Cree as a young man, and internalizes the negative stereotypes he learns at school about Métis people, who "weren't Indians at all, but Frenchmen pretending to be Indians," and about Louis Riel, a "traitor to the Canadian government" (64). He recounts "the shame my grandfather carried throughout his life for being Métis. Perhaps it goes back even farther, back to his mother, my great-grandmother" (6). He describes his grandparents' "marriage of secrets" whose multiple silences exacted a heavy price on the family's descendants: "the denial of [my grandfather's] heritage has left hundreds of unanswered questions and I strongly believe deeply affected each generation of my family" (11). He connects his family's sense of displacement to a larger Aboriginal history in Canada: "To some degree, we were all displaced people, survivors who had either been through foster care, in jail, or on the streets" (110).

Yet as much as Scofield directly confronts these multiple dislocations, he is wary that his readers might overinterpret the rootlessness of Métis identity, and impose a ready-made critical apparatus of perpetual displacement. He is understandably dismayed when his life is wrongly translated as a pat narrative of *"the poor Métis boy who had turned his horrible life into a success story"* (194, emphasis in the original). After publishing *The Gathering: Stones for the Medicine Wheel* (1993), which won the Dorothy Livesay Poetry Prize, Scofield became aware of the toll produced by his narrative of diasporic unbelonging when he encountered "a certain article that read, 'Scofield grew up in a family of drunken half-breeds ...'" (190). Scofield is not alone among Native writers who distrust their critics' interpretations; Cree writer Janice Acoose, for example, talks about the "Wiintigo like forces of western literary criticism and its accompanying critical language" (37). I would argue that Scofield's and Acoose's apprehensions arise, to some extent, from the difficulty in critically navigating the differences between immigrant and Indigenous histories and experiences. Indeed, most critics are cautious about unproblematically conflating a diasporic critical model with an Indigenous one. James Clifford acknowledges some of the fundamental incommensurabilities between diasporic and Indigenous critical approaches at the outset of his landmark article, "Diasporas," stating that "[d]iasporas are caught up with and defined against

(1) the norms of nation-states and (2) indigenous, and especially autochtho-
nous, claims by 'tribal' peoples" (250). Clifford argues that "diasporist and
autochthonist histories ... do come into direct political antagonism" (253),
and that "[t]ribal cultures are not diasporas; their sense of rootedness in the
land is precisely what diasporic peoples have lost" (254). Clifford's delineation
of the differences between diasporist and autochthonist histories is contentious: it is not at all evident that diasporic peoples have lost their sense of
rootedness, or that all tribal cultures are rooted in the land in the same way.
Furthermore, as Wilson and Peters argue, Clifford approaches Indigenous diasporas as a form of internal migration, which he assumes does not unsettle or
challenge settler state norms and identities, and which only minimally allows
for the possibility of Indigenous nationhood (398). Nevertheless, his point is
valid that diaspora's emphasis on rootlessness, mobility, and migration risks a
certain complicity with a settler, colonial-capitalist hunger to continually seek
out new territories. And the long-standing antagonism between diasporic and
Indigenous histories, as Métis-Salish writer Lee Maracle has argued, reasserts
itself in the language of academic debate, especially when scholarly writing on
Indigenous issues does not acknowledge a longer history than one of contact
with Euro-American communities ("Oratory" 55–56).

   Theories of diaspora have to a large extent emerged from postcolonial
theory, which itself has an uneasy relationship with Aboriginal studies. The
"post" in "postcolonial" has been a much disputed term, and critics in Aboriginal literary studies, following Thomas King's well-known article, "Godzilla
vs. Post-Colonial," often point out the shortsightedness of critics who either
(1) fail to recognize that colonialism is ongoing in Canada, or (2) persist in
using European colonial incursion as a starting point in their analyses, thereby
ignoring the complexity and persistence of tribal traditions. The erasure of
Native agency, "first by colonial force, then by postcolonial analyses," as Julie
Cruikshank puts it (139; qtd. in Weaver, "Splitting" 26), is a real concern,
even though postcolonialism has produced a number of politically enabling
critiques of the settler-nation.

   One concept that reveals the fault lines between postcolonialism/diaspora
studies and Indigenous/sovereigntist studies is the question of hybridity. In
postcolonial and diasporic approaches, hybridity is often used as ammunition
against essentialism, which is viewed as a politically dangerous valorization of
purity, while hybridity is aligned with heterogeneity, openness, and a politics
of difference.[4] Yet in Indigenous studies, claims to hybridity are treated with
some suspicion.[5] As Métis critic Emma LaRocque argues, "recent postcolonial

emphasis on 'hybridity'..., 'crossing boundaries' or 'liminality' can serve to eclipse Aboriginal cultural knowledges, experiences ... and ... the colonial experience" ("Teaching" 222). LaRocque expresses a certain frustration with what she frames as a demand to become cross-cultural or hybrid in contemporary critical approaches at a time when Aboriginal communities are attempting to forge a stronger sense of a nation-specific identity in an era of land rights and self-government. Jace Weaver, Craig Womack, and Robert Warrior in *American Indian Literary Nationalism* also speak forcibly against hybridity as a conceptual tool, clearly demarcating Aboriginal sovereigntist positions from the "footloose, rootless, mixed-blood hybridity" of postcolonial theory (Preface xx).[6] For these critics, postcolonial theory has closer ties to "doctrinaire postmodernism" (xx) than to either viable theories of decolonization or meaningful engagement with the cultural and social contexts of Aboriginal communities. Another complicating factor in the debate over hybridity is the extraordinary weight of discourses of authenticity in Aboriginal studies. Colonial legislation, such as the *Indian Act*, as well as its modern-day correctives, such as Bill C-31,[7] continue to pit "real" Indians against "others," as Mi'kmaq scholar Bonita Lawrence compellingly explains in *"Real" Indians and Others: Mixed-Blood Urban Native Peoples and Indigenous Nationhood*. She argues that the very concept of "Indian status" is more about who is excluded than who qualifies.

In Scofield's work, the hybrid or half-breed individual is forced to negotiate discourses of authenticity that underpin identity categories such as "status" and "non-status." In *Thunder through My Veins*, Scofield includes a revealing conversation between himself and a welfare worker that illustrates the precariousness of the hybrid figure. Scofield, in desperate financial straits, having just moved to Saskatchewan from a small reserve in northern British Columbia, is seeking social assistance. After reviewing his file, the welfare worker asks questions specifically designed to underline Scofield's ineligibility and lack of belonging to any governmentally recognized Aboriginal community in Canada:

> "Why are you coming here instead of Indian Affairs?" she asked.
> "I'm not status," I mumbled.
> "But it says here you were collecting social assistance on a reserve in British Columbia."
> "I don't have status," I repeated. [...]
> "Then what are you?" she asked indignantly.
> "Half-breed," I whispered....

"Then why were you getting welfare on an Indian reserve?... I don't
know if I can help you. You're not a resident of Saskatchewan—you're
not a treaty Indian—besides, you should have just stayed on the reserve."
(156)

The episode precisely illustrates Lawrence's point that Aboriginal peoples
who lack status fall through the cracks that governmental policies have created between "half-breed" and "Indian." Scofield must navigate the deep
divides not only between White and Native worlds, but also between the
colonial labels of half-breed, status, non-status, off-reserve, on-reserve, urban,
rural, etc., that continue to shape Native communities.

In spite of these and other difficulties, diaspora as a critical tool potentially opens up new spaces in debates pertaining to Aboriginal literary and
cultural criticism. Clifford insists that "the tribal-diasporic opposition is not
absolute" (254); indeed, "there are significant areas of overlap" that need to
be examined (253), particularly if one assumes that the territories of Aboriginal nations underlie national, provincial, and state borders in North America. Diasporic and Indigenous communities share common experiences of
loss, uprooting, and adaptation; they emphasize in a comparable manner the
importance of maintaining the homeland and dreaming of one day "returning" to the homeland; and they strategically "bypass an opposition between
rootedness and displacement" (254). A diasporic-Indigenous perspective
potentially foregrounds the experiences of migrant Indigenous peoples whose
routes and roots, whose losses and persistent connections, have not been well
documented, understood, or even noticed. Furthermore, diaspora represents a
new phase in the ongoing critique of the nation in an era of globalization that
can simultaneously address Indigenous sovereigntist concerns. Claims to First
Nations' sovereignty are often on the front line of resistance to the pressures of
transnational corporatism, as is clear in disputes over oil and gas development
in western Canada today.[8] As Lily Cho argues, reading Lee Maracle, there
is a clear need for more nuanced approaches to diaspora that "differentiates
it from the transnational and situates it inextricably within long histories of
dislocation including ... the dislocation of First Nations peoples of Canada"
(28n). For these reasons, it is productive, even urgent, to discuss how and to
what extent diasporas are "caught up with and defined against" (Clifford 250)
the rights of First Nations peoples.

Scofield's work, which grounds Métis nationhood within the reality of
Métis diasporas, offers a useful starting point to address some of these critical

lacunae. Like Maria Campbell in the first two chapters of *Halfbreed* (1973), a book that Scofield acknowledges has had a profound effect on his development as a writer, Scofield emphasizes the history of the Métis people by narrating some details of the Red River Resistance of 1869, the establishment of a provisional government, and the creation of the "Road Allowance people" who became "squatters on their land" (Campbell 8) following the second Resistance of 1885. As mentioned, Scofield initially believed he was Cree and was unwilling to accept his Métis heritage. In *Thunder through My Veins*, Scofield relates how Cree guidance counsellor, Alana Daystar, took him to the yearly Métis celebration, Back to Batoche Days. She says: "'Greg, pekewe,' [come home].... 'It's time you came home'" (164). What Scofield grows to realize, as he learns to "come home," and as he feels his "heart sink into the very landscape" of Batoche and the Prairies (166), is that the Métis-people are "*Katipâmsôchik*," which translates as "The People Who Own Themselves" (Scofield, *Native* 55).

Scofield's defiant statement of autonomy resonates with much Native North American literary criticism today, which focuses on self-determination, sovereignty, and nation-to-nation relations to counter the debilitating effects of a colonial history of dislocation and diaspora, as well as to meaningfully engage with tribal forms of governance. If, according to Muscogee Creek Cherokee writer Craig Womack, who published the influential monograph *Red on Red: Native American Literary Separatism* in the same year as Scofield's memoir, postcolonialism assumes that the main aim of Native American writers is to "challenge Eurocentric discourse" ("The Integrity" 99), then Aboriginal literary sovereignty provides a powerful antidote to this limited and limiting prescription. In contrast, Womack "seek[s] a literary criticism that emphasizes Native resistance movements against colonialism, confronts racism, discusses sovereignty and Native nationalism, seeks connections between literature and liberation struggles, and, finally, roots literature in land and culture" (*Red* 11). Womack imagines an activist, socially engaged criticism whose aim is to build knowledge networks within Aboriginal nations, rather than continually responding to and countering dominant Euro-American epistemologies. Womack's work is cited positively in many studies of Aboriginal literatures. Like Womack, Acoose also connects "literary sovereignty and political nationhood" (52), arguing that "Exercising sovereignty, we must name/define our own literatures and take control of the Indigenous-literary territory" (46–47). She links her work as a literary critic to current political struggles over land and sovereignty.

Womack's and Acoose's construction of a one-to-one relationship between literature, land, and culture is highly contentious in diasporic and postcolonial theory. Rooting literature in land and culture, naming and defining one's own literatures, taking control of the Indigenous literary territory: all of these goals are anathema to diasporic studies, which remain distrustful of cultural or Romantic nationalist claims. However, though Indigenous literary sovereigntists often do rely on a type of Romantic nationalist ideology, they are also careful to differentiate their tribal-specific notions of nation from those of dominant settler nation-states. Abenaki writer Lisa Brooks claims that her notion of Abenaki nationhood has little to do with industrialized nation-states.[9] Rather, she argues for a tribal nationhood that enacts a more participatory form of citizenship and that more flexibly accommodates democratic processes.[10] Similarly, the co-authors of *American Indian Literary Nationalism* resist the stereotypical characterization of nationalism as necessarily xenophobic. For example, Weaver makes the case for the value of a "pluralist separatism" (Weaver, "Splitting" 46), insisting that Indigenous nationhood is at its best when it is "processual" (38) and resistant to a singular, one-size-fits-all definition. Warrior, reading Edward Said, rejects the usual oppositions between the nationalist and the cosmopolitan, the tribalist and the humanist, claiming that it is possible to be at once "a critic, a nationalist, a cosmopolitan, and a humanist" ("Native Critics" 192). Each of these models insists that American Indian literary nationalism is not a thing but an active process of community building across a broad spectrum of social hierarchies and differences.

While a wholesale rejection of sovereigntist positions is clearly misguided, an uncritical acceptance is also a problem, and, according to Warrior, pressure can build to present unanimous support for sovereigntist positions.[11] Daniel Heath Justice asks: "[W]hat happens ... when a concept like sovereignty shifts from indigenous empowerment and responsibility and is instead used as a hammer to stifle dissent within the community?" ("'Go'" 154). Justice provides some provocative examples in which mixed-blood identity and Indigenous nationalism have been on a collision course.[12] He refers to a proposal from his own Cherokee nation, in which the tribal government sought to disenfranchise mixed-race African American Cherokee people in violation of established treaty rights.[13] Womack also acknowledges that the role of mixed-race, off-reserve Native peoples is an unresolved tension in Indigenous nationalisms: "I'm somewhat ambivalent about the whole notion of celebrating mixedblood identity.... It's not the issue of mixedblood identity that bothers me since, for better or worse or a combination of the two, this is a contemporary reality for many Indian people, including myself ... [but] I'm wondering if identifying as mixedblood, rather than as part of a tribal nation, diminishes sovereignty?" ("Howling" 32). Clearly, Womack is reacting against the tendency in critical scholarship to privilege the individual subject's negotiation of his or her hybridity at the expense of asking questions that engage with community-based, tribal-specific social contexts. Yet the fairly strong distinction that he makes between nationhood and mixed-blood identity poses a problem for discussing the Métis nation and subjectivity within a sovereigntist framework.

Debates informing Indigenous nationhood and diaspora are brought into focus with respect to the historical struggle of Métis people to both establish a nation and to reinvent the concept to accommodate the rootedness and the displacements of disparate communities that now call themselves "Métis." Emma LaRocque grapples with the diverse origins of Métis people, describing her family as a distinct Métis community that is not always recognized as such because her family never owned land and eschewed settlement. Like Scofield, LaRocque writes that her people are known as *Otehpayimsuak*—an alternative spelling of *Katipâmsôchik*[14]—which she translates as "the independent and self-reliant ones." As hunters, trappers, and fishers, "[r]eserves and residential schools were anathema to *Sagaweenuak*, or bush people, as we also called ourselves" ("Native" 389).

LaRocque argues that one reason for her community's invisibility is the tendency, in postcolonial critical approaches, of broadening the term "Métis" to the extent that it becomes synonymous with mixed-race identity. For LaRocque, the focus on mixed-race identity elides engagement with history and what she calls "our unique Red River Cree-Métis roots" ("Teaching" 222). Yet LaRocque's privileging of the Red River Métis is contentious. In September 2002 the Métis National Council, which Canada recognizes as the primary organization for Métis people, adopted a new definition of Métis identity based on the Red River community, which is causing tensions with other Métis communities in Canada.[15] This move is part of a larger trend in which western Métis organizations have attempted to restrict Métis history to western Canada. In 1984, the Métis National Council proposed using upper-case M to refer to those Métis "originally of mixed ancestry who evolved into a distinct indigenous people," and lower-case m to describe all other people of mixed ancestry who identify as métis (LaRocque, "Native" 382). This typographic denotation not only distinguishes but also hierarchizes Métis communities.

For Lawrence, as for LaRocque, the solution is not to broaden the label "Métis" to refer to any and all mixed-race Native peoples. Lawrence's purpose is not to challenge the special history of the Red River community or to undermine any Métis group's history. Rather, she is concerned with how the *Indian Act* has "arbitrarily externaliz[ed] from Indianness an entire category of Indigenous people, designated as 'half-breeds' and now called 'Métis'" (*"Real"* 82–83). The thrust of Lawrence's argument is that the *Indian Act* has produced separate and unequal categories of identity, stemming from the cleft between "half-breed" and "Indian," thereby allowing Canada "to deny its fiduciary obligation to any community that lacks Indian status" (93). This in turn has forced non-status individuals "to rally themselves, in contemporary times, as Métis in order to survive as Indigenous people at all" (93). The label "Métis" in turn papers over the at times contradictory nature of mixed-blood identity, with its "different spaces of marginality and privilege" (10) relating to class, level of education, social opportunity, region, and skin colour.

In Scofield's writing, the multiple meanings of "Métis" do not cancel one another out, nor do they assert a sharp distinction between Aboriginal and Métis subjectivity; I agree with Qwo-Li Driskill, who argues that Scofield's poetry "maintain[s] a sovereign mixedblood identity" that "claims Métis identity as sovereign from both 'fullblood' and white contexts" (232).[16] Yet as much as Scofield imagines and brings into being a sovereign Métis nationhood, he does not retroactively romanticize its origins; rather, like Lawrence, he cannily outlines the "different spaces of marginality and privilege" (Lawrence, *"Real"* 10) that continue to stratify Métis communities. For example, in the poem "Policy of the Dispossessed," Scofield outlines how the Métis people were swindled of land through an unethical manipulation of scrip (a cash payment or a piece of land); at the same time, he also shows how the scrip system interpellated the Métis people and rendered their survival as a community complicit with the extinguishment of Aboriginal rights. Scofield opens the poem with a citation from Section 31 of the *Manitoba Act* of 1870, which specifies that "the extinguishment of the Indian Title to lands in the Province" would be secured by appropriating "one million four hundred thousand acres ... for the benefit of the families of the halfbreed residents" (qtd. in Scofield, *Native* 53). On the one hand, the *Manitoba Act* recognized the legitimacy of half-breed land rights; on the other, it used the category of half-breed as a means of extinguishing Aboriginal title to land. Scofield resists the temptation, in the face of this history of dispossession, to construct a simplified narrative of victimization; indeed, he warns his readers that "there are some deceptions left unmentioned" (54). The first deception is how mixed-race individuals were granted scrip in exchange for silencing their claims to collective indigeneity (Lawrence, "*Real*" 84). The second is how "the children's scrip" was "sweet-talked / for chocolate bars or candies. / My *Cheechum* was born clutching prairie dust" (Scofield, *Native* 54). Scofield implies that unscrupulous land dealers, Métis and White alike, participated in the children's and future generations' dispossession. Thus, in his articulation of the Métis nation and its history, Scofield paints a complex picture of resistance and complicity. His fierce identification with the Métis people as *Katipâmsôchik* does not lead him to forget the Métis history of displacement and its relationship to a larger Aboriginal history of uprooting. In the last stanza of the poem "Policy of the Dispossessed," Scofield writes:

> *In that part of the country*
> *we were always Katipâmsôchik—*
> *and our displaced history*
> *is as solid as every railroad tie*
> *pounded into place, linking*
> *each stolen province. (Native 55)*

The oxymoron of a "displaced history / ... as solid as every railroad tie" rebuffs a narrative of nation based on manufactured origins while simultaneously evoking Canada's history of colonial-national expansion through the use of the railway. Scofield, in linking this history of displacement to "each stolen province," is imagining a(nother) confederacy that might create affiliations between Native nations and mixed-race Aboriginal communities across Canada.

In *I Knew Two Métis Women*, Scofield further explores the possibilities of a Métis-Cree confederacy through his matrilineal ancestry. Like *Thunder in My Veins*, *I Knew Two Métis Women* is a searing exploration of homelessness and displacement in which the speaker describes constantly moving from one apartment or shack to another during his childhood. These painful memories of forced diaspora are held in tension with his remembrance of homes created by Dorothy Scofield, his mother, and Aunty Georgina, a Métis woman who adopts Scofield when he is about seven years old in Maple Ridge, British Columbia.[17] In the poem "True North, Blue Compass Heart," the Cree territory of Wabasca in northern Alberta operates as an imagined homeland to which the diasporic subject longs to return, if only through story and memory. Aunty Georgina grew up in and around Wabasca before she was sent to St. Martin's Convent School, a Catholic residential school (*I Knew* 140):

> Twenty-eight years, drenched to the bone
> she talked about Wabasca,
> the old days, mud-caked roads
> and muskeg forever
>
> a blue compass heart
> pointing north, lost
> like moose tracks
> in the snow (105)

"Home" in *I Knew Two Métis Women* is always "home on the range" (55), associated with travel, roads, and the impermanence of borders, "lost / like moose tracks / in the snow" (105). Though Wabasca, as part of the Cree nation, has a specific location, it is not static; it is associated with the movement that informs the storytelling exchange between the young Scofield and Aunty Georgina: "the Wabasca, the people, / the wild roses of her childhood, / became stories / that skipped across the kitchen table" (106). And Wabasca is not incompatible with Métis identity. It is Aunty Georgina who teaches Scofield his first Cree words, and it is also she who tells him he is "*Awp-pee-tow-koosan*, like me ... a half-breed" (*Thunder* 41–42). Much of Scofield's work is concerned with stitching together the severed histories of the half-breed and Cree people.

Just as nation is represented as an active process of nation-building within and between communities, home in this text is a process of home-*making* that continually unfolds, even on moving days. Scofield's mother and Aunty Georgina make homes wherever they go by putting up "handmade curtains / trimmed with lace" (*I Knew* 11) and "spreading scatter-rags" (64). The text is full of images of sewing, braiding, patching, quilting, and mending, emphasizing the skills of Métissage of these two women who ceaselessly reinvent home. While Dorothy sews "old slacks, sweaters / and blouses / that no longer fit, that hemmed / and altered became like new" (12), Aunty Georgina would "fluff the pillows, / spread and tuck / her homemade quilts / under my chin, / count the patches in Cree" (28). In all of his work, Scofield emphasizes the rich possibilities of cultural exchange and borrowings. He moves fluidly between

Cree and Road Allowance English to create a re-territorialized Métis poetics that both acknowledges and defies his childhood experiences of homelessness and his family's denial of Aboriginal heritage. Code-switching, wordplay, and partial and asymmetric translations are hallmarks of his poetry.[18] Through techniques of Métissage, his work provides an opportunity to forge a diasporic-Indigenous-sovereigntist critical framework. Cynthia Chambers, Dwayne Donald, and Erica Hasebe-Ludt, from the Faculty of Education at the University of Lethbridge, write that Métissage "is a site for writing and surviving in the interval between different cultures and languages; a way of merging and blurring genres, texts and identities; an active literary stance, political strategy and pedagogical praxis" (par. 1). Métissage, which derives from the French word "Métis," "a person of mixed ancestry,"[19] is associated with mixed-race identity, and it operates as a strategy of reappropriation that spins settled assumptions about cultural difference to different political effect. Métissage is also associated with auto-ethnographic and autobiographical writing, which drives much of Scofield's work. Finally, it functions as a means of reconnecting severed histories, such as those of the Cree and Métis peoples.

As is clear from the examples above, nationhood in *I Knew Two Métis Women* is strongly associated with Scofield's matrilineal heritage (by birth and by adoption) and, as such, is gendered in the feminine. This counters the masculinist bias that often haunts dominant settler nationalisms (and indeed some American Indian nationalisms).[20] However, Scofield is less concerned with correcting ideas about Indigenous nationhood than he is about redressing the incompleteness of the history of the Métis people, in which records of Scottish, Irish, English, and French fathers are relatively detailed, yet all information about their Cree "country wives," even their names, are missing. In *Singing Home the Bones*, Scofield names his foremothers and his forefathers, tracing his ancestry five generations back to the 1860s and the Red River settlement, where his maternal great-great-grandmother Mary Mathilde Henderson lived (102), as well as to Kinesota, Manitoba, where his great-grandparents and grandfather lived (104). Upon finding fairly detailed records of his great-great-grandfather James Peter Whitford, while his great-great-grandmother is described as "Wife: Sarah, an Indian woman" in the Hudson's Bay Company archives, Scofield responds: "I am certain my châpan [ancestor] Sarah, my kayâs ochi nikâwî [my mother of long ago] ... came to my ancestor/grandfather carrying a name too sacred for him to pronounce" (106). The first part of the collection, "Conversations with the Dead," is dedicated to this project of naming his Cree foremothers, and "repatriating [their] bones" (105) in an act of Métis nation-building. Through this matrilineal heritage, then, Scofield crafts his sense of Métis nationhood, and through his father's lineage he confronts the multiple absences of colliding diasporic histories. It is through their combination that a reader glimpses the possibilities of developing a diasporic-Indigenous-sovereigntist perspective.

Scofield's father represents an absence that continually haunts Scofield, and in the second series of poems, "Conversations with the Missing," Scofield addresses his perpetual sense of loss for not knowing, for most of his life, who his father was. Some time before 2005, Scofield discovered that his father, Ron Miller, who had vanished when Scofield was six months old and who died in 1998, was Jewish (Scudeler, "The Song" 141). In the poem "If," Scofield speaks a one-sided conversation with a father he never met. Syntactically associated with the conditional and the negative, as well as with the poet's own complicated self-projections, the father is a wavering after-image: "If / I am a Jew [...] / I could cover the mirrors, ghost / your reflection / I've never seen" (*Singing* 42). Here Scofield is evoking traditions of Jewish mourning by covering the mirrors and honouring his paternal ancestry. Yet his uncertain feelings about what his biological inheritance means, as June Scudeler argues, lead Scofield to observe other Jewish cultural traditions in "unconventional and personal" ways (Scudeler, "The Song" 141). After all, Scofield remarks in another poem, his "father's throwaway chromosomes" have never amounted to fatherhood (*Singing* 92).

But it is when Scofield connects an Aboriginal history of displacement, homelessness, migration, and forced relocation to a Jewish history of diaspora and genocide that his work demands special critical flexibility. This controversial yet important act of relational history-writing moves within and between the fraught discourses of indigeneity and diaspora. The poem "If" opens with an epigraph from Miklós Radnóti, a Jewish Hungarian poet who was shot, along with twenty-one others, by SS guards and buried in a mass grave in 1944 (Scofield, *Singing* 108). In citing a poem that was discovered along with Radnóti's identification card in the mass grave, Scofield is clearly suggesting that his own repeated question, "If / I am a Jew," is implicated in the history of the Jewish Holocaust:

If

I am marked by the Star of David,
if I am to carry
the terrible weight of the dead,
the dead, Papa
who were forced into shower rooms
naked and gasping
the thin air of life. (43)

Taken in the context of the first series of poems "Conversations with the Dead," which deals with the erasure of the Cree and feminine heritage of Métis people in the Hudson's Bay records, the second series, "Conversations with the Missing," creates a parallel between genocidal practices and policies in Nazi Germany and those endured by Aboriginal peoples in North America. In making this parallel, Scofield is implying that the violence, dispossession, and sense of homelessness that have marked his life narrative can be traced to state-organized policies of genocide that forced him, his mother, and other Aboriginal peoples to leave their homes and set up new ones countless times. Lawrence, in making the case that the experiences of mixed-blood Native peoples in Canada have been "shaped by a legacy of genocide" (*"Real"* xvii), quotes from Raphael Lemkin, who defined genocide at the United Nations Genocide Convention in 1944. According to Lemkin, genocide "does not necessarily mean the immediate destruction of a nation"; however, it does "signify a coordinated plan of different actions aimed at destruction of the essential foundations of the life of national groups, with the aim of annihilating the groups themselves" (qtd. in Lawrence, *"Real"* xviii). Once again, Scofield is engaged in a process of becoming an identity, this time Jewish, just as earlier in his life he grew to accept a process of becoming Métis. Indeed, *Singing Home the Bones* documents Scofield's process of becoming both Métis and Jewish, and there is no way to smooth over or downplay the disparate genocidal legacies of both ancestries.

Yet Scofield's point in experimenting with a connection between Aboriginal and Jewish diasporas is not solely to "prove" that genocide has occurred in North America, or to dwell on the pain of Métis diasporas; rather, he is seeking to honour and give a place to the missing. In the series "Conversation with the Missing," Scofield links the unsolved murder of his Aunty Georgina, "all sixty-nine years / of her / lost in the translation / of a policeman's report" (60), with other acts of feminicide and violence against women. In "No Peace," Scofield writes a poem about the murdered and missing women from the border town of Juarez, Mexico, and connects this scene of horror with Vancouver's and Edmonton's missing women, many of whom were (and are) Aboriginal: "But you must know, Señorita / two countries away / my own dark-skinned sisters / turn in a grave of silent rages" (63). The next two poems in the sequence, "The Unread Letter" and "Strange Request," both reference the death of an unnamed woman, addressed in the poem as "you." Read together, the poems in "Conversations with the Missing" suggest a connection between the ideologies that inform genocide in many parts of the world with violence against women, the loss of matrilineal heritage, and the need for a renewed sense of Indigenous nationhood, inscribed in the feminine. By suggesting that the policies directed at Native peoples amount to genocide, Scofield is asserting the reality and persistence of Indigenous nationhood: in other words, the effort to destroy the institutions of a nation asserts that nation's existence. In this way, Scofield's work offers an opportunity for Indigenous sovereigntist critics to take into account the historical crossovers between Indigenous and diasporic histories, and diasporic critics to more meaningfully engage with histories of displacement within and between Indigenous nations.

Singing Home the Bones concludes with a moving series of homoerotic love poems, "Conversations with the Living," in which the speaker expresses some peace and resolution in his search "to finally come / home" (70). In "Prayer for the House," Scofield describes a house that he shared with his lover, where he "learned to feel safe," and where he lived for "the longest [he'd] ever lived in one place" (109). Paradoxically, the poem is about packing up and leaving the house. Throughout this series of poems, Scofield interweaves images of bones and homes. At times, the bones of the missing make up the frame of the house. At other times, it is his partner's six-foot "frame" that undergirds their shared home: "Then there is you, / the ribs of the house / in the house of the life we created, / all six unmoveable feet of you" (78) Scofield also locates belonging in the travelling home of his own bones, both cursing and paying tribute to "the splintered / bones I've moved from house to house / unpacking you, spine" (91). As in all of his work, home and diaspora remain in tension, producing a complex understanding of Métis nationhood. What I find enabling about Scofield's work is how he articulates a hinge between diasporic and Indigenous-sovereigntist viewpoints: he explores the thematics of internal displacement and marginalization within the borders of the Canadian nation-state, he re-territorializes the western Canadian landscape into what might be thought of as Cree/Métis confederacies, and he transforms the historically loaded associations with "half-breed" from a term of abuse into a term of pride, through a poetics and politics of Métissage. By bringing into conversation theories of diaspora with theories of Aboriginal sovereignty, we might address diaspora's deep-seated suspicion of nationalism, settler or Indigenous, as well as the interdependency of diaspora and nation. Likewise, we might create new approaches to Native sovereignties that speak to the experiences of those who, in "repatriating [the] bones" (Scofield, *Singing* 105) of their ancestors, create belonging in more than one place, time, memory, and body.

NOTES

1   My thanks to June Scudeler and to my co-editors, who read earlier drafts of this chapter and made some helpful suggestions. Thanks also to M.A. graduate Cristy Thomson, whose excellent paper on Scofield's poetry helped clarify my own perspective. Finally, my appreciation goes to my undergraduate and graduate students in seminar classes in 2008 and 2009 respectively who led some stimulating conversations.

2   Sociologists and cultural geographers Kathi Wilson and Evelyn Peters, in their study based on interviews with Anishinabek people living both on and off the reserve, argue that the majority of their interviewees maintain strong ties to their nation's territory. Though the researchers initially expected that the urban dwellers would express a different, and perhaps less intense, sense of connection to the land compared to those living on reserves, "[i]n hindsight, this assumption reflected the naiveté of the researchers' understanding of the significance of relationships to the land for Anishinabek, regardless of their place of residence" (402).

3   Nativism overlaps with Romantic nationalism, which, as Margery Fee has argued, forms the basis of the settler national ideal. In Romantic-nationalist discourses, the search for and appropriation of "Ab-original" traditions paradoxically brings about the birth of the "new" nation. See also Glenn Willmott's "Modernism and Aboriginal Modernity: The Appropriation of Products of West Coast Native Heritage as National Goods."

4   For the most part, as Bill Ashcroft, Gareth Griffiths, and Helen Tiffin argue in the "Introduction" to the section entitled "Hybridity" in *The Post-colonial Studies Reader*, "most post-colonial writing has concerned itself with the hybridized nature of culture as a strength rather than a weakness" (137). However, it should be noted that several postcolonial and globalization theorists such as Aijaz Ahmad (1992), Robert Young (2006), Don Kalb (2006), and Timothy Brennan (2006) have expressed concerns about the theoretical and ideological underpinnings of dominant approaches to hybridity.

5   Peter Kulchyski, who writes about Dene communities in the Northwest Territories and Inuit communities in Nunavut, has little patience for critical approaches that "[c]elebrat[e] insurgent hybrid forms solely or merely for the fact that they are hybrid" (53), especially if this results in sidelining political projects pertaining to communities rooted in traditional territories and deemed somehow non-hybrid (54).

6   Here the co-authors are specifically critiquing Elvira Pulitano's *Toward a Native American Critical Theory*, which analyzes the work of six American Indian literary theorists

(Paula Gunn Allen, Craig Womack, Robert Warrior, Greg Sarris, Louis Owens, and Gerald Vizenor). According to the co-authors, those whom Pulitano characterizes as in favour of hybridity—Owens, Sarris, and Vizenor—are deemed to be progressive; in contrast, those arguing in favour of tribal sovereignty—Womack, Warrior, and Allen—are represented as retrograde and exclusionary. In *American Indian Literary Nationalism*, Weaver and Womack devote the greater part of their chapters (each of which run over eighty pages) to disputing Pulitano's analysis, indicating the high stakes that animate the discussion. Pulitano's championing of hybridity and her disparagement of Indigenous sovereignty, as well as Weaver's and Womack's passionate refutation of her claims, provide a clear example of the divide I am talking about between "diasporic/postcolonial" and "Indigenous/sovereigntist" positions in Native American literary criticism.

7   While Bill C-31, passed into law by the government of Canada in 1985, corrected the gender bias in the *Indian Act* (which stipulated that Native women who married non-Native men could not pass down their status to their children), it perpetuates the very problem it sought to rectify because, after three generations, those Native peoples who were reinstated as "Bill C-31 Indians" will no longer be able to pass on their status to their children.

8   Recent articles published by *Tar Sands Watch: Polaris Institute's Energy Program* have reviewed some of the claims made in western Canada by First Nations, who have argued that traditional lands are being destroyed for tar sands exploration and extraction, and that they are not being properly consulted or compensated for their damaged lands and water supplies. According to one editorial, the various legal and political challenges from First Nations in the region threaten "the very basis of Alberta's oilsands industry." See the many articles listed under "Aboriginal Rights" at the Tar Sands Watch website for more.

9   Brooks writes: "I'll admit that talk of nationalism makes me wary. For me, like many, it calls to mind the setting of boundaries, both physical and cultural, and defending those boundaries with force" ("Afterword" 244). Cherokee scholar Daniel Heath Justice also argues that "Indigenous nationhood should not ... be conflated with the nationalism that has given birth to industrialized nation-states" ("Go'" 151). He continues that whereas "[n]ation-state nationalism is often dependent upon the erasure of kinship bonds in favor of a code of assimilative patriotism," Indigenous nationhood is "an understanding of a common social interdependence within the community, the tribal web of kinship rights and responsibilities that link the People, the land, and the cosmos together" (151). Justice's emphasis on relationality and kinship ties is also evident in Womack's understanding of Indigenous nationhood: "Since sovereignty, by definition, has to do with government-to-government relations, it has everything to do with intersections and exchanges between inside and outside worlds" ("The Integrity" 111).

10   According to Brooks, in the Abenaki language, the word for nation is *Mizi Negewet kamigwezoi*, which she translates as "families gathered together" ("Afterword" 229). In this model, "the activity of nation-building ... is not a means of boundary-making but rather a process of gathering from within" (229). "Families gathered together" is not a noun, but a process that requires active participation. And family gatherings, which can be full of strife, require nuanced negotiations of divisions and alliances.

11   Warrior offers an insightful discussion of the work of three well-known Aboriginal
     critics: Taiaiake Alfred, Mohawk theorist of Native governance, Laura Tohe, Diné
     researcher of Diné matriarchal traditions, and Linda Tuhiwai Smith, Maori historian
     and applied anthropologist. In the work of Alfred and Tohe, Warrior submits, "[t]he
     need for disagreement and dissent ... [is] seemingly subsumed by adherence, participa-
     tion, and belonging" ("Native" 213). Meanwhile, Smith's argument, which supports
     Indigenous scholars researching Indigenous communities to counteract the centuries
     of research by outsiders, can be used to justify abuses of power by institutional review
     boards (IRBs), which may attempt to determine the results of research on reserves
     (214–15).

12   Justice cites the well-known and at times bitter debate between Crow Creek Sioux
     scholar Elizabeth Cook-Lyn, who champions critical perspectives dedicated to sover-
     eignty and tribal land rights, and mixed-blood Choctaw Cherokee writer Louis Owens,
     who focuses on mixed-bloodedness and American Indian stories of migration and dis-
     placement. Justice validates both their perspectives, but also suggests that they both
     assert too sharp an opposition between tribalist and diasporist points of view in Native
     North American contexts ("'Go'" 161–65).

13   In his contribution to the roundtable discussion, "Canadian Indian Literary National-
     ism?: Examining Literary Nationalist Approaches in Canadian Indigenous Contexts,"
     Justice referred to a vote in March 2007 by the Cherokee nation to revoke the tribal
     citizenship of an estimated 2,800 African American Cherokee members whose treaty
     rights were secured in the mid-nineteenth century.

14   My thanks to June Scudeler, who pointed out this connection between the two Cree
     words (personal communication).

15   Scudeler, a Métis Ph.D. candidate who formerly worked for the United Native Nations
     (UNN) and is on the board of the Vancouver Métis Community Association (VMCA),
     has supplied some examples of the tensions between Métis communities, suggesting
     that Métis Nation British Columbia (MNBC)'s "use of the historic homeland is causing
     many problems in the community." For example, MNBC is pressuring Métis Family
     Services (MFS) to follow the Métis National Council's definition of the Métis nation.
     However, "MFS has a Protocol Agreement with [VMCA] to protect Métis children
     who don't follow MNBC's definition and may not receive Métis services under their
     definition" (Scudeler, personal communication).

16   Driskill relates his discussion of sovereignty and mixed-blood identity to sexuality, argu-
     ing that Scofield's work "demands that Two-Spiritedness, the erotic, and mixedblood
     identity be seen as sovereign" (222). In this he is following the lead of Scofield, who
     asserts that as much as his writing has focused on discovering his Métis heritage, "the
     issues and struggles of gay Native people ... were just as important and relevant to my
     poetry" (*Thunder* 192).

17   In adopting Gregory, Aunty Georgina as mother did not supplant Dorothy as mother.
     In "Conversation with the Poet" in *Singing Home the Bones*, Scofield describes how he
     "came to be her [Aunty Georgina's] son," adding that "[m]y own mother ... did not mind
     this arrangement, for it was good for me to have two mothers" (57).

18   For a more thorough discussion of Scofield's strategies of code-switching, wordplay, and
     variations in translation, see Andrews and Stigter.

19 According to *Le petit Robert*, the word "Métis" first appeared in the early 1600s and "Métissage" in 1834.

20 In contrast to the American context, strong feminist perspectives have shaped Aboriginal literary nationalism in Canada. Campbell (1973), Maracle (1996), Armstrong (1998), and Acoose (2001) are just some of the critics who skilfully interweave Indigenous-nationalist and feminist analyses. It should be noted that Womack, Warrior, and Justice are aware of the potential for a masculinist bias in American Indian nationalism, and offer a range of feminist antidotes.

Canadian Indian Literary Nationalism?
Critical Approaches in Canadian Indigenous Contexts—
A Collaborative Interlogue

Kristina Fagan, Daniel Heath Justice, Keavy Martin, Sam McKegney,
Deanna Reder, and Niigaanwewidam James Sinclair

OPENING THOUGHTS: CANADIAN INDIAN LITERARY
NATIONALISM—A CRITICISM OF OUR OWN?
Niigaanwewidam James Sinclair (Anishinaabe)

AMERICAN INDIAN LITERARY NATIONALISM—what we will refer to in this
chapter as Indigenous Literary Nationalism—is an intellectual movement
that marks a range of committed critical responses to the calls throughout the
1980s and early 1990s for Indigenous-centred literary scholarship.[1] Because
mainstream critical approaches—including those indebted to formalism and
post-structuralism—proved somewhat incapable of relating to grassroots Indigenous struggles or of engaging adequately with particular tenets present in
Native literatures (such as elements of tribal community histories, politics,
and subjectivities), calls were made by both Native and non-Native literary
critics to consider the specific contexts and aesthetics of Native literary production. This resulted in an explosive critical movement advocating specific
spheres of Indigenous literary study in English and Native studies departments,
as well as innovative definitions of Native literary criticisms. Indigenous Literary Nationalism is one such theoretical response.

Indigenous Literary Nationalism is one of the most dynamic, controversial, and broadly defined critical approaches emerging today. Simply put, this
movement is interested in illuminating the intellectual histories, experiences,
and knowledge structures available in Native (tribal/pan-tribal) nations' creative and critical expressions, and embedding these in the history and politics
of those nations' community existences. Literary Nationalism examines stories, poetry, songs, non-fiction works, and autobiographies as processes deeply

invested in the continuance of a people; it seeks to identify a political (and at times polemical) subjectivity at the centre of Native literary endeavours, while at the same time celebrating the interconnectedness of Native peoples with other cultures through treaties, nation-to-nation sovereignty struggles, models of cultural adaptation, and linguistic exchanges. It is also deeply invested in articulating histories, aesthetics, and expressions in political and historical moments while placing Native voices at the core of critical thought in relation to Native literatures (with their accompanying complex knowledges and experiences privileged). Following Robert Warrior's 1995 call in *Tribal Secrets: Recovering American Indian Intellectual Traditions*, this privileging ensures that Native peoples are treated not only as storytellers and creative thinkers but as intellectuals with abilities to articulate and devise dynamic, complex, and sustaining philosophies, theories, and approaches to their own lives, literatures, and laws (xviii–xix).

As many literary nationalist critics have argued, Indigenous nationalisms tend not to be predicated on the historical "nation-state" model, which depends upon unifying patriotisms, coercive policing of perceived deviance, and hegemonic allegiance to the structures of the state at the expense of kinship and other loyalties. As Daniel Heath Justice indicates in his 2006 book *Our Fire Survives the Storm: A Cherokee Literary History*,

> Indigenous nationhood is a concept rooted in community values, histories, and traditions that ... asserts a sense of active sociopolitical agency, not simply static separatism from the world and its peoples....
>
> Indigenous nationhood is more than simple political independence or the exercise of distinctive cultural identity; it is also an understanding of a common social interdependence within the community, the tribal web of kinship rights *and* responsibilities that link the People, the land, and the cosmos together in an ongoing and dynamic system of mutually affecting relationships. (24)

For the most part, however, Indigenous literary nationalist critics have remained focused on Indigenous struggles in the United States, with American Indian critics becoming the movement's dominant voices and Native experiences and histories south of the 49th parallel being cited most regularly.[2] This is most easily evidenced in one of the movement's seminal texts, co-written in 2005 by Jace Weaver, Craig Womack, and Warrior, and aptly entitled *American Indian Literary Nationalism* (hereafter *AILN*). In this book, while broadly conceived notions of Indigenous global sovereignty and intellectualism are used, clearly identifiable Indigenous struggles in the United States become linchpins for discussion.[3]

Such US-centrism, however, has not stopped many scholars from utilizing literary nationalist tools to interpret Indigenous creative and critical endeavours in Canadian contexts. Native critics in Canada like Emma LaRocque, Thomas King, Basil Johnston, Lee Maracle, Maria Campbell, Armand Garnet Ruffo, and Jeannette Armstrong have all made what might now be considered literary nationalist arguments in the past and can be viewed as contributing to the intellectual climate in which this movement has developed. Today, several scholars working at Canadian universities reference American Indian literary nationalist critics in their own work to make persuasive interpretations of Indigenous literatures in Canada.[4] Some also critique the movement's potential pitfalls or weaknesses, including two critics in this interlogue.[5] This all leads to several interesting and crucial questions regarding locality, inheritance, transportability, transnational-tribalism, language, colonialism, continental Indigenous resistance, and possible areas of development. These, and more, are what this chapter seeks to engage.

RENAMING A DOUBLE-EDGED NATIONALISM
Keavy Martin (Treaty 6 settler)

Indigenous Literary Nationalism is in many ways a project of renaming. Instead of myths and oral traditions, instead of the early writing of letters, diaries, and treaties, instead of crafts or material culture like beadwork, sewing, carving, and map-making, and instead of a Native American literary renaissance, we may now speak more gracefully of Indigenous intellectual traditions. It is not that the old names were necessarily bad; rather, like any names, they represent an inheritance and carry a set of connotations, and these had been both troubling in their paternalism and limiting in the perspectives that they convey. Womack writes in *Red on Red* that Literary Nationalism "attempts to find Native literature's place in Indian country, rather than Native literature's place in the canon" (11); however, an important (and not unrelated) side effect of this task is that it rephrases Indigenous traditions in terms that the academy can recognize and engage with. Myths are easy for the university to sideline, but *intellectual traditions* it must contend with.

Nationalism is another term known to the Western tradition, but as a label it is somewhat less benign than intellectual traditions. As Sinclair notes above, Indigenous scholars have been careful to differentiate between the nationalism of Indigenous peoples and the nationalism of nation-states; Justice stresses "the ability of Indigenous nationalism to extend recognition to other sovereignties without that recognition implying a necessary need to consume, displace, or become absorbed by those nations" (*Our Fire* 24). Yet although it has been resignified, the term "nationalism" cannot escape troubling connections to the excesses of nation-states. Like Womack's initial term for his methodology—*Literary Separatism*—the signification of Literary Nationalism hovers within reach of militarism or at least of militancy. Indeed, these connotations are an important part of the term's usefulness in Indigenous literary criticism: nationalist literatures or literary theories are by implication autonomous and worthy of recognition—even if that recognition is tinged with wariness. As Warrior writes of one of his intellectual forebears: "[Edward] Said understood nationalism as something problematic, but also something necessary to the mobilization of groups of people toward political goals" (*AILN* 180).

The term "nationalism," then, is a double-edged sword. On one hand, it fulfills a strategic purpose—it draws attention sharply back to the political origins and impacts of Indigenous texts. On the other hand, it forces critics to grapple with a set of lingering and troublesome connotations. Ernest Renan, in his seminal 1882 address "What Is a Nation?" stated that "[f]orgetting … is a crucial factor in the creation of a nation…. [T]he essence of a nation is that all individuals have many things in common, and also that they have forgotten many things" (11). And although Indigenous nations should not be confused with nation-states, the dangers of nation-state nationalism (such as the creation of totalizing narratives or the suppression of internal diversity) can act as a caution for Indigenous Literary Nationalism, a warning that rings every time the methodology is named.

The study of Inuit literature, though somewhat peripheral to both Canadian and North American Indigenous criticisms, embodies many of the challenges facing Indigenous Literary Nationalism today. Inuit political and cultural history is distinct from other Indigenous histories in Canada and the United States—the Arctic homeland, for instance, never attracted large numbers of European settlers, and the *Indian Act* does not apply to Inuit. For these and other reasons, Inuit literature has remained somewhat underrepresented in Indigenous literary studies. In a 2004 *Windspeaker* article, Inuk leader Zebedee Nungak writes about the challenges Inuit writers face in distributing their work. "With nobody actively seeking such material," he says, "any number of journals, diaries, and manuscripts gather dust in many an obscure shelf" (26). While literary nationalist approaches would certainly help to rectify this omission and would honour the uniqueness of Inuit history and politics, they also seem to require the pre-existence of an Inuit nation and an Inuit literary tradition, notions that are problematic in their singularity. After all, the Inuit homeland reaches from Greenland across the Canadian Arctic to Alaska and Siberia, and its many regions are naturally distinct in their language, culture, history, and politics. While organizations like the Inuit Circumpolar Council and the Inuit Tapiriit Kanatami strategically emphasize Inuit unity, scholars and elders often comment on the inappropriateness of overarching theories (of the style of the generalized knowledge so beloved by the Western academy).[6] As Iqaluit elder Lucassie Nutaraaluk said when asked by a group of Inuit students to tell the story of Sedna, "I'll tell you the story as I heard it. I think our stories vary from community to community even though they are the same *unikkaqtuat* [classic stories]. I want you to know there are variations" (qtd. in Laugrand, Oosten, and Rasing 188).

Indigenous literary nationalists, including collaborators in this chapter, are now grappling with ways to honour the diversity within their nations and literatures while still contending with intellectual and political systems that seem to equate viability with ideological unity (or homogeneity). As Justice writes, "no community is monolithic and without dissent or even conflicting ideas about what exactly constitutes the group" (Womack et al. 153). In order to resist the more troublesome connotations of its powerful name, then, Indigenous Literary Nationalism must entertain and even value this dissent; it must celebrate the slippages—the texts and histories that are unruly, that do not fit, or that cause discomfort and healthy disagreement.[7] Literary Nationalism values historicization; like literary history, it maintains an interest in origins and intellectual heritage. The term "nationalism" may conjure an energy that is useful to Indigenous literatures, critics, and communities, but this zeal—as history demonstrates—can obscure as much as it inspires. Indigenous Literary Nationalism may benefit, then, from chasing its tail, or becoming its own text—from acknowledging the historical and political complexities of its own terminology.

THE RAGGED EDGES OF LITERARY NATIONHOOD
Daniel Heath Justice (Cherokee Nation)

As a graduate student at the University of Nebraska–Lincoln beginning to seriously engage nation-specific understandings of Indigenous literatures, it never occurred to me to consider myself a "nationalist"; while certainly a proud citizen of the Cherokee Nation, my graduate education had familiarized me with a rich archive of scholarship that was sharply critical of national-ism—indeed, of any essentialist ideological structure—along with its legacies. Though never entirely comfortable with some of the amorphous, middle-class White assumptions of so much that was lumped together without much dis-tinction as "theory," I'd certainly encountered enough work by such varied, big-name theorists as Anderson, Pratt, Butler, Foucault, and Derrida to be equally uncomfortable with claims of collective identity that too often ignored the coercion and exclusion by which such claims were enabled.

It was under the tutelage of one particular mentor, Malea Powell, an East-ern Miami-Shawnee rhetorician and literary critic, that I encountered Vize-nor, Bhabha, Spivak, Fanon, and other theorists who, in varying ways, articu-lated both the intellectual defensibility and the rich interpretive possibilities of other diverse knowledges. Powell is a strong Native woman, a vigorous defender of Native rights and a brilliant advocate of Indigenous intellectual traditions, a scholar who sees no necessary contradiction between being theo-retically savvy and committed to the study of Native literatures on their own terms. She's equally comfortable grappling with the arguments and ideas of French philosopher Jacques Lacan and Paiute intellectual and activist Sarah Winnemucca Hopkins.

From Powell I was able to understand theory as something more than a weapon used by insecure (and often very privileged) graduate students to avoid taking any real intellectual stand or actually risking an opinion. She shares with other international theorists whose work I've come to admire (among them Warrior, Stuart Hall, Hortense Spillers, and my fine colleagues Linda Hutcheon and J. Edward Chamberlin) a passionate belief that theory, at its best, is expansively affirmative of intellectual and ethical values rather than defensively rejectionist in its advocacy of a single, monolithic, and rigid understanding. For those committed to social justice and the dignified par-ticipation of marginalized peoples and knowledges in the realm of scholarly inquiry, theory is an *opening up* of dialogue that, to some degree, forges and develops important intellectual and interpersonal relationships, and rethinks established and too often myopic creeds without silencing diverse voices, per-spectives, or ways of knowing that dare to speak truth to power.

In Native literary studies I'm now firmly established as a literary national-ist, a designation I share with a diverse range of scholars, both Native and non-Native, in the US, Canada, and elsewhere.[8] Though there's no single def-inition that any of us uses (I much prefer "nationhood" to "nationalism," but the latter terminology is the one that's most widely used, so that's the one we work with, imperfect as it may be), in general Indigenous Literary National-ism involves a firm commitment to understanding Indigenous literary expres-sions in part through their relevant Indigenous intellectual, cultural, political, cosmological, and historical contexts. Yet it's a term that's caused us no end of trouble as commonly held scholarly assumptions about "nationalism" are barriers that take a long time to overcome, even though Literary Nationalism as a theoretical movement offers important and nuanced distinctions from the nation-state nationalism that has given rise to some of the most offensive and brutal political ideologies of the last two centuries (issues that Sinclair, Mar-tin, and others address in their contributions to this conversation).

There is vibrant energy in the field today, and the provocative and some-times contentious debates between theorists of Literary Nationalism and other scholars speak to the health of our scholarly community. Amazing work is being produced by emerging and established theorists, both Native and non-Native, in Canada as well as the US, that asks and often compels us to reconsider our comforting understandings of—to borrow the title of Warrior's recent book on Native non-fiction—both "the people and the word." Indeed, the work being done today by graduate students and younger scholars is as forward-thinking and rigorous as anything done to date, and this gives me much hope for the future of our field.

Yet, while we have much to celebrate, there are also challenges to the future health and development of both the critical lens of Literary Nation-alism and the field of Indigenous literary criticism, in general, that demand intervention—the "ragged edges" to which I refer in my title. If, as suggested above, the best theory is that which creates a more expansive, inclusive, and engaging critical discourse, we must be vigorously attentive to both inadver-tent and intentional exclusions that diminish our interpretive perspective. Among these are three that seem to me most pressing:

1 There is a dominance of male perspectives in Literary Nationalism. Although we're seeing an important shift in this area, the most cited voices in Literary Nationalism are men, and this should cause us all to reflect on both the reasons for and the consequences of male critical overrepresen-tation. Indeed, there may well be some uncomfortable soul-searching if these anecdotal observations of sexual bias are (as I suspect would be the case) borne out by more detailed analysis.

2 There is a lack of attention to or substantive engagement with the nation-hood and peoplehood specificities of urban, pan-Native, or multi-tribal literary traditions and writers.

3 There are the dangers of literary nationalists failing to challenge dehu-manizing community politics in the misguided cause of an intellectually and morally vacuous version of "sovereignty."

·I don't have room here to address all three important issues—and my col-leagues do some of this work in their contributions here—so I'll focus on the last one, which has been particularly in my thoughts and recent work, as it emerges from some of the nasty politics taking place in the Cherokee Nation right now, where the same-sex marriage ban and the disenfranchisement of the Cherokee Freedmen have brought the issue of tribal sovereignty into a new and not particularly flattering light.

To be both viable and ethical, sovereignty can't be just about our *rights* as Indigenous peoples and nations. It must also be about our *responsibilities*: to one another, to the Earth, and the web of kinship that binds us to the human and other-than-human world; to the ancestors and the spirits; to rational thought that is tempered with respect and an appreciation for mystery and the unknow-able; to the cause of truth and the purpose of balance and growth; to ourselves and our intellectual, spiritual, and moral integrity. As such, it's incumbent upon literary nationalists to bring not only the political and aesthetic to the conversation but also the historical and the ethical because the concept of sov-ereignty cannot be treated as the end point of analysis or even as the final goal of necessary political action. After all, every tyrannical government, dictator-ship, or despotism exercises its brutality as part of its "sovereignty." So what do we mean by the term, and what is the role of the literary critic in articulating a *sustainable* Indigenous sovereignty of mind, spirit, body, and community, one that attends to the historical relationships of integrity, accountability, and kin-ship that are at the beating heart of the communitist ethos?

Whether in Canada, the US, or elsewhere, literary nationalists need to become, to some degree, intellectual activists for the very *best* Native intel-lectual traditions, not simply for those traditions for their own sake. While community knowledge is invaluable to our understanding of Native liter-ary production, it's important to remember that, along with those traditions that bring healing and connection, bad medicine and witchery are very much traditional knowledges in Indigenous communities. Yet we'd be fool-ish to argue for the corrosive latter traditions to be the critical foundations of community-specific analysis. "Tradition" alone neither can nor should be the sole measure of our work's articulation of Native communitism, any more than an unfettered, free-for-all idea of sovereignty can or should be the end goal of our nations' continuity and self-determination. Responsibilities *must* be paired with rights; without that connection, we have either tyranny or chaos, but not true community.

As an intensely self- and community-reflective theoretical approach to the expressive arts of the People, the best Literary Nationalism is not only embedded in the intellectual, political, historical, and cultural matrix of localized communities and contexts, but it directly engages principles of accountable kinship within that constitutive matrix. In doing so, it demands of its practitioners the responsibility of challenging—respectfully, but unequivocally—the material and imaginative failures (both those imposed by colonialism without and para-colonialism within) that keep the People from participating in communitist relationships and responsibilities in a healthy way. By attending to the specificities of history, expression, and political action, maybe even spirituality, the literary nationalist is to some degree obligated to "speak truth to power" with health and wholeness as the end purpose of that action, even when it's controversial or difficult to do so. To be committed to a sustainable political and intellectual Indigenous sovereignty is necessarily to be committed to the responsible exercise of that sovereignty and its full integrity. With care and attention, and no small degree of humility, the best Literary Nationalism seems well placed to do this in a good way.

COMMITTING TO INDIGENOUS COMMUNITES WHILE KEEPING THE "LITERARY" IN LITERARY NATIONALISM
Sam McKegney (Canadian settler scholar of Irish/German descent)

Near the beginning of his contribution to *American Indian Literary Nationalism*, Weaver invokes a lengthy passage from Blaeser's "Native Literature: Seeking a Critical Center" to outline some of the movement's political goals and ethical commitments, quoting approvingly Blaeser's assertion that she has been "'particularly ... alert for critical methods and voices that seem to arise out of the literature itself (this as opposed to critical approaches applied from already established critical language or attempts to make the literature fit already established genres and categories of meaning)'" (qtd. in Weaver et al. 3). Literary Nationalism at its best—in imaginative, sophisticated, anti-hegemonic, and self-reflexive iterations like those envisioned by each of my

collaborators—responds enthusiastically to Blaeser's call by employing critical strategies that emerge from Indigenous communities while resisting the
uncritical application of externally constructed Western theoretical tools
(like those identified by Sinclair, Martin, and Justice above) to Indigenous
literary studies.

In the spirit of this chapter's collective investment in the development
of what Justice terms "the best Literary Nationalism" and what Fagan calls
"a truly inclusive and expanding form of Indigenous Literary Nationalism," I
wish to analyze in my brief remarks the potential for the movement's political goals to overshadow and de-emphasize literary analysis such that the din
caused by its inspired critical machinery might actually obscure what Blaeser calls "voices" within "the literature." As Literary Nationalism develops
its "critical language" and "categories of meaning" (even if that language and
those categories are non-prescriptive and evolving), its application to particular iterations of Indigenous literary production might reflect less and less
an active response to critical cues present in the texts themselves. Just like
postmodernism or any other -ism, Literary Nationalism can be imposed on
a piece of literature in a manner that forwards the critic's agenda—however
ethically laudable, politically generative, or socially empowering that agenda
might be—while disregarding the creative autonomy of the piece itself. For
"the best Literary Nationalism," I wonder if critics of Indigenous literatures
might need to retain a literary (or storytelling) focus along with our commitments to community; in fact, I want to suggest that true commitment to "the
literature itself" is a commitment to community, nationhood, and sovereignty.

In AILN, Womack observes: "What is, in fact, becoming apparent to me
is that two schools have emerged: those who teach Native literature as NAS
[Native American Studies] practitioners and those who teach Native literature
from English department perspectives" (Weaver et al. 153). Womack cham-
pions, and views Literary Nationalism as emerging from, NAS perspectives in
which the primary commitment of the researcher, critic, or teacher is to the
healthy continuance of Indigenous communities. Unlike English department
perspectives, which conceive of Indigenous literature as a discrete field of
critical inquiry that can be addressed adequately without recourse to its interconnectedness with the lived experiences of Indigenous individuals, communities, and nations, NAS perspectives employ literary analysis in the service
of political goals like decolonization, sovereignty, and self-determination. On
the one hand, the shift to NAS perspectives is crucial to understanding how
Indigenous stories build from, represent, and potentially affect Indigenous

lives. On the other hand, while philosophical commitments to Indigenous intellectual traditions remain essential to ethical criticism of Indigenous literatures,[10] we need to be cautious about *literary* criticism in which literature is valued foremost for its utility. In other words, we risk doing violence to the literature when we *require* it to be a tool for political action. The danger involves approaching literature with predetermined goals and agendas, the urgency of which encourages us to be less responsive to the literature's creative insights, thereby disregarding Indigenous artistic agency. Stories and storytellers seek to move us in unique and unpredictable ways—such is their power—and Indigenous literary criticism needs to maintain an active posture through which it can respond to writers' creative interventions.

Another complicating factor is the potential ambiguity of the term "Indigenous Literary Nationalism," which is designed to reflect commitments and strategies on the part of *critics* of Indigenous literatures, but can also be applied to a *literary* movement. For this reason, literary nationalists risk indicating not just what critics should do in the service of "an ethical Native literary criticism" (Womack et al. 94), like that theorized by the critics in *Reasoning Together*, but also what Indigenous creative writers ought to create. This terminological slippage is evident in Womack's contribution to *AILN*. As one of his "flexible tenets for ... literary nationalism" (Weaver et al. 168), Womack argues that "the compassionate nationalist cannot simply walk away from those things that are killing us in Native communities.... It should be obvious by now that casinos ... are not going to save us; thinking must save us, and this is where critics come in" (170). With this call out, Womack identifies the critic's role in dealing with crises befalling Indigenous communities;[11] however, he goes on to argue in the same paragraph that "a major strategy for the compassionate literary nationalist is commenting on social policy and articulating community strategies for increased health, in *one's art*, while *keeping it artful*. While finding ways to increase his or her commitment to social realism, the compassionate literary nationalist will also strive for *artistic excellence and experimentation*" (170, my emphasis). Using the same term he had applied to critics of Indigenous literatures—"compassionate nationalist"—Womack here seems to describe producers of Indigenous literature; how else to explain the repeated uses of "art" and "artful"? The categories of "artist" and "critic" are, of course, not mutually exclusive, as evidenced by Sinclair's list above of Indigenous critics in Canada, each of whom is also a renowned creative writer.[12] Yet Womack's conflation of categories can be unsettling insofar as it posits a definition—a flexible one, but a definition nonetheless—of what makes Indigenous art valuable: "comment[ary] on social policy," the articulation of "community strategies for increased health," and "commitment to social realism."[13]

Literary nationalists need to encourage the writing and publication of politically relevant texts, while studying, teaching, and reviewing favourably Indigenous texts that align with sovereigntist goals. However, I worry about the inference that Indigenous texts that are themselves literary nationalist are the texts of primary value to Indigenous communities and the idea that critics should suggest to writers what the content of their work ought to be. When I interviewed Taiaiake Alfred in 2007 about the state of Indigenous literature in Canada, he lamented, "Unfortunately, now I find most [writers] disengaged.... They're just not politically committed." "[W]hat's been written lately," he asked, "that's ... alive in terms of the political struggle?" (personal interview). Janice Acoose explains along similar lines: "With great expectations, I fervently search the pages [of Indigenous texts] for reflections of an author's nation of origin, ancestors, language, and expressions of national sovereignty. Often I am saddened to 'discover' natives ... who have ceded not only vast territories of land, but also the territories of imagination and voice" (Womack et al. 221). These are real and urgent concerns. And critics have a role to play in validating texts like those Alfred longs for with identifiable political goals and those Acoose desires with discernible connections to ancestry, culture, and language by teaching and studying them. However, these are by no means the only Indigenous texts we should be teaching and studying in Canada or elsewhere, nor are they the only texts that serve the needs of Indigenous nations.

When asked at a conference what he saw as "the future of Native American literature," Womack reportedly replied, "'More and funkier'" (qtd. in Weaver et al., *AILN* 74). In the same book, Womack argues that literary critics "have a role in facilitating the work of Indian writers who are innovative, subversive, [and] deviant" (93) and states that he is "interested in the kind of work ... that continues to function as a catalyst for new forms of Native literature" (168). I worry that a literary nationalist movement that neglects to "chas[e] its tail," in Martin's terms, could encourage literary conformity that is actually antithetical to the "more and funkier" Womack and others desire (particularly if it devalues works that are not socially realist, for example). This is why I feel that ethical critical work in this field, while building from a solid foundation of the critic's commitment to Indigenous communities and sovereignties, needs to be committed simultaneously to the autonomy of Indigenous literary production and attentive to Indigenous voices as manifest in literary art. Going back to

Womack's earlier distinction, while we may not want to approach Indigenous literatures from English department perspectives, it remains significant that critics of Indigenous literatures remain open to the insights of literary artists; in those insights new pathways will be mapped out, political strategies envisioned, subjectivities validated, and roles and responsibilities reimagined. My own hope for a compassionate Indigenous Literary Nationalism foregrounds ethical commitments to the continuance of Indigenous nations, to historicization, and to communitist activism, but remains guided in various ways by Indigenous artistic creation. Respecting Indigenous voices by truly engaging with the cues to criticism embedded within texts themselves *is*, it seems to me, among the myriad ways of respecting and catalyzing Indigenous sovereignties.

THE STRATEGIC POTENTIAL OF INDIGENOUS LITERARY NATIONALISM
Deanna Reder (Cree/Métis)

I write from the perspective of somebody, who—while a relatively junior scholar—has been in the field, it seems, since its inception. I don't think this is an exaggeration. Throughout the 1980s I started and stopped and restarted my studies, depending on my income, first at the University of Alberta and then at the University of British Columbia, only to be finally successful at Concordia (aided, I might say, by the tuition freeze and Montreal's relatively cheap cost of living at that time). Indigenous literature, as far as I can remember, was never on the curriculum. However, because I had never studied the work of an Indigenous author (other than Pauline Johnson's famous "The Song My Paddle Sings") in all my years of public school education, this absence at university didn't strike me as unusual. It wasn't until the late 1980s, when Anne Cameron's *Daughter of the Copper Woman* (1981) made its way to women's studies syllabi, accompanied by controversy, that I began to recognize the need for change.[14]

Of course, what I understood to be my personal conclusion was in fact a realization being made across the country. With the advent of postcolonial studies, scholars began to ask about the function of the image of, and then of work by, the *indigene*. Others relied on discussions in postmodernism to identify Indigenous challenges to nationalist metanarratives and, influenced by Gerald Vizenor, the role of the trickster. By the 1990s, anthologies were compiled, Native literature courses were developed, and a "first generation" of doctoral students produced dissertations in the field (including such scholars as Sophie McCall and Kristina Fagan; I would call their work *groundbreaking*, except I don't want to employ a term so rife with colonial implications).

The fact that a mere decade later it is now considered legitimate in departments of English literature to use Indigenous frameworks to examine Indigenous literatures suggests a transformational moment in the academy, and to this I credit the influence of Native American Literary Nationalism.[15] This is not to ignore the fact that, as my colleagues have pointed out, these new approaches have tripwires and flaws. All theoretical models act as lenses that help clarify an area of focus, while at the same time obscuring other aspects of a scene, and this movement is no different. But before we jump to point out the blind spots of this approach, I would encourage us to take a long and leisurely look. Indigenous Literary Nationalism offers a way to shift the focus of research away from the effects of colonization to the contributions and potential of Indigenous world views. It also offers a strategic position from which to critique and alter the structure of English studies.

Even at this present date, literature departments across Canada offer courses for almost every century of writing in Britain, while at the same time offering only one or two catch-all Native literature courses that are somehow supposed to cover the entire literary output of all of Native America's disparate nations over time.[16] As a result, most curriculums offer only a cursory glance at a few token texts. But Indigenous Literary Nationalism celebrates the variety of specific national or tribal interpretations of the world, a point that suggests unlimited possibilities. Imagine creating courses that, for example, discuss the differences between Coast Salish and Anishinaabe literary traditions and perspectives. This is not to insist that every author fits perfectly into a national tradition or that epistemes are easily evaluated and adaptable for comparative work. But Richard Atleo's *Tsawalk* (2004), a Nuuchahnult analysis of traditional stories, and Basil Johnston's many volumes on Anishinaabe culture are rich and often untapped sources that can help us understand everything from George Clutesi's early work to Drew Hayden Taylor's recent young-adult vampire novel. Of course, Taylor's *Night Wanderer: A Native Gothic Novel* (2007) begs to be compared to Bram Stoker's *Dracula* (or at least the *Twilight* franchise), and considered, as Eden Robinson's *Monkey Beach* has been, as an example of Canadian Gothic. But just as *Monkey Beach* is situated in a Haisla context and formed out of a Haisla imaginary, *Night Wanderer* can productively be examined as Anishinaabe. Instead of the inevitable discussions of the subversiveness of heteroglossia when the reader comes across a non-English word, scholars can focus on the words—whether they are Haisla,

Anishinaabe, or whatever language encountered—attempting to understand the word in its context. Instead of the now conventional conclusions about agency or intersubjective hybridity, scholars can focus on the literary traditions specific to each nation or develop evaluative techniques and vocabulary to discuss such things as the role of ceremony or challenges to genre.

Furthermore, the relevance to community inherent in literary nationalist critical approaches could attract Native students to the study of literature. As someone who is housed in both a First Nations studies program and a Department of English at Simon Fraser University, it seems to me that a key factor differentiating students of the two programs is ethnicity. While the majority of my students in FNST (otherwise known as NAS) are Native, almost none of the students in my English courses are, which has profound implications for the future of the field. Jo-Ann Episkenew, an English professor and former dean at the First Nations University of Canada, recalls being approached by a Canadian university recruiting for a Tier 1 Canada research chair in Aboriginal literature; they contacted her looking for names of potential candidates who not only had a Ph.D. and an eminent record of scholarship, but were also members of an Indian nation in Canada. She laughed when recounting this story and asked me, as she asked them, "How many Indigenous scholars has your department produced?" The number of Indigenous faculty trained by Canadian universities is one way to evaluate the infrastructure that supports the study of Indigenous literatures in Canada.

While this seems to be a plea for inclusion of Indigenous scholars, it is in fact a call for changes to improve the status quo in our field. Right now, whether I am teaching a second-year course or a graduate course, I always have to allot some time to go over "the basics" for reasons that have nothing to do with the intelligence of my students (they are very bright) but rather speak to their woeful preparation. For example, I can never take for granted that students have ever read a text by a Native author or have even a simple understanding of "status Indian" or the *Indian Act* of Canada. Even the most elementary of literary conversations is hampered by this lack of basic information. In a recent fourth-year class, I planned ambitiously to discuss the influence of Cree literary genres and Cree concepts of family in Gregory Scofield's *Thunder through my Veins*. While introducing the text, I made a simple gesture about influence, citing Maria Campbell's *Halfbreed*, one of the most seminal texts in the Native literary canon and the model on which Scofield's autobiography is based. Before I could proceed with Scofield, however, I discovered that few students knew who Campbell is, and even fewer had even a cursory understanding of Métis history. This made my contextual claim of a historical trajectory of Métis literary output in Canada—positioning Scofield's text as emerging from a generation influenced by Campbell—meaningless to them. Of course, in our teaching we need to go over key points (and I did); at the same time, however, most English professors do not have to explain the significance of Shakespeare or Virginia Woolf to their students and by fourth year can expect some familiarity with the field.

There is great potential in the approaches of Indigenous Literary Nationalism, not only because of its call to rethink Indigenous intellectual history but also because of the emerging generation of critics, both Native and non-Native, engaging in conversations that hopefully will support creative production. Eventually, I predict that the next generation of literary critics will return to pan-Indian approaches in the discussion of literature, not because they wish to return to a monolithic, homogeneous notion of "Indian" but because such approaches hold within them possibilities to theorize aspects of common experience and common aesthetics, especially given the growing presence of urban Native populations with little connection to home communities, languages, or cultures. That being said, my hope is that they will be inspired to study in literature departments, that there will be various course offerings giving them options to consider, that they will be able to study their languages and literature in their languages, that they will have the chance to study with Indigenous professors as well as non-Indigenous experts, that their perspectives will be respected, and that they will be mentored. Also, I hope that the knowledge base about Indigenous literature and Native history in Canada increases, so that the basics that we need to repeat in university become common knowledge routinely taught in public school, thereby creating room and imagination at the university level for deeper analysis.

CONCLUDING THOUGHTS: DOING THEORY AND DOING COMMUNITY
Kristina Fagan (Labrador Métis)

In his contribution to this collaborative essay, Justice writes that, as a graduate student, he considered himself to be a "proud citizen of the Cherokee Nation," though not, at that time, a "nationalist." I want to consider this distinction between the experience of being part of an Indigenous nation and the theoretical position of nationalism. The latter has grown out of the former, and yet they are not the same. The Indigenous Literary Nationalism movement has been largely driven by Indigenous scholars seeking to relate their academic practice to their sense of what it means to be part of an Indigenous community. But what happens when we try to turn the complex experience of community into academic theory and practice? Or, as Womack concisely puts it, "What is the relationship between our theories and the people we are theorizing about?" (Womack et al. 369). I would argue that there is a tension between Indigenous experience and Indigenous Literary Nationalism that, while perhaps inevitable, needs our ongoing attention if we are to create nationalist work that is inclusive and engaged.

Indigenous Literary Nationalism aims to understand Indigenous literature within its Indigenous contexts—that is, to understand how stories work within communities. But as we move to define Indigenous communities in an institutional context, pressures to delineate the borders of the nation and its relevant forms of expression arise. I would like to illustrate these pressures with a brief story from my own experience as an Indigenous nationalist researcher. I am currently working on a project with my own people, the mixed-blood Inuit of Labrador (sometimes called the Inuit Métis). To carry out this work, I applied for an Aboriginal SSHRC, which requires collaboration with an Aboriginal organization. There are two political organizations in Labrador that represent the Inuit Métis: Nunatsiavut, which calls its members Inuit, and the Labrador Métis Nation, which calls its members Métis.[17] My decision to partner with the Labrador Métis Nation has had profound implications for my study. For example, one day I sat down with Max Blake, an Inuit Métis elder, in his kitchen over bowls of caribou-heart soup. As is customary among Labradorians, the conversation began with Blake figuring out who I was and how I fit into the interwoven Labrador families. After some discussion, he declared with satisfaction, "Sure we're related!" and he launched into a story of one of our mutual Inuit ancestors. It is in part through these kinds of stories that the Indigenous peoples of Labrador remember and maintain their relationships with one another. Yet, despite our relatedness, and despite the fact that Blake was one of the founders of the Labrador Métis Association (now Nation) in the 1970s, he is now an official member of Nunatsiavut rather than the Labrador Métis Nation. As a result, he is neither "Labrador Métis" nor part of the group represented by the Labrador Métis Nation. This presents a real dilemma for me as I imagine the scope and purpose of my research project because my experience of Labrador Métis community and the official definition of who is Métis are at odds.

This example is meant to show, in the simplest of terms, the ways in which defining an Indigenous nation is a complicated and contentious task. And I would argue that our understandings of Indigenous nations must be based in Indigenous experiences of community rather than in institutionalized definitions. Yet interpreting the experience of nationhood is no easy task. To belong to a community involves many forms of connection: shared identity, relationships, emotional and physical support, shared work and responsibilities, and rich cultural and linguistic inheritances. Yet it also involves conflict, difficult relationships, pressures, feelings of exclusion, and inheritances that we would often rather do without. Of course, by focusing closely on particular Indigenous communities and moving away from pan-tribal generalizations, Indigenous Literary Nationalism is more likely to see the complex ways communities define and express themselves. It is for this reason that Reder, in her contribution to this chapter, asks us to take a "long and leisurely look" at the advantages of Indigenous Literary Nationalism before poking holes in it. So, for instance, a nationalist approach can potentially reveal the variety of ways in which we can understand Labrador Métis identity as a form of kinship, as an official designation, as a response to historic influences, etc. This is the kind of complexity that Justice is getting at when he says that his study of Cherokee literature explores "varied understandings of what it is to be Cherokee" (*Our Fire* 6).

The potential problems with Indigenous Literary Nationalism arise when it becomes detached from this experience of community. Institutionalization of a particular theoretical approach leads, perhaps inevitably, to efforts to define and stabilize it. And to work with the concept of nationhood means that we must, on some level, define the nation. However, this defining process can, as Tol Foster writes, work to "close off voices that do not obviously seem to be part of the tribal community and to privilege the more conservative voices in that community" (Womack et al. 270). Moreover, funding agencies, ethics boards, Aboriginal organizations, and other institutions can exert stabilizing influences on how Aboriginal communities/nations are defined. Several of the contributors to this chapter discuss the dangers of defining Indigenous nations and nationalism too narrowly. Martin warns, for instance, that when analyzing literature from the massive Inuit homeland, notions of a unified Inuit nation and literary tradition are "problematic in their singularity." Justice calls for a Literary Nationalism that considers the experiences of Indigenous women, urban, pan-tribal, and multi-tribal Indigenous peoples and those excluded or oppressed by Aboriginal community politics. And McKegney worries that

Indigenous Nationalism will exclude or obscure particular texts or aspects of texts that do not fit the nationalist agenda. What these contributors have in common is a concern that nationalism not lose touch with the complexity of Indigenous experience and literature.

Experience of Indigenous community, with all its trouble and richness, can act as a corrective to any overarching theory and to the academic tendency to define and conclude. Some recent and exciting examples of Indigenous Nationalism have pushed toward opening up our ideas about Indigenous community rather than putting boundaries around them. Justice suggests in *Reasoning Together* that we look to the practice of kinship as a way of understanding how Indigenous communities create and maintain themselves. Foster advocates paying greater attention to the relations among communities within a region and "acknowledging dissent within the community in a muscular fashion, as well as pointing out unsavory elements of our home community's practice openly" (Womack et al. 273). I would also suggest that we reflect on our own experiences of Indigenous community and allow those experiences to inform our work. As Womack writes, his views of Muskogee Creek experience are built, not only on research, but on "a lived relationship that is a lifelong process and never an easy one" (Womack et al. 369). In emphasizing experience in this way, I do not exclude non-Indigenous scholars. Experience includes not only the theorist's personal experience (though I believe such personal experience has great value and should be more often acknowledged) but the experiences of others, past and present, near and far. While we cannot completely know the experience of another, it is surely part of our human gifts to seek to know and to try to understand. And we can all look to the literature, where the diversity and complexity of Indigenous community is reflected and explored. As Chamberlin writes, "Culture is *always* threatened by anarchy, as belief is by doubt. That's the essential nature of both conflict and belief.... Conflict is at the heart of the way language works, and therefore the way stories work as well" (25). If we acknowledge the tension between connection and conflict that is inevitably part of the experience of community, then we can move toward a truly inclusive and expanding form of Indigenous Literary Nationalism.

NOTES

Originally published as part of a special issue entitled *What We Do, What We Are: Responsible, Ethical, and Indigenous-Centered Literary Criticisms of Indigenous Literatures*, co-edited by Niigaanwewidam James Sinclair and Renate Eigenbrod, *Canadian Journal of Native Studies* 29.1 and 2 (2009).

1   Some timely examples of this would be Geary Hobson's ethical choice to combine critical and creative Native-authored works in his 1979 anthology *The Remembered Earth: An Anthology of Contemporary Native American Literature*, Paula Gunn Allen's illuminating forays into a pan-tribal, Native-centred "gynocentrism" in Indigenous literary output in *The Sacred Hoop: Recovering the Feminine in American Indian Traditions* (1986), and Kimberly Blaeser's calls for a "tribal-centered criticism" in her 1993 article "Native Literature: Seeking a Critical Center." Other scholars of this time who made similar calls included N. Scott Momaday, A. LaVonne Brown Ruoff, Gerald Vizenor, Simon Ortiz, Arnold Krupat, Elizabeth Cook-Lynn, Emma LaRocque, Lee Maracle, Marie Annharte Baker, and Jeannette Armstrong.

2   Such texts include: Warrior's *Tribal Secrets: Recovering American Indian Intellectual Traditions* (1995), Jace Weaver's *That the People Might Live: Native American Literatures and Native American Community* (1997), Craig S. Womack's *Red on Red: Native American Literary Separatism* (1999), James Cox's *Muting White Noise: Native American and European American Novel Traditions* (2006), Lisa Brooks' *The Common Pot: The Recovery of Native Space in the Northeast* (2008), and Sean Kicummah Teuton's *Red Land, Red Power: Grounding Knowledge in the American Indian Novel* (2008), and the collectively authored *Reasoning Together: The Native Critics Collective* (2008).

3   Such struggles include US Supreme Court decisions and Native American confrontations with the United States government, while models of Indigenous cultural productions by such tribal nations as the Cherokee, Muskogee Creek, Acoma Pueblo, Crow Creek Sioux, and Osage become focal points of the study.

4   See, for example, Sam McKegney's *Magic Weapons: Aboriginal Writers Remaking Community after Residential School* (2007), Kristina Fagan's article "Tewatatha:wi: Aboriginal Nationalism in Taiaiake Alfred's *Peace, Power, Righteousness: An Indigenous Manifesto*" in *American Indian Quarterly* 28.1 and 2 (2004), and the contributions of Cheryl Suzack and Janice Acoose in *Reasoning Together*.

5   See Fagan and McKegney's co-authored article entitled, "Circling the Question of Nationalism in Native Canadian Literature and Its Study" in *Review* 41.1 (May 2008): 31–42.

6   See Nunavut Arctic College's invaluable five-volume *Interviewing Inuit Elders* series. The introduction to the first volume, by Alexina Kublu, Frédéric Laugrand, and Jarich Oosten, contains a very useful discussion of the highly specific and contextualized "nature of Inuit knowledge" (Laugrand and Oosten 8).

7   This includes stories that represent the rich and occasionally less-than-idyllic political lives of Indigenous nations; see, for instance, the Inuit stories of displacing the Tuniit (Dorset) people in the eastern Arctic.

8   An emerging scholar from India, Nilanjana Deb, has done a remarkable nation-specific study on Anishinaabe literatures.

9 Jace Weaver's neologism "communitism" is a term particularly responsive to Native expressive contexts. As he describes in *That the People Might Live: Native American Literatures and Native American Community*, "[communitism] is formed by a combination of the words 'community' and 'activism.' Literature is communitist to the extent that it has a proactive commitment to Native community, including what I term the 'wider community' of Creation itself. In communities that have too often been fractured and rendered dysfunctional by the effects of more than 500 years of colonialism, to promote communitist values means to participate in the healing of the grief and sense of exile felt by Native communities and the pained individuals in them" (xiii).

10 I use the term "philosophical" here in gratitude to the intellectually sophisticated yet clear and accessible discussion of Literary Nationalism on Justice's publicly accessible website, http://www.danielheathjustice.com/scholarship.html, which contains the following definition: "Indigenous literary nationalism is a philosophy that places Indigenous intellectual and cultural values at the center of analysis, rather than the margins."

11 I invoke here the term "call out" from Sean Kicummah Teuton's book *Red Land, Red Power*, which he employs to describe the moment in which "American Indian scholars awaken politically and begin putting their ideas to work" (161).

12 Womack is himself the author of a profoundly nationalist Creek novel, *Drowning in Fire* (2001), and Justice has authored the Indigenous epic fantasy trilogy *The Way of Thorn & Thunder*, which is heavily influenced by Cherokee intellectual traditions and history.

13 I must stress that Womack is careful, here and throughout his critical *oeuvre*, to be neither prescriptive nor limiting, as noted in the emphasis above on "experimentation." The admission in Womack's groundbreaking work *Red on Red* that its critical methodology "is merely a point" on the spectrum of "legitimate approaches to analyzing native literary production" and "not the spectrum itself" (2) resonates with his articulation of "*flexible* tenets for a compassionate American Indian literary nationalism" in *AILN*. Also, it must be noted that between the initial composition of my element of this chapter and the publication of the present collection, Womack has published an important work entitled *Art as Performance, Story as Criticism: Reflections on Native Literary Aesthetics* (2009); in its nuanced attentiveness to the creative and the aesthetic, this work complicates many of the issues discussed above in ways I haven't the space to engage adequately here.

14 It was only once I began my master's that I discovered the work of Penny Petrone whose *First People, First Voices* appeared as early as 1983. Still, my English professor at the time, a Canadianist, was also unfamiliar with this text.

15 This is not to contradict Sinclair's chronology of the influence of Indigenous literary nationalism as early as the 1970s; while he traces the continuance of such nationalist ideas by Indigenous intellectuals, I am commenting on the uptake in the canon and in the classroom, particularly by (almost unilaterally) non-Indigenous academics in Canada.

16 I attribute this point to Jennifer G. Kelly, who made it to me in conversation.

17 This division of the Inuit of Labrador is a result of a series of political decisions that have left a single, culturally unified and related community sorted into different categories, a process that is beyond the scope of this article to explain. In some cases, one sibling is Inuit while another is Métis, depending on their place of birth.

Breaking the Framework of Representational Violence
Testimonial Publics, Memorial Arts, and a Critique of Postcolonial Violence (the Pickton Trial)

Julia Emberley

IT'S ALL ABOUT WHITE MEN

IN DECEMBER 2007, CANADIAN NEWSPAPERS were full of the Pickton trial. Robert William Pickton, arrested in February 2002, was found guilty of six counts of second-degree murder. He is a white man often referred to derisively in the media as the "greasy-haired pig farmer" because his victims, all women, were murdered on his pig farm. The women he "killed and dismembered" occupied, at one time or another, Vancouver's Downtown Eastside, a poverty-stricken area known for its "drugs and prostitution" (Mickleburgh A16). Thus, newspapers such as *The Globe and Mail* and *The Vancouver Sun* indiscriminately refer to the murdered women as "drug-addicted prostitutes" (Matas A1). The name and the location are irrevocably tied together in media representation of these women, who were also, in some cases, Indigenous, poor, mothers, sisters, and daughters.

The news coverage of the Pickton trial brought to national attention the violence Indigenous women face in Canada. Major newspapers such as *The Globe and Mail* and *The Vancouver Sun* supplemented the coverage of this event with Internet websites.[1] From these websites emerge a series of testimonial practices that I will discuss in this chapter. One site includes a photographic slide show of the evidence found on Pickton's farm in Port Coquitlam, British Columbia, and used in the trial (see *The Globe and Mail*'s "Slideshow: The Trouble with DNA"). Another space of testimonial significance includes "victim-impact statements" made by family members of the murdered women, transcribed and published on the news media websites for *The Globe and Mail* and *The Vancouver Sun*. The third site can be found in a small unassuming garden created close to the courthouse by and for Indigenous women. This space was mentioned in various news articles, but was neither photographed nor its precise location revealed. Journalists were asked to respect this space for use by the Indigenous women who were attending the trial. It was understood that the garden provided a space of healing from the trauma of the trial itself. A fourth testimonial site consists of two letters written by Pickton in prison and sent to a pen pal that reveal his identification with the Christian figure of Jesus.

I have located these testimonial sites in order to analyze the ways in which they disclose the violence directed specifically toward Indigenous women, but I am also interested in how testimonial practices might contribute to a fundamental transformation in how Indigenous women's bodies are viewed as objects of violence. How, in other words, can testimonial practices *decolonize* the perception that sexual difference, aboriginality, and violence are so inexplicitly intertwined that their interconnections appear inevitable and unchangeable? To answer this question it is necessary, I argue, to trace the circulation of cultural economies of affect in testimonial practices; to attend, for example, to how feelings of racial hatred, love, benevolence, and empathy emerge in these testimonial sites. The production of cultural economies of affect within testimonial practices can tell us something about how categories of human and non-human are made and unmade, and furthermore, how such identitarian processes are constitutive to forms of cultural, biological, and human genocides.

Today, we might view the making and unmaking of human and non-human categories in terms of the larger field of bio-capital productivity. Consider, for example, what happens when associations between humans and animals emerge as forces of dehumanization. In her diary, written when she was in hiding from the Nazis in the occupied city of Amsterdam during the Second World War, Anne Frank observed such a process:

> Rauter, some German bigwig, recently gave a speech. "All Jews must be out of the German-occupied territories before July 1. The province of Utrecht will be cleansed of Jews [as if they were cockroaches] between April 1 and May 1, and the provinces of North and South Holland between May 1 and June 1." These poor people are being shipped off to filthy slaughterhouses like a herd of sick and neglected cattle. But I'll say no more of the subject. My own thoughts give me nightmares! (134)

In Pickton's trial, the pig farm inevitably reinforced the connection between the murders of these women and the slaughter of pigs, especially because the photos of evidence included the very machines used to butcher the pigs. The pig farm was intended as an industrial site to process animals for human consumption. Bio-capital refers not only to the production of Pickton as a labourer on this site, a point to which I will return in the examination of his letters, but also to its products, animal food. The significance of the refrain of the "drug-addicted prostitute," which runs throughout the news media coverage of Pickton's trial, comes to light here because both drug addiction and prostitution are conventionally thought of as non-productive labour. In actual fact, the prostitute and the addict are highly productive figures, not of labour in the narrow sense with which Marx, for example, characterized the male labouring body, but of desire (further to this point, see Emberley "Economies"). Desire is an essential product for all kinds of commodity and non-commodity consumption. The product of desire, however, is not generally recognized as a legitimate or official aspect of human capital but rather as a subspecies of bio-capital or non-human capital. Thus, the prostitute and addict's bodies are marginalized as by-products of labouring practices, and as non-value-added by-products they are synonymous with wastage.

The non-human differs categorically, however, from both human and animal; rhetorically speaking, the non-human is a catachresis because it signifies something for which there is no referent. There is a disturbing transparency to how "catachresis" mirrors its own defining characteristic in the very meaning of the non-human, as if the non-human represented the limit case of rhetoric, the end of speech or, let's say, of having a say. That the non-human is a catachresis in the figure of the "non-human" in no way, however, diminishes the performative power that is *enacted* when it is used to do the work of referentiality, of distinguishing the human from those who are apparently not human. I wonder if such a distinction is necessary, materially and rhetorically, for genocide and other forms of extinguishment to take place. The association of particular people who are also socially identifiable groups—such as Jewish and Indigenous peoples—with the "non-human" facilitates the violence of identity, a representational violence, or, on another register, a semiotic violence. It doesn't matter how you say it, the effects are the same. In occupied Europe during the Second World War, Jewish people were required to wear a yellow star so that the authorities could identify them. As what? As Jewish or as something else? Something that is unsaid, but nevertheless transparent.

The marking of Indigenous women's bodies as objects of embodied violence and extinguishment constitutes a racial order of difference. In the case of
Jewish people, socialists, gypsies, gays and lesbians, the unspoken, yet noticeable association of these specific groups of people by Nazis as "non-human"
led to genocide; in the case of Indigenous peoples, including First Nations,
Métis, and Inuit, a noticeable silence, a public secret, created the historically
and geopolitically specific conditions for the murder of Indigenous women as
a way to commit both human and cultural genocide. Relegating Indigenous
peoples and their way of life to the charred remains of the past occurred, as
the colonial record attests, by rendering illegal Indigenous ceremonial practices, severing children from their kinship and communal affiliations through
the implementation of residential schools, and creating specific clauses in the
Indian Act (1876) and subsequent amendments that would also disentitle status Indian women from kinship affiliations by superseding established kinship
and community affiliations, and also by the dehumanization of Indigenous
children, youth, and women's lives through the institutionalization of sexual
violence in the family, schools, definitions of legality, and cultural economies
of violence.

For analytical purposes, the creation of identities of non-humanness means
that the question of violence must also be opened up to problems of referentiality and of the historical shifts in representational technologies and institutional techniques used to produce and circulate identities of the non-human.
I am not suggesting that representational referentialities and the identitarian
codes of the non-human are transhistorical features of a technological deter-
minism; rather, it is the case that the emergence of colonial referentialities
is constitutive of a matrix of geopolitical and historical processes, including
institutional contexts, technologies of representational violence, and libidinal
and affective economic and political pressures used to produce (non-)human
bio-capital.

THE TRIAL: TESTIMONIAL SITE #1

Just as the women's bodies were scattered across the farm in bits and pieces,
so too do the photo galleries of evidence represent objects in a somewhat disconnected and fragmentary way. A link from the <http://v1.theglobeandmail.
com/picktontrial/> website titled "Slideshow: The Trouble with DNA" takes
the viewer to a visual box that displays some forty-two photographic images
for approximately three seconds each. The slide show begins and ends with

courtroom sketches of Pickton himself. If the viewer chooses, she or he can access captions and photographic credits. There is a voice-over delivered by Robert Matas, the principal reporter covering the Pickton trial for *The Globe and Mail*. His text narrates the trouble with DNA evidence. There is no direct connection to the images in the voice-over narration, except to suggest that the evidence photographed was subject to DNA testing. What connects the collection of images is the inclusion of forensic signs and measurement.

From reading articles in and around the websites on the Pickton trial I connect some of the images to other narrative sites. For example, on *The Vancouver Sun* website there is a diagrammatic representation "Inside the Pickton Farm," which contains figures of the trailer, motorhome, animal slaughterhouse, and workshop.

Arrows point to specific places in the buildings where evidence of "body parts, blood and belongings of missing women" were found. One reference notes: "Four of Abotsway's inhalers [found] in a garbage can." There is a photo of the garbage and the dirty inhaler in the slide show. Now it can be situated in relation to a place and a person. In another note: "Mona Wilson's severed remains found inside a garbage pail in the pigpen." I look at an image of the

Figure 1 Police search Robert Pickton's property in Port Coquitlam, east of Vancouver, May 22, 2002. Photo by Andy Clark. Courtesy of Thomson Reuters.

white plastic pail in *The Globe and Mail* slide show and wonder if this was the garbage pail that contained her body parts, but I have since learned from *The Vancouver Sun* photo gallery that it is not. I can only speculate about the mechanical tools, instruments, and knives used as instruments of torture. I am struck with how my body reacts to these images. My breathing becomes shallow and the space in my lungs contracts. When did I realize that I was writing from different parts of my body?

There is one more image in the photographic sequence I want to discuss. This image is of the Pickton site with a wired fence in the foreground and a female RCMP walking behind the fence. In front of the fence, and where I believe the RCMP officer's gaze is directed, are several artifacts, including flowers, images of women surrounded by text, oil-light burners leaning up against the fence, and a heart-shaped wreath. Without question I know that these objects testify to the memory of the women who disappeared from the Downtown Eastside. This unofficial testimonial space emerged on the polluted grounds of a serial killer. The flowers and the pictures are the only source of beauty and colour in an otherwise lifeless domain. Someone is thinking about the women—when they were alive—and not just their bits and pieces.

I am looking for a narrative thread or coherent framework to understand the images of evidence in the slide show because the chaos of violence is overwhelming. The empirical evidence presented in the trial would, of course, provide such a framework. The juridical narrative will probably be the only narrative to matter in the end, but nevertheless I am skeptical as to how the legal testimony of these photographed objects can contribute to memorializing the lives of these women: How will they be remembered? How will Serena Abotsway, Marnie Frey, Andrea Joesbury, Georgina Faith Papin, Mona Wilson, and Brenda Wolfe's be re-membered in the aftermath of such unaccountable and indiscriminate violence?

THE TRIAL: TESTIMONIAL SITE #2

The victim-impact statements from the trial consist of comments made by the victims' family members on the effects of the victims' deaths on themselves, their families, and their communities. These statements are delivered on the day the court is to determine Pickton's sentence for six counts of second-degree murder. The statements were transcribed and made available through the newspaper websites. The victim-impact statements have a great deal to tell us about the trauma of representation, especially media representation of the victims. Consistently, family members take issue with the persistent reference to "drug-addicted prostitutes" or "crack-addicted prostitutes." Underscoring the representational violence of news media are its effects not only on immediate familial relations and their ability to mourn the deaths of the victims, but also on Indigenous communities.

The interplay of absence and loss emerges from these texts in a radically opposed discourse; on the one hand, those of the identity markers "drug-addict and prostitute," and on the other, "loved one," "mother," and "daughter." In the case of the images of drug addict and prostitute, family members felt that this mode of identification resulted in a focused attention on the murderer and not the murdered women, who were loved and cherished by their families and communities. Representational violence in the media identification of the murdered women registered at the level of their non-humanity, their figuration as objects of social wastage, deserving no better than to be absented from the reader's or viewer's consciousness, as was also the case with the abject indifference toward the murder of Helen Betty Osborne. This tension between the way the murdered women are rendered as signs of social debris by news media and felt as a loss in the lives of their birth families and Indigenous communities (foster parent statements were not recorded) persists throughout the narratives. I want to focus here on the telling remarks by Rick Frey, Marnie Frey's father:

> From the day we reported her missing until this day, over ten years later, our emotions and the impact this case has had on our families has impacted us greatly in many different ways.
>
> It was not just Marnie's death that affected us so strongly. Our emotional anguish was made even made worse by having to deal with the issues around the police investigations, like traveling from our home to the Vancouver area for meetings. We were troubled by so much of the focus being on the man charged with murdering our loved one, rather than on Marnie herself and her family. We had a lot of difficulty finding counseling for ourselves. And we felt frustrated by not having our proper forum for expressing our concerns. We felt ignored and brushed aside. And we felt Marnie was being brushed aside because people just saw her as a drug-addict and a prostitute, not a mother and a daughter....
>
> Marnie disappeared in 1997 and we didn't find out for sure what had happened to her until well into 2002. And now it has been more than five more years for the trial to finally come to an end. All this waiting has taken a terrible toll on our mental well-being.

Marnie's daughter Brittney, whom we adopted in 1993, has had to endure cruel taunts at school, such as on hot dog day she was asked what it is like to eat her mother. I was asked on one occasion to pick her up from school because three girls were picking on her about her mother. She had to leave school as a result of this. Having to deal with Brittney's school in relation to their handling of this bullying was very difficult for me and my wife, Lynn.

Our family will be forever tormented by visions of what happened to our loved one, our daughter and mother Marnie, who was just an innocent woman caught in the wrong time and place. ("Victim Impact Statement")

In another statement, a young girl, age fourteen, speaks about the mother she never knew but came to know in the worst possible terms via media coverage of the trial. She says that she grew to hate her mother because of how news media "sensationalized" the last year of her mother's life. A social worker, speaking on her behalf, comments that "she does not want her mother's life story to be that of a crack-addicted prostitute but as one whose life was cut short by Robert Pickton" ("Court Hears from Victims' Families").

Embedded in the victim-impact narratives is a critique of how media representation served to separate the murdered women from the social world, which include their familial and communal associations, by persistently identifying them as drug-addicted prostitutes. It is as if news media dis-membered the women from society, from membership in a society that determined the value of human capital on the basis of certain forms of labour and productivity. The media dismemberment of the murdered women and Pickton's dismembering of the women's bodies are structurally similar in their treatment of the women as human wastage. Pickton and the women he murdered were pieces of a similar economy of bio-capital, one that includes the labour of animal dismemberment for human consumption and the dismemberment of "unproductive" female bodies due to their connection to alcoholism, drug addiction, and prostitution for consumption by the media. These pieces of the economy of bio-capital straddle the opposition between so-called productive labour and non-productive, expendable wastage. What media coverage of the murder trial reveals is how bio-capitalism implicates women and animals in a similar economy of dismemberment.

The drug-addicted prostitute signifies the subject of non-productive labour, a subject who does not work for the ends of capitalism, even as she is seemingly necessary to the comfort of militarized bodies and offshore labourers (see Yoshiaki). As a gendered subject, the drug-addicted prostitute defines non-productivity when she is situated in relation to human reproduction and domestic production. In reality, however, she is enormously productive of desire, a force of productive power located in sex, violence, and addiction. That "desire" is the product should not detract us from the need for tangibles, which are everywhere evident in the amount of money accrued through the entrepreneurs of such desiring machines. Prostitution and drug trafficking are billion-dollar industries and thus an integral part of transglobal economic exchange. From an analytical perspective, the fact that the drug-addicted prostitute does not contribute to the gross national product as a productive worker who can earn a living and support herself means that it is necessary initially to account for the oppressive conditions that monopolize the productivity of desire in female Indigenous bodies, and that this mode of productivity must also be seen to contribute to an economy of non-human bio-capital.

The drug addict is an unprincipled subject in capitalist terms dwelling vicariously but persistently within a sphere of "desire," the most extreme and intense form of non-productive and non-deferred desire. This is not the desire determined by a commodity culture of leisure, nor the same level of social absorption into the pleasure dome of video games and uninterrupted access to the Internet, for example. This is an embodied experience of a desire that serves the interests of an "other" economy, which is supposedly not factored into the nation's GNP but nevertheless out-markets the so-called normative economic "systems" manufactured and maintained by officially sanctioned capitalists and transnational enterprises.

THE TRIAL: TESTIMONIAL SITE #3

Violence is an historical object. What counts as violence, for and to whom, changes over time, especially in relation to economic modes of exchange and their cultural politics. Although a body may bear the signs of brutality, it is not always *read* as a body to which violence has been done. Modern violence is largely defined by public institutional structures—juridical, medical, social services, educational—and their socially sanctioned experts—lawyers, doctors, social workers, and, of course, educators. Reparative textualities are paradoxical in that to heal or repair relations that have been torn asunder due to violence, terror, or fear, the text must recount or reproduce the stories of violence. This is important, however, because not all forms of violence are necessarily recognizable as such. Sometimes the story and its healing may be precisely about acknowledging that violence has taken place.

Not only is it a question of recognizing the many forms that violence can take, but also it is vital to address the materiality of violence in the field of representation itself. In the colonial context, representational violence incorporates several modes of "aboriginality."[2] It includes, for example, the forms of violence that developed with representational technologies during the twentieth century to manage and maintain boundaries in the oppositional duality of savage/civilized. Regardless of the arbitrary relationship that exists between labels such as "drug-addicted prostitute" and the reality of the life of an Indigenous woman, the power of such labels to inscribe themselves into the very flesh of existence is real. In this way, "representation" is understood from the point of view of its effects in categorizing and rhetorically managing, stereotyping, and regulating identity for the purpose of generating a so-called individual subjectivity. These effects rely on the iterability of the image as if its repetition becomes part of the process of attempting to secure particular meanings and fix them as canonic and binding: the "truth," in other words. Representational technologies, from the printing press, film, and photography, to digitalization and other forms of virtual reality, supply the means and mechanisms of such iterability. However, the use of technologies of representation for the purposes of generating techniques of representational violence is neither inevitable nor immaterial. These techniques of representational violence are *contingent* upon and interwoven with historical, political, and social forces. They are also part of the cultural materialities of the twentieth century and work hand in hand with other materialities of violence, such as the physical violence of rape, domestic abuse, urban warfare, and war itself, as well as the economic violence of impoverishment, alienation, and marginalization.

In the cultural economies of colonial affect, paternalism, protectionism, and benevolence figure significantly. Notable in Robert Pickton's letters, written in prison while awaiting the commencement of his trial, is his use of Christian references to characterize his "benevolent" intentions to "rid the world of there [sic] evil ways." Pickton's misspelling of the possessive pronoun "their" is only one grammatological "error" among many in his narrative prose that *dispossess* Indigenous women of *their subjecthood*.

Pickton's letters test the limits of paranoid and reparative readings because they disclose his paranoia and his attempt to *repair* his relationship to the "world" through the murder and dismemberment of women's bodies. Reaching the limit of what can otherwise be used in the productive contexts of the political struggles of new social movements and their claims for equality, recognition, and acknowledgement, the reparative reading in Pickton's hand gives way to its historical opposite, the phantasmatic reading of the world that reproduces with a distinctly Oedipal regularity and repetitiveness, the generational passing on of an affiliative kinship of male violence:

> THE POLICE GOT SO MUCH MONEY INVESTED—IN THIS CASE, THERE WILL BE MANY, MANY LIES THROUGH-OUT AS MANY THINGS ALL COME TO SURFACE. THE POLICE HAVE PAID MANY FOR THEM WHAT TO SAY WHEN THEY ARE ON THE STAND.
>
> I LIKE WHAT THE JUDGE HAS SAID IN COART [sic], "HE SAID" THAT I WANT TO GIVE THIS CON-DEMN-MAN [sic] A HALF DECENT-TRIAL AND I SMILED AND SAID TO MY-SELF MY FATHER ALSO WAS A CONDEMNED MAN OF NO WRONG DONG, AND FOR THAT I AM VERY PROUD TO BE IN THIS SITUATION FOR THEY ARE THE BIGGEST FOOLS THAT EVER WALKED THE EARTH, BUT I AM NOT WORRIED FOR EVERY THING ON EARTH WILL BE JUDGED INCLUDING ANGLES [sic]. I MY-SELF [sic] IS NOT FROM THIS WORLD, BUT I AM BORN INTO THIS WORLD THROUGH MY EARTHLY MOTHER AND IF I HAD TO CHANGE ANY-THING [sic] I WOULD NOT, FOR I HAVE DONE NO WRONG. I DO KNOW I WAS BROUGHT INTO HIS WORLD TO BE HEAR [sic] TODAY TO CHANGE THIS WORLD OF THERE [sic] EVIL WAYS. THEY EVEN WANT TO DISREGARD THE TEN COM-MAND-MENTS [sic] FROM THE TIME THAT MOSES IN HIS DAY BROUGHT IN POWER WHICH STILL IS IN EXISTENCE TODAY. (Letter dated 20 February 2006; "The Pickton Letters: In His Own Words" 3)

Pickton's paranoia is represented in both his letters and in conversations with inmates recorded in prison and transcribed in news media in terms of how he is being *framed* by the authorities: "FOR THEY ARE NO CLOSER NOW AS THEY WERE FOUR YEARS AGO AND SADLY TO SAY THEY, 'THE POLICE' GOT ME AS THE FALL GUY FOR THAT THEY LOOK GOOD ..." (Letter dated 20 February 2006; "The Pickton Letters"). Within the institutional limits of the law, he describes how the amount of time and money ("EIGHTLY [sic] MILLION DOL-LARS") invested in the legal practice of his trial is such that it is inevitable that he will be found guilty and convicted. Like the police, he, too, detects his guilt as the inevitable finding of an already initiated investigation. The compelling nature of these perceptions makes them difficult to ignore. Nevertheless, the existence of his paranoid reading of the state of his imprisonment does not in the final existence discount the court's finding that he was guilty of killing the women. There is no logical inconsistency with the rationality of a paranoid reading of the world and actions taken that counter the deployment of a paranoid reading. The paranoid reading also seeks to expose the workings of institutional powers such as those operating in the juridical system. What the paranoid reading also does is strategically mobilize a reading with and by particular political interests that speak to and may even compete with other paranoid readings; in other words, paranoid readings are not disconnected from the historical and political contingencies in which they are produced. In Pickton's case, to be framed by one paranoid reading is to liberate himself from one set of contingencies while leaving others in their place. Pickton sees himself as a victim of the juridical system, the self-appointed saviour of the women he murdered, and as a man who, in his phantasmatic view of the world, sees himself above the law and in a context of religious salvation, as a Christ figure with the duty to rid the world of violence. That he committed violent murder in order to carry out this act of salvation is what situates his phantasmatic relation with the world as one that disassembles the worldly frame of what constitutes cultural belonging and, thus what constitutes recognized forms of violence that cannot be enacted without repercussions, and distinguishes those forms of violence from ones that can be enacted because (1) they are not recognized as part of a cultural system of socially unacceptable violence and (2) they simultaneously embody and re-present violence.

In her account of reparative readings, Eve Kosofsky Sedgewick acknowledges that

> No less acute than a paranoid position, no less realistic, no less attached to a project of survival, and neither less nor more delusional or fantasmatic, the reparative reading position undertakes a different range of affects, ambitions, and risks. What we can best learn from such practices are, perhaps, the many ways selves and communities succeed in extracting sustenance from the objects of a culture—even of a culture whose avowed desire has often been not to sustain them. (*Paranoid Reading* 150)

In his need to locate a site of nurturance, Pickton resorted to extracting the life sustenance from the so-called "objects" of one culture in order to achieve the recognition from another culture. Pickton complains that he is a worker on a pig farm, that he has worked his whole life and received nothing for his self-perceived "honest labours" ("The Pickton Letters: In His Own Words"). As with many reparative practices, Pickton's overattachment to fragmentary, marginal, waste, or leftover products, his all too literal dismemberment of women's bodies, is an attempt to assemble and confer plenitude on an object that will then accrue the resources to offer coherency to his otherwise inchoate self. In this farcical tragedy of reconciling his working-class "self" within an exploitative and oppressive capitalist culture via the cultural economies of the benevolent violence of Christianity, Indigenous women's bodies became the object of his reparative impulse to anchor himself to "the world." What needs to be done to stop the spurious equation between the loss of working-class male plenitude and Indigenous female absence is to build a bridge between class, colonial, anti-racist, feminist, and sexual politics such that it becomes impossible to think of imperialism without also thinking of gender, race, sexuality, and class. Such might be the reparative impulse behind an analytical approach that seeks to break the frame of violence as the all-compelling containment of Indigenous women's lives and livelihood.

OUTSIDE THE TRIAL: TESTIMONIAL SITE #4

It is interesting that many of the women killed were foster-parented and taken from their original birth families, and yet it is the birth families who give testimony in the form of impact statements. Some of those statements are also acts of mourning as well as declarations of loss. Elana Papin, Georgina Papin's sister, states that

> all we had was bone fragments. We couldn't even have a funeral for her. The memorial was hard enough to take in but the idea of court was even more surreal.... I love you Georgina and I pray for the sake of your children that there is complete justice done on your behalf. And all the people, all the beautiful spirited victims, may the great spirit carry you through to your next great adventure and may he always love you and gently guide you in kind ways and take all these flowers to a nurturing garden and replant Georgina Papin. ("Court Hears from Victims' Families")

Although there is no prelapsarian paradise of wholeness and totality to comfort the living for the losses of trauma and violence, in the case of the Pickton trial, a garden was established by the Indigenous women to mourn the loss of the murdered women. At the time of the trial a public memorial site did not exist for these murdered women, but a special space was created in a secluded place not far from Vancouver's skid row. It was created by the families of the women killed by Robert Pickton and other members of Indigenous communities:

The families have been reluctant to speak about the site. They hope to keep it as a somber place to remember those who have no graves. They have been trying to shelter the area from the public eye in order to maintain its peaceful, meditative atmosphere. *The Globe and Mail* was allowed to visit the site this week on the promise of respecting their privacy.

The area is dominated by mementoes from the so-called healing tent that provided refuge to the families in 2002 and 2003 while police investigated the suburban property. Posters and heartfelt tributes are tacked to a wooden bench made from fence that was previously on the edge of the property. A weather-beaten poster of 31 missing women, a faded missing-person's poster for Helen Mae Hallmark and a loving remembrance of Cindy Feliks are among the postings. Some of the tent's original plantings are in planters in the area. ("A Peaceful Place to Mourn")

Such memorial sites ask us to engage with history, to understand the social, political, and economic conditions that could possibly lead to the murder and dismemberment of a group of dispossessed, struggling, and loved Indigenous women. How can the history of colonization in Canada ignore the incredible violence done to these women and what this violence means to the writing of such a history? The testimonial sites in the case of the Pickton murder trial present the possibility of reading history differently, of moving such sites out of the shadows of "history's Other" and putting them in the way of colonial historiography and representation. In a word, it would be to put historical representation on trial.

BREAKING THE FRAMEWORK OF REPRESENTATIONAL VIOLENCE

In recounting a crisis that developed in her university classroom, the literary critic Shoshana Felman noted the way in which the experience of watching a Holocaust survivor's testimony necessitated a break in the framework of the class (Felman and Laub 47–49). The students were able to break from and break apart whatever it was that had led to their self-censorship, silencing, and denial. Breaking the framework of the class described, for Felman, the students' liberation from silence. Dori Laub also discusses an event in which a Holocaust survivor's testimony became the basis for reconceptualizing the value of testimony in what counts, or not, as historical truth. At a conference on Holocaust testimony, which brought together historians, literary critics, and psychoanalysts, a particular fragment of a survivor's testimony invited debate over its historical value and, in more general terms for Laub, the actual meaning of historical truth in the testimonial narrative. The event the woman recounted included a moment when the Jewish captives in Auschwitz mounted a rebellion. In telling her story, the woman mentioned that four chimneys were blown up. The historians questioned the value of this women's testimony because, in fact, only one chimney was blown up (Felman and Laub 61). Laub recounts the historian's reaction as follows:

> "Don't you see," one historian passionately exclaimed, "that the woman's eyewitness account of the uprising that took place at Auschwitz is hopelessly misleading in its incompleteness? She had no idea what was going on. She ascribes importance to an attempt that, historically, made no difference. Not only was the revolt put down and all the inmates executed; the Jewish underground was, furthermore, betrayed by the Polish resistance, which had promised to assist in the rebellion, but failed to do so. When the attempt to break out of the camps began, the Jewish inmates found themselves completely alone. No one joined their ranks. They flung themselves into their death, alone and in desperation." (61)

The historians expressed their concern that if testimony did not accurately reflect the historical record, then it could potentially play into the revisionists, who would like to discount altogether the realities of the violence of the Holocaust. Equally, if not more problematic, is how the historians characterized the event as a failed attempt to resist the death camps of the Holocaust. But Laub, a psychoanalyst with years of clinical experience working with Holocaust survivors, insisted that this testimony had a different value and contribution to make to "historical truth." He argued that the woman

> was testifying not simply to empirical historical facts, but to the very secret of survival and of resistance to extermination.... She saw four chimneys blowing up in Auschwitz: she saw, in other words, the unimaginable taking place right in front of her own eyes. And she came to testify to the unbelievability, precisely, of what she had eyewitnessed—bursting open of the very frame of Auschwitz.... She had come, indeed, to testify, not to the empirical number of the chimneys, but to resistance, to the affirmation of survival, to the breakage of the frame of death.... It is not merely her speech, but the very boundaries of silence which surround it, which attest, today as well as in the past, to this assertion of resistance. (62)

This breaking of the all-compelling frame of Auschwitz is significant because it speaks to a moment when the violence of fascism, which maintains itself by silencing through terror and fear anyone who dares to speak out against it, is finally broken. The testimony is thus, in and of itself, a significant act *un-silencing* the effects of fascism, especially those of self-denial and self-censorship.

What constitutes an important moment of "breakage" in testimonial practices might also be read within other historically and geopolitically specific conditions of violence. In the case of the Pickton trial, the media text contributed to an already established framework of "knowledge" in which the colonization of Indigenous female bodies generated the naturalization and normalization of those bodies as objects of violence. Such bodies came to *embody* violence. Thus, to break the framework of this representation violence is to rupture the association of Indigenous women with violence. Such a moment occurs, partially, with the testimony of the families of the victims. Within this testimony is a language of love, intimacy, and kinship affiliation that allows the reader to see these women differently and to reduce, in part, the traumatic dimension of the trial.

To read the diverse testimonial sites associated with the trial is to engage in a critical practice designed to disclose the violence done to these Indigenous women. In part, it is also to work toward creating reparative readings based in alternative knowledges and memorializing practices, the point here being to challenge or redefine the meaning of decolonization and the commonly held understanding, at least in other colonial contexts, that it represents a transfer of powers within the institutional limits of the postcolonial nation (see, for example, Ashcroft et al., *Key Concepts*). Rather, I want to suggest that testimonial practices can *decolonize* the institutional limits of the state, including its legal frameworks, judicial forms of incarceration, as well as media industries. To do so, however, involves breaking the frame of the all-compelling violence associated with the lives of Indigenous peoples.

Institutional techniques and representational technologies during the twentieth century introduced a new logic of coercion, separate from and yet interdependent with older forms of physical violence. The attempt to transform the physical realities of violence into new and contradictory modes of regulatory, routinized, and non-physical coercion was only partially successful, however, and perhaps beneficial only to an emerging postcolonial elite and its desire for a homogeneous constituency. Testimonial practices, including documentary films, photography, and life-writings, are also part of those institutional and representational regimes of violence and, thus, recall dominant values of realism, truth, authenticity, and narrative cohesion, but they do not necessarily reproduce those values; they also inhabit the varied media of human regulation dialogically and, thus, turn them to other purposes.

In what I would consider a significant moment of breaking the framework of representational violence toward Indigenous women, Rebecca Belmore enacted a public memorial to the disappeared Indigenous women from Vancouver's Lower East Side through a street performance called "Vigil." "Vigil" was performed on a street corner in Vancouver's Downtown East Side in 2002, the year Pickton was arrested. A video recording of her performance can be accessed through her website, but I would like us to imagine being there on the street with her and a group of people, some of whom are interested viewers, others casual observers (see http://www.rebeccabelmore.com/video/Vigil .html).[3] One of the first things we see her do is invite, significantly, a young white man to light the votive candles. This act of hospitality immediately crosses the identity-difference line and displaces the pain and anxiety that occurs when "race" and "gender" are reduced to fixed and immutable categories. By her invitation, this young white male has become an unwitting member of her performance, but his identity is also only a performance, it is not what defines him. In this context, what define him are his actions and his willingness to become a participant in a public act of memorialization. Belmore, too, is an Indigenous woman. On the street she inhabits a place of enormous pain, poverty, and violence toward Indigenous peoples. Thus, her presence complicates questions of identity and performance, underscoring the need to remember who we are and also how we are represented within and inhabit specific spaces.

In her performance, largely carried out in silence, Belmore changes her clothes and puts on a red dress. She then takes hold of the dress and nails it to a wooden pole or fence, and after having done so, she tears it from the post. She continues to do this until the dress is torn to shreds and torn away from her body. The names of the disappeared are written on her arms and she calls out their names—a moment in which the silence is broken—and rips a yellow rose through her teeth. These acts of tearing are expressions of anger toward the violence done to the women. As she tears apart and is torn by these symbols of desire, prostitution, and love, Belmore generates a fourth dimensional text, in which the spaces occupied by performer, performance, audience, and participant come together to make another spatial entity. As a street performance, this newly formed spatial matrix exists in an ephemeral space–time continuum, but it also exists in the memory of those who witnessed the event. Memorialization becomes possible in the layers of remembering the disappeared Indigenous women that Belmore recalls in the performance itself and in remembering Belmore's performance in which she has created for her audience a position of witness to her rage at how these women's bodies were racialized and sexualized into objects of violence.

Belmore's street performance breaks the frame of representational violence associated with Indigenous women's bodies through a performative enactment of rage and pain. Such cultural practices do more than testify to the violence done to Indigenous women. They work with the violence of postcolonial nationalism in order to show what it is that violence *does* to the lives of people and communities. By ripping and tearing into fabric and flowers, on and through her body, Belmore engages in a visceral dramatization of her rage, which in turn creates a visceral experience for the audience. The audience of Belmore's performance both witnesses the knowledge of the violence done to the Indigenous women and Belmore's own powerful response to such knowledge, leaving the audience-as-witness to reflect on their own "empathic unsettlement" (LaCapra, *Writing History* 38). Testimonies can motivate a range of affective responses. Such a range of affectivities, however, is circumscribed by the material production of feelings generated by historical contexts. In the colonial register of affectivities, pity, for example, taps into the benevolence and protectionism constructed by colonial and postcolonial state policies. In the context of Belmore's street performance, her countermemorial with its unsettling rage, eschews the affective violence of liberal guilt and colonial benevolence. Rather, it produces an ethics of response for the witness, who is invited to inhabit, dialogically, the site of his or her own postcolonial unsettlement.

NOTES

1 Further to the media representation of missing and murdered women, see Stone and Dean, Jiwani and Young, and Jacobs and Williams.

2 For a more detailed account than I can provide here of the relationship between aboriginality and colonial and postcolonial origin stories of violence produced through cultural forms of representation, see my *Defamiliarizing the Aboriginal: Cultural Practices and Decolonization in Canada*, especially "Introduction: Of Soft and Savage Bodies," 6–39.

3 Belmore also presents this video at her video-installation *The Named and the Unnamed*, shown at the Morris and Helen Belkin Art Gallery at the University of British Columbia. For a discussion of this installation work, see Lara Evans, "Rebecca Belmore: Vigil and The Named and the Unnamed," http://travelpod.wordpress.com/2010/05/08/rebecca-belmore-vigil. See also Luna and Townsend-Gault. Further to this installation, see McCall.

"Grammars of Exchange"
The "Oriental Woman" in the Global Market
Belén Martín-Lucas

A LARGE NUMBER OF POSTCOLONIAL and feminist critics of diverse cultural backgrounds, including Edward Said,[1] Gayatri C. Spivak, Arif Dirlik, Kwame Anthony Appiah, Aijaz Ahmad, Arjun Appadurai, Chandra T. Mohanty, Graham Huggan, or Neil Lazarus, have argued that it is most crucial to restore to both postcolonial and/or feminist cultural analyses their political nature since their potential for social reform is being efficiently neutralized by global capitalism. The "current intellectual backlash against postcolonial studies" is carried out through at least two major strategies: Orientalist marketing tactics that exoticize "ethnic" literatures in the international markets in order to raise their economic value while devaluing their political ones; and the co-optation of resistance discourses such as feminism, anti-imperialism, or anti-racism through their domestication within academic institutions (Huggan vii). I will be paying attention here to the first of these two strategies. My position as a foreign Canadianist, writing from Spain, determines to a high degree my own access to Canadian texts. Since academic research is facilitated nowadays by powerful database systems that hold thousands of journals at the distance of a click, the expensive trips to Canada to buy books and copy articles from journals and magazines are less frequent; catalogues and Internet booksellers become a primary source of information on the literary novelties of Canada that replace the pleasurable browsing through bookstores, where you can touch and read excerpts of your own choice. While clearly making Canadian literature more easily accessible to international readers, global trade practices have also limited in important ways the kinds of titles offered to the non-specialist readership. Like me, more and more people buy their books through the Internet. How is Canadian literature promoted to foreign readers? How are Canadian texts sold to the rest of the world? Which Canadian texts get translated into other languages? And how does international reception affect CanLit? These are questions that I intend to address here. Since English is, undoubtedly, the global language, texts in English, whether from Canada, the United States, or any other part of the world, get wider circulation and more chances to get translated into other languages; among the literary genres, narrative fiction is the favourite, "the hottest literary commodity" (Kamboureli and Wah 138): my study here is limited to the paradigmatic case of contemporary Canadian fiction in English.

By looking at the attempts to instrumentalize so-called ethnic literature by the market and the state, I do not mean to suggest that the creative works here surveyed were, in any way, written to satisfy orientalizing drives; many of them present imaginative strategies of resistance to commodification and co-option. Besides, the many works by anti-racist critics and activists in Canada teach us ways of reading that transgress the expected/desired representations of the exotic ethnic. Their theoretical and critical works, together with the ongoing publication of innovative literature by committed small presses and the interventions of distinguished translators within their specific literary systems, constitute important enactments of resistance that I will consider. Nevertheless, to a large extent, a number of economic and political forces determine both the creative production of racialized writers and the critical work on them and shape the conditions of production, circulation, and reception of literature. The publishing industry and its markets beyond Canada, the marketing of "ethnic" fiction and the paratextual elements that wrap the book as an object desirable to potential consumers, as well as translation as a distinctive instrument of public diplomacy, have established the available selection of "ethnic" writing distributed internationally.

THE PUBLISHING INDUSTRY AND ITS MARKET(S)

In the last two decades, we have witnessed an unprecedented appetite in the West (a problematic metaphor that I use here to invoke Eurocentric cultural dominance in a colonial stance toward the Orient) for fiction by "ethnic minority" authors, mostly written in English (or in translation from English). Apparently, readers in the West have developed a taste for the narratives of alterity, hybridity, and difference that are now hitting the market and, surprisingly, making it to the bestseller lists. This recent interest in certain kinds of texts excluded for centuries from the literary canon—most remarkably those written by racialized (lesbian) women[2]—can be understood within the wider context of globalization, which perversely promotes a false image of cultural heterogeneity in a world that is in fact becoming more homogeneous. In this context, literature is, like any other cultural activity, a product that is bought and sold in a market strictly regulated by a few multinational corporations, at a time when cultural capital—that is, in Bourdieu's terms, the impact of a given text in the academic world—and economic capital—the monetary profit achieved—go hand in hand. As part of a general taste for "ethnicity"—like ethnic cinema, food, and clothes—"ethnic" literature is being appropriated as a visible banner of globalized culture.

In this "age of information," living in the new "knowledge societies," we must be aware, as common readers and as academics, of the tight control of a few corporations on cultural production and distribution channels since they effectively determine the circulation of literary texts and their reception, and thus constitute nowadays the primary censorship apparatus. Consider, for example, the power of Random House, "the world's largest English-language general trade book publisher" (Random House Inc. "Our Publishers"): Random House agglutinates over a hundred publishing houses in sixteen countries, together with a whole system of printing companies and distributors, including Internet booksellers and reading clubs. They own, among others, the following publishers of English fiction for adults: in Canada, Random House of Canada and McClelland & Stewart (25 percent of the shares);[3] in the US, Ballantine, Bantam Dell, Crown, Doubleday-Broadway, Knopf, and Random House Adult Trade Group; in Great Britain, Transworld and the Random House United Kingdom Group. Each of these integrates several previous companies; for example, Random House of Canada merged with Alfred A. Knopf Canada in 1991 and with Doubleday Canada in 1999. These companies use diverse imprints for their works, such as Bond Street Books, Anchor Canada, Seal Books, or Vintage Canada. The surname "Canada" in these group names indicates they constitute a branch of an, originally, American company;[4] Random House of Canada was first established in 1986, the period when these huge corporations started to grow. McClelland & Stewart also publishes under several distinct imprints, like Douglas Gibson Books or Emblem. Each of these imprints publishes adult fiction in English. They all belong, completely or partially, to one single company: Random House.[5] Penguin Putnam, their main competitor, is the second largest publishing company in the English literary world, followed by HarperCollins. These three huge

publishing groups, each with a national Canadian branch, are just the literary
sections of much bigger media corporations that control what we read, listen
to, and watch, in every possible format: news, entertainment, and culture,
both popular and high.[6] Beneath an impressive image of plurality and freedom
of choice, there is a grim picture of a real censorship exerted by economic
(and ideological) transnational powers: only through the big corporations do
literary texts (almost exclusively fiction) get widely publicized and distributed
on a global level.

It is in this context that the renewal of Orientalism comes to the forefront
for the exotic ethnic revealed in the selection of titles easily available in the
international sphere.[7] Alongside these corporate giants, the work of a myriad
of small publishing houses, many of them established by feminist and anti-
racist collectives (such as Sister Vision Press, Press Gang, Second Story Press,
Sumach Press, Theytus Books, TSAR, or West Coast LINE, among others)
continues apace. It is important to note that these small activist presses are
usually the promoters of new authors who may later engross the catalogues of
larger multinational presses; despite their tiny budgets, these small publishing houses take economic risks by investing in new authors who are republished by larger corporations once they have proven successful. Thus, Shani
Mootoo's *Cereus Blooms at Night*, first published in 1996 by Press Gang, was
reprinted in 1998 by McClelland & Stewart; and Shauna Singh Baldwin's
English Lessons, first published in 1996 by Goose Lane in Canada, was published again three years later by HarperCollins India. Many other racialized
authors who published their first work with small Canadian presses are now
being published by international firms. This imbalance between investment
and benefit in the production of the literary text has been pointed out by
Christine Kim in reference to the unaffordable extra costs in publicity associated with literary awards: "While small publishers are willing to take risks and
produce texts that might not appeal to a wide market, they are often unable to
reap the economic and cultural rewards when these texts become successful"
and republished by a multinational company (164). In the face of the pressures exerted on the market by the bigger companies with the support of the
NAFTA and the cuts in governmental subsidies, the function of these small
presses—some of them forced to close, as in the cases of Press Gang and Sister
Vision Press—is nowadays even more relevant as they are crucial agents in
the production of innovative and challenging literature. As Kim maintains
in her comparative study of the reception of Mootoo's *Cereus Blooms at Night*
and Lai's *When Fox Is a Thousand*, the circulation of a given literary text as

"bear[ing] the imprint of a major publisher" or as coming from the hands of a specialized one affects significantly the sort of reading practices and critical approaches employed and, consequently, the higher or lower symbolic capital it is finally invested with (171).

Shazia Rahman's comparison of the reception of Anita Rau Badami's first novel, *Tamarind Mem*—one of the first novels by a South Asian woman to be published by a multinational corporation, Viking Penguin—and Rachna Mara's *Of Customs and Excise*, published by the feminist Second Story Press, provides a representative example of this phenomenon. Both texts were circulated as mother–daughter narratives and marketed to a North American readership. While the first one has been widely studied and reviewed both in Canada and internationally, Mara's outstanding short-story cycle has been sadly neglected, receiving only a couple of reviews after its publication. Even so, Rahman points out how the marketing of Badami's book as a nostalgic, romanticized promise of an exotic faraway adventure "is in direct conflict with the book's actual argument, which posits mobile, diasporic, and feminist subjectivities" (90), a contradiction that she later describes as "the incommensurability between the cover and its contents" (95). Although the novel collects the memories of two female narrators, Kamini and Saroja, Badami does not provide a coherent account; rather, as Rahman argues, "Badami uses this motif of mobility to emphasize the instability of memories" (92). Rahman provides a careful close reading of the novel to show that, contrary to stereotypical representations of fixed (ethnic) identities, "the multiplicity of feminisms and narratives [in *Tamarind Mem*] subverts the marketing of the novel" (90). Rahman's reading of Badami through theories of diaspora and feminisms shows that although major publishers may attempt to "manufacture not just a particular kind of taste, but a great equalizing taste" (Mathur 150), alternative readings are not only possible, but also invited by the texts themselves.[8]

MULTICULTURAL LITERATURE IN PUBLIC DIPLOMACY

At a time when postmodernist theory and practice have raised simulacrum to the category of art and automatic reproduction has reached the field of biology in the form of clones, one of the most precious qualities in a cultural product is that of authenticity, a desired characteristic "that the dominant culture either professes to lack or that it claims to have lost, and for which it feels a mute nostalgia" (Huggan 156). Several critics have pointed out this nostalgia for the authentic, together with a colonial voyeuristic fascination for the exotic

Other, as the main factors that would explain the apparently "sudden" irruption of an important number of authors who, under a varied range of generic labels such as postcolonial, ethnic, immigrant, or diasporic, have been rapidly canonized into Western curricula, awarded and honoured, and their works widely distributed in translation in a well-orchestrated operation that Huggan identified as "marketing the margins" in 2001.

CanLit has contributed notably to the creation of such a global taste for the ethnic Other. In Canada, where "visible minorities" have a long history of struggle for visibility, the rise of multiculturalism as an official policy from the 1970s onwards gave place to a "Multicultural Literature" that has effectively been instrumentalized in Canadian public diplomacy, a form of "soft power" that understands that "culture can be used to affect foreign public opinion, and thus can garner support, for a nation's foreign policies" (Maxwell 5).[9] In the 1990s, Canadian culture and international commerce became intimately joined when the supervision of cultural grants, international Canadian studies programs, and the International Institutional Research Program was assigned to the Department of Foreign Affairs and International Trade (DFAIT). Multicultural literature has been employed in nation-branding, a convenient representation of the Canadian state in the international sphere.[10] Prominent "ethnic" authors like Michael Ondaatje or Rohinton Mistry figure in the new Canadian canon that is taught, reviewed, and promoted internationally, both in English and in translation. However, the ongoing internal debates, which date back to the late 1980s in Canada over appropriation, racism, and co-optation, have critiqued this idyllic image of literary Canada, one that Kamboureli has described as the "fetishization of its multicultural make-up" ("Preface" viii). In fact, the commercial exploitation of literary texts marketed as "ethnic" or "multicultural" threatens—which does not imply it manages to erase—their vindicative value at the same time that this capitalist, racist, and sexist system ostracizes racialized artists (Lai, "Corrupted" 43). The commodification of "ethnic" writing in Canada and its negative implications for anti-racist activism have been extensively studied, especially since the late 1990s.[11]

The case of South Asian literature in English is particularly remarkable and tied to the Western taste for anything "Indian,"[12] including South Asian (mostly Indian but not exclusively) fiction in English and of "Bollywoodesque" films, Deepa Mehta's Bollywood/Hollywood (2002) being a representative Canadian example. In the Canadian fiction scene, Rohinton Mistry's international success opened the doors of mainstream publishers to other writers of South Asian origin mentioned above.[13] Since 1991 (when Mistry obtained the Governor General's award), we have witnessed a remarkable proliferation of narratives by women of South Asian origin. Among them, Badami and Baldwin have been especially successful, publishing with mainstream houses, receiving multiple awards and distinctions, and achieving international recognition, reaching further into foreign publishing markets than any other new racialized literary figures from Canada.

This recent attention from publishers, critics, and readers on South Asian Canadian fiction requires a wider contextualization in relation to the above-mentioned "Indian boom" in international cultural markets. The Rushdie affair and Arundhati Roy's Booker Prize were two main catalysts for the contemporary success of Indian fiction in English. Their frequent appearances in the media served to promote Indian fiction in English all over the world, and most especially in the West, a success confirmed by V.S. Naipaul's Nobel Prize in 2001 and the more recent Man Booker Prizes awarded to Kiran Desai in 2006 and to Aravind Adiga in 2008,[14] together with an important number of South Asian novels translated into other languages in recent years. Translation constitutes an important marker of status in the economic and cultural global systems as it determines the range of the circulation of texts and, therefore, their span of reception. It also plays a relevant role in nation-branding and cultural diplomacy, and encourages trade in foreign countries, as Luise von Flotow has convincingly argued in her analysis of translations of Canadian literature into German (2007). The International Translation Grants program of the Canada Council for the Arts subsidizes the publication of Canadian works in foreign languages abroad, covering half the honoraries for the translator, though never the printing, editing, and distribution of the translated text. The program specifically states that "Priority will be given to books that have been short-listed for or have won literary awards (for example, Governor General's Literary Awards [...] and Canada-Japan Literary Awards)" (Canada Council for the Arts website), a condition that can work to favour affluent mainstream publishers over small ones, as mentioned above, and capitalizes on the cultural value already obtained by a book. Despite the help of such institutional programs, the decision to translate texts and authors lies now more than ever before in the hands of the big publishing corporations, which exchange their authors' rights with their sister branches in other countries. Exceptional though hopeful cases are those translations produced by admiring writers and academics who, making use of their contacts within the industry, will convince their own publisher to include some specific text in their catalogue of translations.[15] In Spain, there are few Canadian titles available in translation from racialized writers;[16] the authors whose works are in circulation are mostly award recipients of South Asian origin: Michael Ondaatje, Rohinton Mistry, M.G. Vassanji, Shyam Selvadurai, Shani Mootoo, Anita Rau Badami, and Shauna Singh Baldwin.[17] There is a shameful lack of translations of texts by Black Canadians, and East Asian Canadian fiction is represented by Madeleine Thien's *Certainty*, Nancy Lee's *Dead Girls*, and Lydia Kwa's *This Place Called Absence*. Ondaatje, Vassanji, Mistry, Baldwin, and Badami are available not only in Spanish, but also in Catalan. Mootoo's *Cereus Blooms at Night* was translated into Spanish in 1999 (once its rights had been bought by McClelland & Stewart); unfortunately, it is now out of print, which demonstrates that literary success and commercial interests do not always maintain a long-lasting relationship. It is the destiny of most works of fiction, prizes and awards notwithstanding, to disappear from bookstores in a brief while, which complicates the teaching and therefore the canonization process of contemporary writing. The success (however ephemeral) of these South Asian writers—labelled in our literary systems as "diasporic," "multicultural," or "ethnic"—is in great part due to the work by diverse activist groups that demanded public space and visibility for racialized artists (see Li). However, the commercialization of these writers in the cultural market has exposed a renewed colonial desire for the exotic that some postcolonial theorists had diagnosed decades ago, most notably Edward Said (1978).

MARKETING THE AUTHENTIC ORIENTAL

In the Canadian literary market, as in the rest of this globalized world, "authenticity" is sold and bought, and a good guarantee of true authenticity is the classification of a given story as "based on real events." The fact that auto/biographical texts abound in the postcolonial field has been noted by many critics who have often theorized them as resistance modes. However, due to the Western appetite for authentic exotic products, there is a marked tendency in the recent years to sell them as autobiography, to the point that even when a narrative is not autobiographical, it is most often read and analyzed that way, especially when the author is not White, as Huggan has pointed out:

> Ethnic autobiography, like ethnicity itself, flourishes under the watchful eye of the dominant culture; both are caught in the dual processes of commodification and surveillance. This might help to explain why the work of writers who come from, or are perceived to come from, ethnic minority backgrounds continues to be marketed so resolutely for a mainstream reading public as "autobiographical." (155)

Consequently, the narratives by "ethnic" authors are read as ethnographic evidence and not as literary pieces, devaluing their political and artistic value (the cultural capital in Bourdieu's terms) while increasing their economic one.[18] The case can become more acute with women's texts, since women are often made to "embody" a whole nation.[19] Chinese Canadian writer-activist Larissa Lai has incisively analyzed this marketing strategy and critical reception as a more subtle assertion of White supremacy: "the suggestion is, of course, that we are not creative agents capable of constructing nuanced fictions which address historical situations, but rather mere native informants reconstructing, as accurately as our second-rate minds allow, what actually happened" ("Political Animals" 148). Her creative production is a good example of the complex imbrication of theoretical discourses and conflicting histories at work in some contemporary fiction by transnational authors. The alternative worlds she creates in her dystopic *Salt Fish Girl* and the abject mutant bodies that inhabit her two novels are strategies that foreclose ethnographic or autobiographical readings of her work.

In marketing Asian women's writing, publishers show a preference for those narratives that tell a woman's story of courage and defiance in an old-fashioned context of violent traditions. For example, Baldwin's second novel, *The Tiger Claw*, deals with the violent history of the war in Europe that was taking place in the same span of time of the events in her previous novel, *What the Body Remembers* (1937–1947). On the back cover of her first novel (Vintage Canada edition 2000), the violent conflict of the first Partition war is described in the following dramatic terms: "separatist tensions between Hindus and Muslims trap the Sikhs in a horrifying middle ground." This promotional summary emphasizes the horrors of ethnic and religious violence, while in the book the war occupies only the final section, number 8 (122 pages out of 517), and is treated with subtlety. In contrast, the summary on the back cover of *The Tiger Claw* (Vintage Canada edition 2005) does not include any adjectives in reference to "the Nazi occupation after the German invasion of France in 1940," and the only three adjectives market the plot as a romantic one: "*extraordinary* story of love and espionage," "an *astonishing* search through the chaos of Europe's displaced persons camps," "an *unforgettable* denouement" (my emphasis). The back cover also includes a blurb from *The Gazette* that reads "*The Tiger Claw* muses on the dangers of tribal intolerances"; the use of "tribal" is not innocent when describing the work of an "ethnic" writer.

The title of a book is, obviously, an important element in the marketing process, and publishing houses have professional teams that, in negotiation with the writer's agent, decide the strategies of book cover design. Publishers may even use different titles and different cover designs in different countries for the same literary text. An example of this is Badami's first novel, published in Canada as *Tamarind Mem* (1996), which became *Tamarind Woman* in its American and British editions (2000), keeping the exotic taste of the tamarind while targeting a feminine audience that might not recognize the term "Mem." In France it was published as *Memsahib*, a recognizable foreign word that would make explicit the reference to an "exotic woman."

Anthologies that collect the work of diverse authors of a given ethnic collective—and therefore intend to be highly representative—use iconic words that immediately invoke their culture, as in *Strike the Wok: An Anthology of Contemporary Chinese Canadian Fiction*, *Paper Doors: An Anthology of Japanese-Canadian Poetry*, *Red Silk: An Anthology of South Asian Canadian Women Poets*, *Story Wallah!: A Celebration of South Asian Fiction*, *Shakti's Words: An Anthology of South Asian Canadian Women's Poetry*, and *Voices in the Desert: An Anthology of Arabic-Canadian Women Writers*. In fiction by individual Asian women writers, titles often include similar references to an "exotic" difference that emphasizes a presupposed foreignness—for instance, *Tiger Girl (Hu Nu)*, *Tamarind Mem*, *Belly Dancer*, *Brahma's Dream*, *The Concubine's Children*, *Cereus Blooms at Night*, *The Sherpa and Other Fictions*, *We Are Not in Pakistan*, *Mangoes on the Maple Tree*, *Blues from the Malabar Coast*, *The Forever Banyan Tree*—or allude to spaces typically associated with a community, as is the case of the Chinese restaurants and laundries in SKY Lee's and Judy Fong Bates' books.

The titles emphasize difference and locate stories in faraway times or places; they frequently suggest tragic stories in a foreign context. The visual elements help produce this effect of seductive otherness: pagodas, dragons, Chinese or Japanese scripts, fans, delicate foreign flowers and birds, most often framing beautiful or sorrowful feminine faces with slanted eyes. The lyric and colourful covers tempt the reader with the appeal of Oriental perfumes: azaleas and lotus provide the olfactory stimuli, while silk wraps beautiful bodies of Asian women, who become the main bait for the Western consumer.

In the trendy Indo chic, the woman in a sari has become a sort of trademark and we can easily identify the old nationalist trope of woman as the embodiment of the m(other)-land. Henna-painted hands and feet and silky or cotton saris appear in almost every single book in English from Indian authors (both male and female), and Indian women authors are, perhaps, the most photographed of all. The author's body may indeed become an important factor in the promotion and reception of the literary text as Guy Beauregard has criticized in his reviews of Asian Canadian women's fiction:[20] "repeatedly placing Sakamoto's face on display to promote the novel [does] ... feminize and racialize the author to make her a suitable object of consumption" (191). In *What We All Long For*, Dionne Brand has her protagonist Tuyen (an Asian Canadian visual artist) exhibit her body as part of an installation, a move that exemplifies Beauregard's criticism. Pilar Cuder-Domínguez has read this scene as follows: "In Tuyen's installation, she uses her own racialised body as the medium to make visible how the immigrant body is displayed, exposed, and handled without her consent or control" (7).[21] Yasmin Jiwani has analyzed these strategies in the realm of film, demonstrating the exploitation of the symbolic values of South Asian women's bodies in Western mainstream culture, which, from my point of view, constitute the ideological basis for the use of these visual representations in the marketing of South Asian fiction (45).

ENGAGED READING PRACTICES

The cumulative effect of these marketing devices, with their promotion of tragic and violent stories set in a remote place and/or time, partially veils these authors' strong resistance to specific patriarchal practices in their cultures and to imperialism, reifying their narratives as a product for quick consumption (Lai, "Corrupted" 42). The paratextual elements I have commented on here— promotional blurbs, titles, and iconographic items on the book covers—are a few obvious examples of an ongoing Orientalism, which in my opinion resides at the heart of globalization's hypocritical celebration of cultural "diversity" and hybridity. The cultural market reifies women's narratives of histories of oppression as objects to be consumed and, as Bannerji and Lai have claimed, disguises the violence upon which the Canadian nation is constructed. The artistic value of these novels is thus compromised by the very system that promotes them as it attempts to depoliticize the marginalized voices and experiences that the fictions present (Rahman 90), thus *contradicting* the combative ideological discourses present in the texts. By foregrounding the object (the exotic woman in a sari or kimono), the reader's attention is directed away from the political issues raised by these narratives, such as feminism, anti-racism, anti-colonialism, and of course Asian women's agency as subjects.[22]

It has been my intention here to provoke some thoughts on the projection of Canadian writing by racialized authors in the global market for foreign audiences and for readers of other languages (not English), and to offer some glimpses from abroad of the images of multicultural Canada that governmental

institutions and mainstream publishers promote. While considering the instrumentalization of so-called ethnic literature by the market and the state, I hope
to have made clear that their homogenizing impulses are not totally successful
and resistance is effectively performed on all fronts by small activist presses
that persevere in their commitment to compromised literature; by translators who exert whatever minor influence they might have on their publishers
to have less "profitable" texts also included in their catalogues; by cultural
critics who read against the grain to evaluate the radical cultural capital and
subversive forces operating in the narratives; and by imaginative writers who
envision literary strategies that impede easy digestion of the ethnic delicates-
sen. These constitute important enactments of resistance that encourage hope
that, yes, another reading is possible.

NOTES

Research funded by the Spanish Ministry of Science and Innovation, Project "Globalized
Cultural Markets: The Production, Circulation, and Reception of Difference" (Reference
FFI2010=17282).

1   My title borrows Said's term "grammars of exchange" from his *Culture and Imperialism*,
    where he uses it in reference to the contemporary depoliticization of cultural discourses:
    "representations are considered only as apolitical images to be parsed and construed as
    so many grammars of exchange" (57).
2   The literary production by racialized lesbian and bisexual authors is a major achieve-
    ment of Canadian letters as compared to other national literatures, with well-estab-
    lished writers like Dionne Brand, Marlene Nourbese Philip, SKY Lee, or Shani Mootoo.
3   The fact that the main holder of the major Canadian publishing house, McClelland &
    Stewart, is the University of Toronto, as a result of the donation of the 75 percent of the
    shares by Avie Bennett in 2000, may effect a valuable restraint on the profit-directed
    policies of its more commercially oriented partners.
4   The Doubleday Publishing Group (US) includes the Broadway group, Black Ink, Spie-
    gel & Grau, Nan. A. Talese, and Flying Dolphin Press, while the Knopf group includes
    Alfred Knopf, Vintage, Anchor, Pantheon, Everyman's Library, and Schocken Books.
    Random House Inc. also includes (besides these groups with Canadian branches) the
    Bantam Dell Publishing Group, the Crown Publishing Book, the Random House Pub-
    lishing Group (Ballantine Books among them), and RH International (which includes
    McClelland & Stewart Ltd.). The Random House United Kingdom agglutinates Arrow,
    Century, Chatto & Windus, Everyman, Harvill Secker, Hutchinson, Jonathan Cape,
    Rider, Vermilion, Vintage, and William Heinemann.
5   In Canada, federal measures protect the book publishing industry. Among them, the
    Investment Canada Act, which "requires that foreign investments in the book publishing
    and distribution sector be compatible with *national cultural policies* and be of net benefit
    to Canada and to the Canadian-controlled sector" (Canadian Heritage/Heritage cana-
    diane; emphasis added). Having national branches of the original American company
    allows these publishers to enter the Canadian market. Most books by Canadian authors

are published by "Canadian-controlled" companies; however, the two main publishers, Random House of Canada and McClelland & Stewart, are, as I have noted, financially linked.

6 Random House is only a piece within the much larger corporation Bertelsmann AG: "Bertelsmann produces, serves and markets media. Our content is contributed by RTL Group, the No. 1 European broadcaster; Random House, the world's largest book-publishing group; and Gruner + Jahr, Europe's biggest magazine publisher. Arvato provides media and communication services, while Direct Group is the global market leader in media distribution through clubs and on the Internet" (Bertelsmann AG, "Structure").

7 I am using here Said's well-known definition of Orientalism as a discourse that fundamentally sustains cultural constructions of the exotic and is currently understood as a pejorative term. For an extended discussion of the term "Orientalism" both in Said's seminal text and since, see Amit Ray.

8 In my own reading of Badami's novel in my chapter "Indo-Canadian Women's Fiction in English: Feminist Anti-racist Politics and Poetics Resist Indo-Chic," I point out how Badami's novel offers a subversive reversal of mother-daughter, South Asian diasporic narratives: it is Saroja, the mother, who symbolically breaks the umbilical cord that ties them together and becomes, not the pitiful Hindu widow of traditional narratives, but a free woman with "a room of her own": "I do not belong to anyone now. I have cut loose and love only from a distance. My daughters can fulfil their own destinies" (265–66).

9 See also von Flotow.

10 Frank Davey lamented the, in his opinion, excessive interest of European Canadianists in "minority authors" in a plenary lecture titled "Uneasy Companions: Canadian, Cultural, and Postcolonial Studies in Canada" at the 31st Annual Conference of the Spanish Association for English and American Studies, November 2007). On the use of multicultural literature in nation-branding, see Kamboureli and Wah, as well as Lai, "Brand."

11 See Kamboureli and Wah, Lai "Strategizing the Body," Mathur, Maclear, and Rahma. However, as powerful as the economic and political forces of co-optation are, effective strategies of resistance have been simultaneously devised. Some writers have experimented with innovative, unconventional genres such as speculative fiction and fantasy, hybrid ones like ficto-criticism (consider Yasmin Ladha's "essay" pieces in *Lion's Granddaughter* and *Women Dancing on Rooftops*, for instance) or the short story cycle (Mara's *Of Customs and Excise*, Gupta's *The Sherpa*, Ghatage's *Awake When All the World Is Asleep*, or Warrior's *Blues from the Malabar Coast*). Against fixed racial and sexual stereotyped identities, we find an avalanche of mutants, aliens, hybrid species, and other metamorphosing bodies so fluid that no identity label can be permanently stuck on them (I am thinking here of Lai's *When Fox Is a Thousand* and *Salt Fish Girl*; Hiromi Goto's *The Kappa Child* and *Hopeful Monsters*; Suzette Mayr's *Moon Honey* and *Venous Hum*; and Nalo Hopkinson's *Skin Folk*, among others).

12 See Gita Mehta, Toor, Huggan, Brouillette, and Niessen, Leshkowich, and Jones.

13 See Arun Mukherjee's study of the critical reception of South Asian Canadian writing in Canada in her *Postcolonialism: My Living*.

14 Adiga's win stirred controversy in the Indian media, as he is being accused of re-Orientalizing representations of India.

15 This is a rather frequent case in Spain, where academics have been translators of Atwood, for instance. In Galicia, a former student in my CanLit courses who later became a reputed Galician author, María Reimóndez, translated Rachna Mara's *Of Customs and Excise* (in 1998, out of print now) and Erín Moure's *Little Theatres/Teatriños* (in 2007) into the Galician language. I mention these examples to point out certain fissures in the apparently impenetrable economic system; publishers may be receptive to titles that come with the extra cultural value attributed by the reputed author/academic (and will publicize this collaboration).

16 In a recent article titled "¿Es visible la cultura canadiense?" published in the Mexican literary supplement *Hoja por Hoja*, Graciela Martínez-Zalce laments the lack of translations of Canadian texts in Mexico. She notes that the available translations are distributed from Spain and in peninsular Spanish, implying that the offering of titles is "doubly foreign" to a Mexican reading audience. For a more detailed analysis of the translations available in Mexico, see her article "Exporting Canadian Literature for Mexican Readers."

17 All books published in Spain (in whichever of our four languages, Spanish, Galician, Catalonian, or Basque) are registered by the National ISBN Agency and can be consulted at the following online database: http://www.mcu.es/libro/CE/AgenciaISBN/BBDDLibros/Sobre.html.

18 For an extensive analysis of the co-optation of "exotic" women's life narratives, see Gillian Whitlock's incisive study of the circulation and reception of Middle East texts, *Soft Weapons: Autobiography in Transit* (2006). There are important exceptions, though. For example, some of the articles in the volume *Asian Canadian Writing beyond Autoethnography*, collected by Eleanor Ty and Christl Verduyn, amply demonstrate the variety, richness, and inventiveness of the many different literary modes employed by Asian Canadian authors.

19 Shauna Singh Baldwin voices such "burden of representation" through her character Piya in the story "Toronto 1984" after having confronted her racist boss: "For now I am not only myself, but I am all of India and Pakistan and Bangladesh. I am a million and a half people sitting in one small office in Mississauga. I wear a label and will take pride in being a damn Paki" (*English Lessons* 57). I have elsewhere analyzed the identification of "woman" and the "motherland" in relation to Asian Canadian authors (see Martín-Lucas, "Metaphors").

20 A glance at the South Asian Women's NETwork's section Bookshelf (at www.sawnet .org), specializing in South Asian women's writing, will provide plenty of examples, including those published in Canada.

21 A visit to Anita Rau Badami's and Shauna Singh Baldwin's websites will show the covers of the different editions of their novels, most of them featuring a woman in a sari. In Ryerson Library's "Asian Heritage in Canada: Authors" on the Internet, there are plenty of images of book covers that illustrate my references above.

22 My chapter "Indo-Canadian Women's Fiction in English: Feminist Anti-racist Politics and Poetics Resist Indo-Chic" analyzes in depth these political issues and the strategies of resistance presented in a number of recent literary texts.

II Past Participles

Unhomely Moves
A.M. Klein, Jewish Diasporic Difference, Racialization, and Coercive Whiteness

Melina Baum Singer

THIS CHAPTER BRINGS QUESTIONS of Jewish difference into the contemporary critical grammar of diaspora. These questions might seem unproblematic. Historically diaspora, from the Greek word meaning dispersion, was attributed to the multitude of communities formed as a result of the Babylonian expulsion of Jews from Judea in 587 BCE and characterized these communities' relationship to homeland, as well as the formation of a horizontal (transnational) fellowship. But in the present moment, the definition of diaspora has become paradoxical. In the public sphere, the Jewish resonances have been extended to describe a range of experiences, both the tragic (such as the Hurricane Katrina diaspora) and the ridiculous (such as the Croatian Math diaspora).[1] Whereas in critical commentaries that share an interest in reconceptualizing the category, diaspora's terms of reference have been narrowed. "Diaspora," here, has become not only an interpretative device for literary and cultural analysis, but also a powerful organizing prism that includes and excludes particular identity formations.

In their studies on diaspora, international scholars Brent Hayes Edwards, Paul Gilroy, Stuart Hall, and William Safran, and Canadian scholars David Chariandy and Lily Cho clearly recognize the way Jewish experiences have underscored diaspora's definition. But their proposals for a new grammar of diaspora historicize the relevance and contribution of such experiences: Jews and expressions of Jewishness have been de-linked from the category and thus faded into diaspora's etymological *past*. I believe Jonathon and Daniel Boyarin's worry that scholarship on Jewish diaspora will be "confined to the archives—either sufficiently researched and acknowledged (having nothing

99

to teach postcolonial studies), or worse yet, as *obviated* because there is now, after all, a Jewish state" ("Powers" 11) has in fact already taken place.[2]

In relation to the theorization of diaspora in Canada—and as grounds for an intervention—I seek to draw attention to the reasons Jewish difference has been excluded. I believe the absence of responses is neither a coincidence nor a result of the dilution of the term, but rather a fissure in the way diaspora is read through critical race theory. This chapter tests the limits of the contemporary cultural grammar of diaspora through readings of A.M. Klein's *Hath Not a Jew* (1940) and *The Rocking Chair and Other Poems* (1948). I argue for an understanding of A.M. Klein's poetics under the contemporary rubric of diaspora and identify, in these works, an overlooked narrative, one that makes a unique contribution to studies on racialization and coercive whiteness in Canada. This chapter insists on the importance of looking back at the racialization of Jews, in order to recognize its historic factuality and the way such racialization raises questions about the terms and conditions forming the perceptions of Jewishness today.

POSTCOLONIAL DIASPORA STUDIES

After delivering a public lecture (2004) at the University of Western Ontario, Rinaldo Walcott provocatively proclaimed that globalization studies is a white area of study and diaspora studies is a non-white area of study.[3] Looking around at the audience response, expressions of confirmation far outweighed expressions of incredulity. I found the simplicity of the double opposition troubling as well as useful, for following the logic of Walcott's assertion, expressions of Jewishness seem to be placed outside the material of diaspora studies, and alternatively studies of such material would be situated in a separate field of study. Walcott's comment thus became my point of departure to elucidate the incompatibility between the contemporary understanding of diaspora and Jewishness, an incompatibility, I will argue, that hinges on a relatively recent shift in race, religion, and national identity formation.

In recent years, scholars have begun to theorize diaspora as a category of inquiry in studies about Canada, in terms akin to the assumptions I believe are implicit in Walcott's double opposition. Chariandy and Cho's commentaries on diaspora have emerged as central in the development of that field Chariandy usefully names "postcolonial diaspora studies" in Canada. Significantly, both scholars' work addresses (directly and indirectly) the relationship between Jews and Jewishness and diaspora's reconception of diaspora.

In "Postcolonial Diasporas," Chariandy succinctly puts forth the field's broad concerns as addressing the "profound socio-cultural dislocations resulting from modern colonialism and nation-building." Foregrounding the theoretical possibilities of diaspora, he writes:

> That diaspora studies will help foreground the cultural practices of both forcefully exiled and voluntarily migrant peoples; that diaspora studies will help challenge certain calcified assumptions about ethnic, racial, and, above all, national belonging; and that diaspora studies will help forge new links between emergent critical methodologies and contemporary social justice movements. ("Postcolonial Diasporas" par. 1)

These passages do not necessarily foreclose investigations of Jewish diaspora; such questions could easily fall into the impetus behind the points Chariandy raises. But his subsequent statement—"I want to suggest that the postcolonial diasporas might best be understood not as self-evident socio-cultural phenomena, but as figures which may help us to better read and animate the cultural politics of specific racialized collectivities within the modern West" ("Postcolonial Diasporas" par. 2)—qualifies the subject of the previous points, a qualification that retroactively casts doubt on the fields' inclusion of responses to expressions of Jewishness based on whether Jews and Jewishness are perceived as a racialized community in the present (Western) moment.

The article does not directly answer this question, but it does contend with the relationship between Jewish experience and thought and postcolonial diaspora studies, an exposition that calls attention to the role temporality plays in the field's reconception of diaspora. Chariandy states there is a clear "need to appreciate better the meanings, effects, and epistemologies that have historically consolidated themselves around the term diaspora.... Of crucial importance here is the uniquely robust and compelling articulation of diaspora in Jewish thought, whereby Diaspora (capital D) names specific histories of Jewish exile" ("Postcolonial Diasporas" par. 17). In reference to the work of the central articulators of contemporary diaspora, he ultimately identifies a thread of shared belief in which postcolonial diaspora studies understands the link between singular socio-cultural entities, such as "Jews," and diaspora as historically redundant (confirmed by the title "The Legacies of Diaspora" of the subsection where Jewish thought and experience is considered). In contrast, Chariandy situates the field's designation of diaspora studies as a "figurative" or "metaphorical" politic, a "special agent for social change" responsive to the need to address the material and psychic realities produced by racialization

("Postcolonial Diasporas" par. 32). Postcolonial diasporas are born of new concerns.

In her work on diaspora in Canada, Cho conceptualizes diaspora as a consequence of imperial and colonial processes of racialization. In "Diasporic Citizenship: Contradictions and Possibilities for Canadian Literature," Cho argues for diasporic citizenship "as a mode through which to engage with the demands of minority histories upon Canadian literature" (99). Referencing Black, Asian, and First Nations literature in Canada, she evocatively writes:

> My understanding of minority literatures throughout this essay is thus deeply connected to race. Minority marks a relation defined by racialization and experienced as diaspora. That is, Asian Canadian literature, for example, relates as a minor literature to Canadian literature not because it is less important, valuable, and illuminating, but because it cannot be divorced from the long histories of racialization that mark Asian Canadian communities as being in the minority in relation to a dominant culture. (98)

Cho situates diaspora as an affective structuring of *persistent* minority belonging, a form of belonging that formed through patterns of "racial" categorization. Jewish literature does not figure in this argument, and given the fact that Cho names the formations she believes relate as minor literatures, Jews (represented through Jewish literature) seem, by extension, to fall outside the group of communities she perceives as racialized in Canada.

In "The Turn to Diaspora," Cho draws attention to the way a "critical engagement with experiences of Jewish and Armenian diaspora [has] enable[d] her to form] an understanding of diaspora as a subjective condition bound by the catastrophic losses inflicted by power" (15). Implicitly connecting to her earlier engagement with minority belonging and diaspora, Cho argues that "classical" (17) diasporas "are not simply collections of people.... Rather, they have a relation to power. They emerge in relation to power. This power is both external to the diasporic subject and internally formative" (21). She situates her interest as "contrary to studies of diasporas as objects of analysis where race or religion [are taken as the] defining factor" (21), and theorizes that diasporic subjectivity or belonging is not a birthright claim (one is not born Asian, for example) but rather an affect of social and political forces that emerge through one's relationship to power. Thus she declares, "I want to reserve diaspora for the underclass, for those who must move through the world in, or are haunted by, the shadowy uncertainties of dispossession" (19). Although she foregrounds Jewish diasporic subjectivity, read through the Boyarins' work,

Cho's argument ultimately centres on two categories of racialization: "black and Asian diasporas" (22). This begs the question of whether expressions of Jewishness have a place within Cho's conception of diasporic subjectivity, or whether Jewish experiences have been decontextualized in order to shed light on "the displacement engendered by colonialism" (13). Namely, the displacements, she believes, were produced by racialization.

In order to move toward an explanation for the lack of responses to expressions of Jewish difference in contemporary diaspora studies, I want to turn to a few commentaries on race and racialization that further the understanding of the way Jewishness has been directly and indirectly situated in Chariandy and Cho's work. Roy Miki writes:

> Racialization applies to the imposition of race constructs and hierarchies on marked and demarked "groups" whose members come to signify divergence from the normative body inscribed by whiteness. The subject racialized is identified by systemic categories that winnow the body, according privilege to the glossed with dominance and privation to those digressed with subordination. (*Broken Entries* 303)

His definition emphasizes the oppositional binding of privilege, whiteness, and normativity versus subordination, non-whiteness, and abnormality. For Miki, racialization is centrally a relational construction, simultaneously creating "non-white" and "white" forms of identity formation. Miki lucidly points to the uneven axis between majority–minority relations, an axis that relationally defines white versus non-white and is contingent on one's relation to power. Reading this definition back into Chariandy and Cho's arguments, racialization is a process whereby particular religious/ethnic/national differences are erased and broad generalizations are formed about pre-given "racial" belonging (such as Cho's commentaries on Black, Asian, or First Nations): these categories become endowed with pejorative characterizations used to justify a range of social and political inequities.

Franz Fanon's early commentary on Jewishness can be connected to the way Jews are implicitly situated outside the types of questions postcolonial studies seeks to address. He writes:

> [T]he Jew … is a white man, and, apart from some rather debatable characteristics, he can sometimes go unnoticed … the Jews are harassed— what am I thinking of? They are hunted down, exterminated, cremated. *But these are little family quarrels.* The Jew is disliked from the moment he

is tracked down. But in my case everything takes on a new guise. I am given no chance. I am overdetermined from without. I am the slave not of the "idea" that others have of me but of my own appearance. (115–16; emphasis added)

His characterization of European anti-Semitism as a "little family quarrel" understands the largely successful genocide of European Jewry as an internal "white" war, a war fought to cleanse cultural-ethnic-religious differences from the continent. Fanon reads anti-Semitism not as racism but as prejudice.

This passage does not recognize the complex way in which Enlightenment thought racialized European Jews as a non-white race, nor that proponents of whiteness reserved its formation for northern-central European (Protestant) peoples.[4] European processes of racialization, culminating in the events of the 1930s and 1940s, are bound to cultural/ethnic/religious differences, processes that brought together assumptions about internal (character, belief, practice, etc.) and external signs (skin colour, hair texture, facial features, etc.); in this way, a prominent nose, olive skin colour, and facial or body hair became racial signs. Fanon's comments obfuscate two related but ultimately different processes of racialization: processes that are unique to the modern versus contemporary periods and to European versus European colonial contexts.

In reference to the colonial context, Michael Omi and Howard Winant point out that "[n]ativism was only effectively curbed by the institutionalization of a racial order that drew the color line around, rather than within, Europe" (65). Therefore, the construction of pre-given racial categories pulled back from assumptions about ethnic/religious/national difference and refocused on visible or external signs of difference. Calling attention to this process in Canada, Dionne Brand writes that "[b]uilt around the obvious and easy distinction of colour, 'whiteness' became more and more the way to differentiate the coloniser from the colonised.... [i]nclusion in or access to Canadian identity, nationality and citizenship (de facto) depended and depends on one's relationship to this 'whiteness'" (Bread Out of Stone 187). Brand goes on to argue that Canadian ideas of "whiteness" have a "certain elasticity" (187) that allow it to "contain inter-ethnic squabbles, like that between the English and the French" as well as to "swallow" and "cleanse" (188) Canadians of European descent—albeit, making a point I will return to in my last study, only once assimilation is believed to be fully realized. In the colonial contexts, the so-called "little" differences were largely erased as the perceived clarity of skin colour was held up as distinguishing factor of "race."

Chariandy and Cho's critical impetus for making a connection between diaspora and racialization seems in pursuit of exposing and righting the inequalities racial discourse puts into play in the production of an "underclass" (Cho, "Turn" 19), these inequalities may be born of historical realities, but they continue to take shape in the present. Extending critical race theory, diaspora has become an "agent" (Chariandy) or a "mode" (Cho) to unearth the politics that produce "non-white subjects [as Miki describes] in the Canadian state ... who inhabit a realm of shadows, of chaotic darkness ..." (*Broken Entries* 306).

I share Chariandy and Cho's hope that the theoretical possibilities of diaspora offer a way to consider the psyche and material affects of racialization, but I want to come to this imperative with a different focus. As I noted, religious differences have been downplayed in the redrawing of the construction of Canadian nativism. But in the post-9/11 North American political landscape, there is surely a renewed urgency to consider the play between religion, race, and home/land shaping white and non-white forms of belonging in Canada. Exploring the way the perception of Jewishness forms a pre-given idea of "racial" belonging, this chapter looks at the early modern moment. Modernism is the juncture that situated the complexities of Jewish and Canadian cultural formations, the moment in which the line was redrawn between a "native" Canadian and a foreigner.

I intend to consider the contributions Jewish diasporic difference might bring to this critical conversation. My interest theorizes an understanding through the problematics raised in Klein's moment. Modernism was a paradoxical and yet extremely significant juncture for situating the complexities of Jewish and Canadian cultural formations and, by extension, racialized and national identity formations. I will map two preliminary and initially disparate studies—the first reads racialization in *Hath Not a Jew* and the second explores the way early modern criticism has read *Hath Not a Jew* in relation to *The Rocking Chair and Other Poems*. Under the rubric of "the unhomely," these questions converge in a final reading that proposes a methodology that accounts for the complexities of "Jewishness" within a contemporary understanding of diasporic difference. My purpose is not to reinsert the centrality of Jewish experience, but rather to point out possible trajectories from which Jewish diasporic difference can extend the conversations taking place in postcolonial diaspora, Jewish, and modernist studies.

RACIALIZED DIFFERENCE

Hath Not a Jew brings together a collection of first-person poems, written in the 1930s and 1940s. Ranging from reflections on religion, language, and village social life to meditations on history and politics, the poems offer a wide-ranging exposition of Jewish diasporic culture. Although they do not follow a singular narrative thread, the poems come together in the production of a particular scene of inquiry, a scene that raises questions about Jewish diasporic difference, race and racialization, and place-based politics. These questions are first raised in the title of the collection and the corresponding epigraph.

Taken from the most recognized and controversial expressions of Jewish alienation, the title and the epigraph to the collection reference Shylock's plea for equality in Shakespeare's *The Merchant of Venice*: "... *Hath Not a Jew* eyes? *Hath Not a Jew* hands, organs, dimensions, senses, affections, passions? Fed with the same food, hurt with the same weapons.... If you prick us, do we not bleed? If you tickle us, do we not laugh? If you poison us, do we not die?" The proto-humanism of Shylock's contention (that Jews and non-Jews are the same biologically) calls on mainstream culture to accept a common human bond with Jews, and disavow the pejorative discourse about "the Jew."

The title and the epigraph do not name to whom Shylock directs his plea,[5] but the second epigraph, to the first poem, "Ave Atque Vale," names "Christian" as the mainstream culture being addressed. Taken from Shakespeare's *Two Gentlemen of Verona*, the epigraph reads: "If thou comest with me to an alehouse, so. / If not thou are a Hebrew and a Jew, and not / worthy the name of Christian" (3). The preceding poem takes up this division: "No churl am I to carp at the goodly feres / In the Mermaid tavern, quaffing the lusty toast; / Myself twanged Hebrew to right English cheers" (112–13). Far from historicizing this passage, the poem calls attention to the speaker's perception that the opposition between a Jew and a Christian is used for a greater purpose than religious distinction.

> *No churl am I to carp at the goodly feres*
> *In the Mermaid tavern, quaffing the lusty toast;*
> *Myself twanged Hebrew to right English cheers.*
> *Though now I do bid farewell to mine host*
>
> ...
>
> *To you I turn, and eke to Jabna town,*
>
> ...

Towards the town of scholars, towards the lean Reb Zadoc,

...

When he forsakes you, Shakespeare, for a space,
Or you, Kit Marlowe of he four good lines,

...

This Jew
Betakes him to no pharisaic crew ... (3–5)

In relation to those who speak "right English," the speaker relates his expression of English as accented. The speaker says his Jewish identity, "twanged Hebrew," marks his difference from the way English belonging has been shaped. The speaker's argument, one that picks up on the resonances of the poem's epigraph, is that if he were not a Jew he would be granted invitation to reside within the bounds of English identity formation.

This image of "English" as a built structure emerges through the parallel between the "alehouse" of the epigraph and the "Mermaid Tavern" of the poem; the "Mermaid Tavern" was the name of the meeting place for artistic and intellectual discussion in Shakespeare's time. The "tavern," then, literally and figuratively houses English community and culture and the denial of Jews from the tavern speaks to the censor not only of Jews from English identity formation but also of autoenthographic expressions of Jewishness within English culture. If the key to the house of English belonging were a sound, the speaker's Jewishness would be as dissonance. The speaker acknowledges the social and cultural exclusion of Jews as an ongoing problematic. But he states, "This Jew['s]" poetic intention is to make a home for expressions of Jewish experiences and discursive thought and practice inside the English language and by extension play a role in the community of articulators of English community and culture (as previously noted, "Shakespeare," "Kit Marlowe," "Jonson" [5]), a canon that henceforth included only largely pejorative representations of Jews by non-Jews (in direct representations, such as Shakespeare's Shylock, and indirect, such as phrases and figures of speech belying assumptions about Jews).

The poem "Childe Harold's Pilgrimage" asserts that the exclusion of Jews is the normative transgeographic and transhistoric experience. The speaker relates: "Always and Ever / Whether in caftan robed, or in tuxedo slicked, / whether of bearded chin, or of the jowls shaved blue, / Always and ever have I been the Jew" (6). Using clothing (caftan or tuxedo) and facial appearance (bearded or shaved) to relate temporal (pre-modern or modern) and spatial (East or West) differences, the speaker evokes one of the clearest consequences created by the persistence of the discourse of "the Jew."

> *To Easperanto from the earliest rune—*
> *Where cancellation frowns away permission,*
>
> …
>
> *For they have all been shut, and bared, and triple-*
> *locked, The gates of refuge, the asylum doors;*
> *And in no place beneath the sun may I*
>
> …
>
> *Sit down to rest my bones …*
>
> …
>
> *Aye, but they fell is somewhat safe in Muscovy!*
>
> …
>
> *Provided*
> *I cast off my divine impedimenta,*
> *And leave my household gods in the customs house.*
>
> …
>
> *Seig heil!*
> *Behold, against the sun, familiar blot;*
> *A cross with claws!*
>
> …
>
> *He likes me not.* (6–8)

The speaker notes the multitude of locations Jews have settled—"Allmany"
(6), "Madagascar" (7), "Muscovy" (7), and indirectly to Germany through the
reference to Hitler and Fascism—since the dispersion from "Palestine, my own
/ Land of my fathers, cradle of my birth" (7), and in so doing connects mainstream cultures' rejection and persecution of Jews, ranging from exclusionary
rules and laws to pogroms and genocide, as the conditions from which the long
history of Jewish migration has occurred.

   In relation to these points, a secondary narrative emerges, a narrative that
links the speaker's exploration of what the Boyarins call "rediasporification"
(*Powers* 11) to ideological assumptions of the discourse of "the Jew."

> *What it is, then,*
> *That ghostly thing that stalks between us, and*
> *Confounds our discourse into babel speech?*
> *Perhaps I am a man of surly manners,*
> *Lacking in grace, aloof, impolitic*
>
> …

And that is false.
For on occasion and in divers lands
I have sojourned, set up abode with you,
   ... uttered the
Very same language, thought a similar thought,—
And still you have sneered foreigner ... (9–10)

Picking up on the earlier references to clothing and facial hairstyles, these passages relate the speaker's belief that the adoption of mainstream norms and behaviours—assimilation being the traditional litmus test of "belonging"— does not alter the perception that Jews remain "foreigners." The caftan and the tuxedo, so to speak, are figured as interchangeable facades, facades that do not penetrate a foundational or essential matter that remains, singularly, "the Jew": the discourse thus reads Jews as lacking an organic identification or connection to broader regional or national formations. Whether or not their histories are long or short in a given place, Jews are believed to be permanently "alien," fixed in a figurative and literal time lag—"always and ever" just arrived. Severed from the local, "the Jew" thus does not literally or figuratively *dwell*, and, in consequence, the grounds of diasporic Jewish existence are pried apart.

There is a connection to be made between the speaker's indignation that diasporic Jews have been read as placeless and his commitment to figuring Jews and expressions of Jewishness in relation to broader forms and practices of identity and community formation. These two concerns make an argument akin to the Boyarins' call for maintaining the "contradictory propositions" of a figure like "the early medieval scholar Rabbi Sa'adya ... an Egyptian Arab who happens to be Jewish and also a Jew who happens to be an Egyptian Arab" ("Diaspora" 721). The Boyarins' point is extremely important, for it is only by drawing out the question of how the identifications they cite have come to be contradictory that light might be shed on the ideological grounds of the discourse of "the Jew" the speaker seeks to highlight. Perhaps as a consequence of the geopolitical politics informing the relations between Israel and Palestine (post-1948), the division between Jew and Arab has been made to seem contradictory and thus surprising. Yet, in the same way, the speaker's reference to caftan and tuxedo, as signs of belonging, has been endowed and thereby reflects the conservative/nationalist connection between geography/ soil (Mediterranean/Middle East and England/North America) and ethnic/ blood formation (Arab/Muslim and Anglo-Saxon/Protestant).

If we follow the logic that Jews have no foundational connection to local forms of belonging, we find an answer to both the speaker's question regarding what is that ghostly thing that separates Jews, and to the question I want to pose to the Boyarins' reference to contradictory forms of identification embodied by Rabbi Sa'adya. For on the basis of geographic origins ("And there is also Palestine, my own, / Land of my fathers, cradle of my birth" [7]), genealogy ("Of my much too-Semitic heart" [10]), and religious doctrine ("My father's heresy, his obstinate creed? / That is the sword between us?" [9]), the speaker brings together the overlapping assumptions that construct Jews as a pre-given "race." The source of difference between "the Jew" and the Arab (the Boyarins' point) and "the Jew" and the Christian (the speaker's point) is found in the *organic* disconnection of Jews from the "caftan or tuxedo" because these metaphors of belonging are equally bound to other racial formations: the caftan to southern European/Mediterranean/Semitic Arab and the tuxedo to Anglo-Saxon/white. As the speaker carefully points out, however, Jews have long histories in Europe as well as non-European locations: thus the racialization of "the Jew" is obviously problematic, for Jews are not only transnational, but transracial (white Jews, black Jews, Semitic Jews, Mediterranean East Asian Jews, South Asian Jews, and so on).

Recalling his point about the mutability and interchangeability of Jewish forms of identification, the speaker draws attention to the intersection of two contradictory and yet mutually dependent discourses, discourses that pertain to race and racialization and place-based politics. Arif Dirlik has suggested that contemporary diaspora studies negates place, and calls for diaspora to be situated through a "place-based politics" (*Postmodernity's Histories* 195). I agree with his sentiment, insofar as it confirms the argument *Hath Not a Jew* makes that mainstream cultures have normalized the rupture or negation between diasporic communities and place to such an extent that the blame or responsibility is placed on such communities themselves.

The speaker notes that while Jews are constructed as pure, "That in your gospels you so character / Me and my kin, consanguine and allied" (9), they are simultaneously defined as "polluted" and "ill-bred" (8). The contradictory sentiment of "the Jew" as at once a pure and contaminated "race" makes dispersion central to the discourse, and calls attention to the way the characterization is a consequence of the derogation and suspicion of mobility or migration. The concern is that diasporic Jewish culture absorbs geography and genealogy, and the fear is that "the Jew" does not remain in his or her proper "place"—two sentiments reflected in 1930s and 1940s popular avowals to Jews to "go home" to Palestine.

Recalling the last line of the first poem, the speaker's statement that he is not beholden to singularities (Jewish or English), that "This Jew / Betakes him to no pharisaic crew" (5), can be read as an alternative view of Jewish contamination, one that I want to contextualize through the Boyarins' reading of Jewish diasporic culture. They write: "diasporic cultural identity teaches us that cultures are not preserved by being protected from 'mixing' but probably can only continue to exist as a product of such mixing … diasporic Jewish culture lays it bare because of the impossibility of a natural association between this people and a particular land—thus the impossibility of seeing Jewish culture as a self-enclosed, bounded phenomenon" ("Diaspora" 721). The Boyarins' point is exactly one that Klein's poems take up in relation to the speaker's insistence that mainstream cultures create an essential character, "the Jew," who depends on the disconnection between Jews and the local.

BECOMING WHITE

Shifting tracks, this study traces the critical reception of Hath Not a Jew specifically for the way a line of thought in early to mid-modern commentaries shaped a progressive and periodic relationship between Hath Not a Jew and The Rocking Chair and Other Poems, a collection of third-person vignettes about French Canadian social and political life that won the author the Governor General's award and was hailed as a Canadian modernist masterpiece. It is my contention that Hath Not a Jew was mobilized in such a way not only to ensure its critical neglect and The Rocking Chair's immediate and ongoing canonization, but also to normalize a historic and profound shift in the construction of Jewish and Canadian form and content and establish the terms and conditions of a new racial grammar—the racial grammar that postcolonial diaspora studies seeks to address and challenge. I seek to draw attention to the assumptions and implications within this narrative of a poetics of evolution.

In one of the earliest reviews of Hath Not a Jew, Earle Birney makes a foundational critique. He argues that the collection is too esoteric, archaic, and significantly Jewish to be understood. He writes: "It is where Mr. Klein is striving to be most 'Jewish' that he is least poetical and most turgid…. Unfortunately, it is necessary to wade through such obscurantism … to arrive at the real poetry of the volume—the writing which speaks to all men" (55). Following the publication of The Rocking Chair and Other Poems, the reception of Klein's poetry takes up Birney's polarity of poetics, obstensibly dividing Klein's poetics into what does or does not "speak to all men."

John Sutherland, in 1949, describes *The Rocking Chair* as his "best" collection, characterizing it as a "correct[ion of *Hath Not a Jew's*] nose-dive into antiquity by realizing the poet in his contemporary setting" (59). Louis Dudek, in 1950, remarks that Klein's "growth … [has been] away from the Hebrew religious core of his poetry toward a realistic and cosmopolitan view of things" (68). M.W. Steinberg, in 1965, comments that Klein's "preoccupation with Jewish matters … is reflected in the fact that he chose for his first volume of poetry, *Hath Not a Jew*, only poems dealing with Jewish" concerns (109), whereas his second collection reflects the "releas[e] from his burden of responsibility as Jewish spokesman" (116); *The Rocking Chair* "turn[s] to new themes" (115)—Canadian, specifically "French-Canadian life" (116). John Matthews, in 1965, characterizes Klein's work in "five clearly marked periods of poetic development" (136); the earliest period, to which *Hath Not a Jew* belongs, is bound by the interchange between autobiographical elements, Jewish history and religion, and English literary references, "all pressed into the service of a Hebraic theme" (136), and "contain[ing] no poems which are specifically Jewish" (142). E.A. Popham, in 1978, writes that "[t]here is an obvious progression in [Klein's] poetry … from the 'Jewish' group … to the 'Canadian' group" (5).

The criticism does not only remark on the collection's obvious and substantial differences. Stemming from the modernist opposition between personal and impersonal poetics and their related assumptions, the criticism places a progressive value on the differences themselves. As defined by Brian Trehearne, "[a]n 'impersonal' poem will suppress content that would alert the reader to a particular poet" (106), content that otherwise could highlight or suggest the poet's personality or particularity. Thus the criticism picks up on and contrasts the auto-enthnographic Jewish voice of *Hath Not a Jew* and contrasts it with the generalized public voice of *The Rocking Chair*. The theory of impersonality, however, is not ideologically free. Inaugurating the tenet, T.S. Eliot's assertion that "the progress of an artist is a continual self-sacrifice, a continual extinction of personality" (1094) naturalizes the form's internal evolutionary logic: progression unfolds through erasure or loss. Evolution, as such, is a stage narrative about advancement; what has been lost is figured as no longer useful and valued versus what remains, or moves into the foreground, which is figured as relevant and valuable.

Taking the tenet as a barometer from which to read across Klein's poetics, the criticism situates impersonality's construction of progressive temporality to situate Klein's poetics as moving beyond personality and progressing toward the adoption of impersonality. *Hath Not a Jew* and *The Rocking Chair* are read relationally and developmentally as early/particular versus mature/impersonal works: "growth away from Hebrew religious core ... toward a realistic and cosmopolitan view ..." (Dudek); "antiquity ... [versus] ... the contemporary" (Sutherland); "releas[e] from ... Jewish ... [and] turn to new themes (French-Canadian)" (Steinberg); and "obvious progression from Jewish group ... to ... Canadian group" (Popham). And recalling a critique frequently levelled at representations of racialized difference, *Hath Not a Jew* is thereby swept into the dustbin of autobiographical and traditional poetics and *The Rocking Chair* emerges as a new testament of depersonalized poetics that speaks a common language and for a common community—free of obligation, debt, or responsibility to "arcane" beliefs and practices.

These assumptions have a clear consequence for the way the criticism situates Jewishness. The criticism blurs the belief that *Hath Not a Jew*'s form and content is contrary to modernist tenets with the belief that Jewishness itself is anti-modern as the formation overlaps with antithetic and pejorative characteristics, such as "antiquity" (Sutherland), anti-realist (Dudek), and anti-cosmopolitan (Dudek)—characteristics *The Rocking Chair* is figured to have superseded. The periodic reading of Klein's poetics relies heavily on the presumption of the second collection's adoption of impersonality as a sign of Klein's social and cultural assimilation of "nationhood."

In terms of form and content, *The Rocking Chair* is resoundingly characterized as Canadian. And in spite of its argument for the reconnection between Jews and the local and, by extension, for the redefinition of "English" to include "the Jew," *Hath Not a Jew* is read in singular terms as Jewish; Jewish Canadian or English-speaking Jew do not figure as possibilities. The thematic categorizations "Jewish" and "Canadian" are imposed on an evolutionary trajectory, with the scale tipping heavily toward the latter period in approval and recognition. The language of progressive evolution makes a clear link between *the loss* of Jewishness and, by extension, the frame of reference of diasporic Jewish difference as the contingency for *becoming* Canadian. The critics situate the loss of "the Jew" as a convenient circumstance or positive precondition for the realization of a true Canadian poetics: early, personal, and Jewish versus mature, objective, and Canadian periods. The deployment of impersonality as a process of depersonalization—a narrative about loss as much as improvement—begs the question of whether the critics situate modern poetics not only as *free* of Jewishness, but also as the conscious erasure of Jewishness? And, by extension, the question arises: If *Hath Not a Jew* had not been written, would *The Rocking Chair* have been so quickly and easily championed as a Canadian poetic achievement? The literary reception seems to make the case that without the former, the latter would not have the grounds to become representative of Canadianness.

While the application of modernist poetic theory uses impersonality to reduce the universal to the Canadian, I recognize that "Canadian" functioned as a new common or universal identification, one that held up a utopian promise to override parochial regional or ethnic particularities that were, during this period, being taken to an extreme conclusion in Europe. Given these high stakes, the definition of Canadian ought to be free of particularities. But as Daniel Coleman has persuasively argued, whiteness, masculinity, and Britishness lie at the heart of the formation of Canadian identity: he writes that the "whole civilizing mission of the British Empire assumes that not just Natives but also 'backward' eastern Europeans will be improved when they internalize the superior scientific and social practices of British civility" (*White Civility* 175). The developmental prism conceptualizing Klein's two collections as Jewish/racialized/archaic versus Canadian/white/modern periods speaks to a larger colonial project, one that lines up with the modernist reduction of "universality" to not only Canadian but also, significantly, to whiteness. Recalling Omi and Winant and Brand's arguments about the creation of nativism, racialized poetics are instrumentalized as the border, blocking entrance into Canadian forms of belonging.

UNHOMELY MOVES

Taking as its frame of reference the literary reception of Klein's poetics, my concluding section reconfigures the narrative reifying *Hath Not a Jew* and *The Rocking Chair and Other Poems* as expressions par excellence for modernism's cultural and political project. Bringing together questions regarding racialization, whiteness, modernism, and temporality, this study proposes a methodology called *unhomely moves*, a way of reading the contemporary cultural grammar of Jewish diasporic difference that accounts for absence.

As I have argued, Jewish experiences, practices, and narratives have come to be read outside the parameters of a contemporary definition of diaspora on the basis of the perception that Jews are white and thus connected to mainstream power and political and social discourse: expressions of Jewishness are situated as diaspora's histories rather than its present and future indicatives. But the perception that Jews have arrived fails to recognize the coercive politics of what Brand perhaps too simply describes as "swallowing"—a process of whitening, and not a benign process but one that is at the heart of managing difference. As Bhabha writes, there is a "difference between being English and being Anglicized" (118) or "not quite" white. My reading seeks to reclaim the complexities I believe are inherent to Jewish diasporic difference, complexities that Avtar Brah's argument for diaspora as "a multi-axial performative conception of power [that] highlights the ways in which a group constituted as a 'minority' along one dimension of differentiation may be constructed as a 'majority' along another" (193) relates. It is my belief that the de-racialization of Jews should not be considered a privilege, although socially and politically it has such an effect, but as a coercive swallowing or crossing that facilitates the early modern terms and conditions necessary to the relational construction of Canadian nativism and racialized "scandalous bodies" (Kamboureli).

Parallel to the way mainstream culture coercively encourages the removal of racialized signs of identity from the social realm, signs that remain ghostly in the poetic realm—traditional and visible markers of identity such as yarmulkes, side curls, wigs, and religious attire—have been replaced with what Coleman calls "the manners and behaviors" of *white civility* (*White Civility* 21): such a modernist impersonality, played out over Klein's poetics, allows his poetics the opportunity to move up the very same hierarchy that was historically a hindrance to Canadian forms of belonging. The literary reception of Klein's poetics directly calls attention to the way ingestion does not engender a benign transformation, but rather a process of macerating difference.

My methodology draws from the articulation of the uncanny in Friedrich Schelling's *The Philosophy of Mythology* (1835), found in a translation in Edward Beach's *The Potencies of God(s)*. Within a larger discussion of historical conditions, Schelling speculates that the creation of Homeric poetics represented a unique achievement. Reversing the Freudian trajectory of the uncanny, he writes that these poetics were a consequence of the Greeks' ability to psychically and socially repress "the uncanny principle" (Beach 228). Schelling suggests the Greeks believed the uncanny, "past," or "irrational principle" were primitive, raw, chaotic forces or fundamental urges (represented by magic, animism, and the occult); traces of an earlier epoch, these principles were out of place in the world the Greeks sought to establish based on reason, order, and form. He adds that the desire to estrange the uncanny and its subsequent fulfillment differentiated the Greeks from "Oriental" (Eastern) cultures, where the uncanny remained visibly dominant and outwardly valued. He feels reason's dominance over the irrational is embodied in the clarity, harmony, and universality of Homeric poetics—aesthetics of the present tense, purified of the outward expression of the "past principle."

Schelling's theory offers a way to reframe the simplicity of progressive erasure that has settled the reception of Klein's poetics into a dogmatic lockstep, for repression obviously is a different formulation than elimination. Schelling writes that the uncanny does not entirely disappear: its "dark and darkening power" (Beach 226) remains in the "interior" of the Greek psychic, social, and aesthetic spheres. It is this interiority that characterizes his perception of the Greek world and consciousness itself: "The Homeric pantheon tacitly contains a Mystery within it, and is as it were built up over an abyss" (Beach 226).

I want to connect Schelling's configuration of the uncanny as absent presence to Nicolas Abraham's reading of the relationship between haunting, visibility, and subversion. His remark that "what haunts are not the dead, but the gaps left within us by the secrets of others" (171) postulates that an individual's repressions form a psychic tomb in the unconscious of subsequent generations. Empowering silence's affective possibilities, he concludes that the tomb is embodied by the figure of a phantom that "is sustained by secreted words, invisible gnomes whose aim is to wreak havoc, from within the unconscious, in the coherence of logical progression" (175). Within this formulation, "the past" does not return to haunt the present; rather, "secreted words" produce an energetic state that drags against the forward march of development, upsetting the dogmatism of progressive linearity and the clarity of superficial representation. It is this unsettling state—a complication to the progressive and periodic classification of Klein's poetics—that I seek to draw out as a methodology, a configuration that forms the basis of an alternative reading of the poetic and social architecture of modernism.

Approaching Schelling's theory through Abraham's thoughts on haunting, this chapter connects the articulation of diasporic difference in *Hath Not a Jew* to the interiority of *The Rocking Chair and Other Poems*, an interiority related through particular passages that relate suffering, alienation, and dislocation. In poems such as "Indian Reservation: Caughnawaga," the speaker asks, "Where are the tribes, the feathered bestiaries?" and finds "This is a grassy ghetto, and no home. / ... The better hunters have prevailed" (11–12); and in "The Portrait of the Poet as Landscape," "He suspects that something has happened, a law / been passed, a nightmare ordered. Set apart, / he finds himself with a special haircut and dress, / as on a reservation" (53); and more specifically we find various words and phrases that recall Jewish experience, iconography, and narrative history, as when the speaker asks, "The blind ark lost and pertrified? ... But even when known, it's more than what it is: for here, as in a Josephdream ... / ... Our own gomorrah house, / the sodom that merely to look at makes one salt? (23), and "O, he who unrolled our culture from his scroll" (50).

From the post-Holocaust contemporary perspective, these passages can obviously be read as Jewish experiences. But I do not want to categorize these passages as "Jewish."[6] Rather, my reading seeks to maintain a focus on the uncertainties, what their definitive lack of "sign" puts into play: an uncertainty that captures the radically disruptive quality of absent presence. *unhomely moves* takes holds of calcified assumptions of what pertains to Jewish versus Canadian poetics and reads *Hath Not a Jew*'s articulation of racialized diasporic temporality as an absent presence within *The Rocking Chair and Other Poems'* timeless universal position, haunting its embodiment as the ideal expression of modernism. Maintaining the ambiguities and ambivalences allows space for the recognition of the collection's limits of acceptable formal and thematic difference and a reminder for what has been left out, overlooked, in the drive for universality. These passages admit to the secret burial of differential principles within the collection itself, a secret buried under the veneer of "Canadian" homeliness.

This chapter reads contemporary Jewish diasporic difference as a process marked by the erasures of cultural displacement necessitated by *white civility*, a process situated within a larger colonial ideological structure, and haunted by the immeasurable losses that are a part of the process of becoming visible (becoming Canadian) itself.

ACKNOWLEDGEMENTS

Early drafts of this chapter were presented at two conferences—"The Poet as Landscape: A Portrait of A.M. Klein" (Concordia University, 2007) and the Canadian Association for Commonwealth Literature and Language Studies (University of British Columbia, 2010)—and I want to thank the organizers for the opportunity and the participants for their questions. I also want to recognize Frank Davey, Jasmin Habib, and Tilottama Rajan for many pertinent conversations, Jeff Derksen for the suggestion of the phrase "unhomely moves," and Christine Kim, Sophie McCall, and Anne Stone for their commentaries in the development of this chapter.

NOTES

1 Hurricane Katrina diaspora: <http://www.nytimes.com/imagepages/2005/10/02/national/ nationalspecial/20051002diaspora_graphic.html>. Croatian Math diaspora: <http://74 .125.155.132/search?q=cache:GtwHEbnuJsAJ:www.croatianhistory.net/mat/cromath .html+%22york+university%22%2Bdiaspora&cd=`&hl=en&ct=clnk&client=safari>.

2 Perhaps due to the new field of inquiry that has opened up through investigations on Israel (such as the work of Ella Shohat and Irit Rogoff) and the Israeli–Palestinian conflict (such as the work of Edward Said and Eyal Weizman) have opened up, specific questions pertaining to the Jewish diaspora are largely absent from the contemporary field of diaspora and/or postcolonial studies. I recognize that the establishment of Israel raises the need to consider a new set of questions about the connection between Jewishness, diaspora, and homeland(s). But I firmly do not believe that "Israel" marks every conversation on Jewish diaspora or that the creation of a modern Jewish nation-state negates or unifies the multitude of diasporic experiences that have continued to be formed since the first dispersion of Jews.

3 The talk was called "Not in My Country: Safe Sex Campaigns, Transnationality, and the Continuing Search for Queer Nation," sponsored by the Faculty of Information and Media Studies.

4 Southern and eastern Europeans and Romani were also perceived as non-white peoples.

5 In the original text, Shylock does name Christian as the mainstream culture to whom his plea is directed.

6 Recent criticism, such as in the work of William Walsh, Zailig Pollock, Miriam Waddington, D.M.R. Bentley, and Brian Trehearne, have suggested that such passages can be read as recalling Jewish experiences.

Asian Canadian Critical Practice as Commemoration

Christopher Lee

> Responsibility annuls the call to which it seeks to respond by necessarily changing it to the calculations of answerability.
> —Gayatri Chakravorty Spivak, "Responsibility" (58)

I

THIS CHAPTER WAS WRITTEN AS a response to the 100th anniversary of the 1907 Anti-Asian riots in Vancouver. On 7 September 1907, the Asiatic Exclusion League held a rally outside city hall that attracted around 10 percent of the White population living in the city at the time.[1] The League was joined by labour unionists from the United States who, two days earlier, had violently driven out some 700 Sikhs from Bellingham, Washington. As the speakers' rhetoric grew increasingly heated, the crowd marched to nearby Chinatown and began to smash windows and vandalize properties. As it moved into Japantown, the mob found Japanese residents armed and prepared to defend their neighbourhood, and a two-day standoff ensued. While there were no known deaths, there were many injuries on all sides and extensive property damage. According to historian Erika Lee,

> By 3:00 a.m. [on 8 September 1907], virtually every building occupied by the Chinese was damaged. In the Japanese quarter, fifty-nine properties were wrecked and the Japanese-language school was set on fire. Two thousand Chinese were driven from their homes [...]. The Canadian government later estimated $13,519.45 and $25,990 in estimated losses for actual and resulting damage among Japanese and Chinese in Vancouver respectively. (31)

Although it was not the first incident of mass violence directed against Asians in British Columbia, the 1907 riots was a watershed event that represents the culmination of over a half century of anti-Asian racism in Canada. When British Columbia joined Confederation in 1871, the new province was a remarkably diverse, albeit already racialized, society that included First Nations (then the majority of the population), White (mostly Anglo) settlers, and other groups such as the Chinese.[2] The completion of the Canadian Pacific Railway in 1885, accomplished in no small part using Chinese labour, facilitated an additional influx of White settlers that would drastically alter the racial demographics and politics of the province. As ideologies of White supremacy, encapsulated by the popular slogan "White Canada Forever," continued to gain dominance, numerous attempts to disenfranchise Asians and restrict their entry ensued.[3] Such measures included the head tax on Chinese immigration (first imposed in 1885 and incrementally raised until the 1923 *Chinese Immigration Act* effectively halted further immigration), the 1908 Gentleman's Agreement by which Japan voluntarily restricted the emigration of its nationals, and the Continuous Passage rule, which stopped all immigration from the Indian subcontinent, passed the same year. These measures exemplify a wider atmosphere of racial terror under which the daily lives of Asians in Canada were marked by mistreatment, exploitation, and violence.

Much more can be said about this history as well as the riots themselves, but the purpose of this chapter is not historiographic. If the history I have sketched indicates the range and depth of anti-Asian racism at the turn of the century, the fact that I am recounting it in the early years of the twenty-first century turns this chapter into an act of commemoration in its own right. The purpose of this chapter is to think through and beyond specific projects of commemoration (including those related to the 1907 riots) in order to address the ethics of commemoration more broadly. How should we understand the responsibility to commemorate, and how is temporality reconfigured through such a call? I pose these questions as a way of framing what I will be calling Asian Canadian critical practice, the constellation of political, intellectual, artistic, and activist projects that have organized (sometimes loosely) around the term "Asian Canadian" in recent years. The stakes of this term has been extensively discussed and debated; here, my purpose is not to insist on its validity and coherence but to simply recognize that it has acquired considerable currency and relevance in contemporary discussions about racialization.[4] With regard to the 1907 riots, which affected South Asians, Chinese, and Japanese, the term is especially useful for drawing our attention to how the history of these groups have been closely intertwined due to the racial hierarchies established in a White settler colony.

In fall 2006, a consortium of arts organizations, academic institutions, labour unions, activist groups, and ethnic community organizations came together under the name "Anniversaries of Change" in order to plan and organize a year of events, as well as an educational curriculum development project, to address and commemorate the 100th anniversary of the riots.[5] In order to stimulate a wider dialogue about the legacies of racism, Anniversaries of Change (hereafter referred to as "Anniversaries") marked three other important anniversaries that also fell in 2007: the 60th anniversary of the 1947 *Citizenship Act* (which finally extended civil rights to minorities, although groups such as Japanese Canadians and some First Nations would remain disenfranchised even after the passage of the Act); the 40th anniversary of the 1967 *Immigration Act* (which finally removed racial and national quotas); and the 10th anniversary of the 1997 handover of Hong Kong to the People's Republic of China (which triggered significant immigration from Hong Kong and other Asian countries in the 1980s and 1990s). Together, these four anniversaries shape a powerful narrative of Asian Canadian history that moves from the era of exclusion, through struggles for civil and political rights, to the recent transformations that have accompanied Canada's participation in the Asia Pacific economy. As a brochure produced by Anniversaries explains,

> Our goals are to underscore the Asian Canadian contribution to diversity in Canada, to reach across generations and cultures to create a broad discussion about how Canadian society achieved diversity, and to learn and apply the lessons of fighting racism. [...] We will remember these important historical moments, honour those who suffered and those who fought against racism, and learn and apply the lessons of the past so that history shall not repeat itself. ("100 Years of Change" 4)

The goal of Anniversaries is therefore to revise Canadian history in order to expose how racism and oppression have been erased from public consciousness. Anniversaries is both commemorative (it forges a specific relationship between those in the present and the past) and activist (its activities are driven by an anti-racist agenda attentive to inequalities in the present); in other words, it takes the occasion of commemoration as an opportunity to reimagine how we might understand nationhood and citizenship. The narrative coherence of this project depends in no small part on the fact that we tend to (arbitrarily) gravitate toward anniversaries that fall in decades. However, the work of commemoration opened up by Anniversaries cannot be contained within the parameters of these four events for even though they resonate powerfully in the lives of Asian Canadians, they provide only a partial snapshot of a long history that, as a whole, urgently calls for recognition and commemoration. The larger project of Anniversaries, then, necessarily exceeds its frame of reference; indeed, we might ask why 2007 should not also be marked as the 122nd anniversary of the first imposition of the head tax, the 93rd anniversary of the *Komagata Maru* incident, the 65th anniversary of the beginning of the internment of Japanese Canadians, and so on.

If Asian Canadian critical practice insists that histories of anti-Asian racism continue to resonate in our present moment, then commemoration reimagines our current conjuncture of time and space as a cipher of these multiple sedimented pasts. Commemoration initiates a particular relationship with these pasts, which we can conceive as a sort of exchange in which we give recognition and attention to the past and receive, in return, a sense of fulfilled responsibility. The *Oxford English Dictionary* defines commemoration as "The action of calling to the remembrance of a hearer or reader. [...] A calling to remembrance, or preserving in memory, by some solemn observance, public celebration, etc." ("Commemoration"). The notion that we are *called* to commemorate underscores our debt to the past, a debt that appears to us most urgently when we can identify those to whom justice is owed—head-tax payers and their families, those who were interned, for example. In such circumstances, commemoration can result in concrete measures to address and redress those injustices.[6]

But nothing guarantees that the measures we enact in the present are in fact adequate to the debt we owe (after all, redress settlements carry a strong symbolic dimension that indicates the inadequacy of material compensation alone). The debt that calls us into commemoration cannot be concretely schematized, let alone repaid. Nor does commemoration guarantee a more just future, although (in the best-case scenario) it may sustain and renew vigilance against the repetition of past injustices. But at the very least, commemoration engenders an ethical relationship between the present and the past that exceeds, even as it animates, concrete actions.

If Asian Canadian critical practice aspires to responsibly engage histories of anti-Asian racism, what happens to this goal when aspects of that history remain unknown and unknowable despite the most meticulous attempts at recovery? I am thinking here of histories that have been ignored in a racialized society and suppressed from public discourse, as well as pasts that have been erased through processes of forgetting, especially with regard to intensely personal experiences that cannot be adequately communicated to those who have not experienced them, nor fully accessible even to those who have. To contend with these absences is to be mindful of Walter Benjamin's distinction between historicism and historical materialism as set out in his famous thesis "On the Concept of History": whereas the former conceives history from the perspective of those in power, the latter confronts the erasure of excluded histories. For the historical materialist, "nothing that has ever happened should be regarded as lost to history," but these lost pasts are not available except as "an image that flashes up at the moment of its recognizability, and is never seen again" (390). Benjamin mitigates the inaccessibility of these pasts by imagining a messianic time of redemption in which the fullness of the past can finally be recovered. Until then, the historical materialist can only confront the impossible task of coming to terms with the unknowable: Benjamin asks, "Doesn't a breath of the air that pervaded earlier days caress us as well? In the voices we hear, isn't there an echo of now silent ones?" (390).

In Joy Kogawa's novel *Obasan*, the protagonist, Naomi Nakane, faces a similar dilemma as she seeks to grasp the elusive personal and collective histories that seem to possess a visceral materiality in her daily life (the novel is set in years prior to the 1988 Redress settlement). "All our ordinary stories," she observes, "are changed in time, altered as much by the present as the present is shaped by the past. Potent and pervasive as a prairie dust storm, memories and dreams seep and mingle through cracks, settling on furniture and into upholstery. Our attics and living rooms encroach on each other, deep into their invisible places" (25). Although a fair amount of this past is revealed in the course of the novel, Naomi never overcomes her feelings of uncertainty unlike her Aunt Emily, who insists that recovery of historical truth is the necessary first step toward justice and reconciliation. When Naomi learns that her mother had died in Nagasaki in the aftermath of the atom bomb, this information, far from resolving a long-standing mystery, only generates new questions: "Silent Mother, you do not speak or write. You do not reach through the night to enter morning, but remain in voicelessness. From the extremity of much dying, the only sound that reaches me now is the sigh of your remembered breath, a wordless word. How shall I attend that speech, Mother, how shall I trace that wave?" (Kogawa 241).

In the absence of adequate knowledge about the past, commemoration inheres in the very temporal relationship between the past and (those of us in the) present. This relationship is fraught with difficulties, but we can at least specify the *form* of this relationship as an ethical one of responsibility. As Gayatri Chakravorty Spivak writes,

> It is that all action is undertaken in response to a call (or something that seems to us to resemble a call) that cannot be grasped as such. Response here involves not only "respond to" as in *"give* an answer to," but also the related situations of "answering to" as in being responsible for a name (this brings up the question of the relationship between being responsible for/ to ourselves and for/to others) [...]. It is also, when it is possible to be face-to-face, the task and lesson of attending to her response so that it can draw forth one's own. ("Responsibility" 61; emphasis in original)

Responsibility calls on us to give our responses, an injunction that takes us from specific acts of commemoration to a larger commitment to commemoration as an unending series of uncontainable projects.

The open-endedness of responsibility underscores Jacques Derrida's account of the gift, a theme that appears frequently in his later writings in which he earnestly engages questions of responsibility and ethics;[7] for the purposes of this chapter, his discussion of the gift provides a theoretical touchstone with which to examine the role of commemoration in Asian Canadian critical practice. In *Given Time*, Derrida argues that a pure gift can exist only where there is "no reciprocity, return, exchange, countergift, or debt" (12). Any trace of exchange annuls the gift by resituating it in terms of obligation and debt. These conditions underscore the impossibility of the gift, which we encounter only as a trace of something that cannot exist in pure form. Derrida suggests that even an awareness of the gift as such would place it back into circuits of exchange and reciprocity. Noting how the gift cannot exist in real time, he insists that it happens "in an instant that no doubt does not belong to the economy of time, in a time without time" (17).

For Derrida, both time and the gift are defined by their uncontainability within conventional circuits of thought. Pheng Cheah explains: "Precisely because time is what we cannot give to ourselves, because time is what we do not have, the giving of time exceeds the certainties and calculations of human reason" ("Obscure" 42). Similarly, "the gift can only appear in its effacement and violation" (43), in our awareness of its disappearance, impurity, and dissolution under demands of exchange and reciprocity. Two important points follow from this: first, the gift exceeds the subject and the social by positing an ethical relationship that cannot be contained through reference to the actual human subjects to whom we would owe something; second, what is left over in the wake of the gift's dissolution (the event that enables us to apprehend a gift in the first place) is the temporal relationship it institutes for as Derrida writes, "The gift is not a gift, the gift only gives to the extent it gives time [...] where there is gift, there is time. What it gives, the gift, is time" (41).

By evoking the gift in this chapter, I want to hone in on how the ethical stakes of commemoration inhere in the forms of temporality it inhabits in order to locate the limits of Asian Canadian critical practice at the very point in which its obsessive engagement with the past dovetails into a politics of futurity. For Derrida, the impossibility of the gift prevents any project of responsibility from achieving closure: justice, in his account, is always a condition to come, never fully actualized in the present. The *urgency* of the demand for justice, however, animates the concrete projects that arise in response to it. Derrida writes:

> the effort to think the groundless ground of this quasi-"transcendental illusion" should not be [...] a simple movement of faith in the face of that which exceeds the limits of experience, knowledge, science, economy—and even philosophy. On the contrary, it is a matter—desire beyond desire—of responding faithfully but also as rigorously as possible both to the injunction or the order of the *gift* [...]: *Know* still what giving *wants to say, know how to give*, know what you want and want to say when you give, know what you intend to give, know how the gift annuls itself, commit yourself [...] even if commitment is the destruction of the gift by the gift, give economy its chance. (30; emphasis in the original)

The point, then, is to embrace concrete acts of giving while recognizing the impossibility of the gift as such. As John Caputo explains, "Derrida enjoins a double injunctive, both to move within the grooves of the existing circles of knowledge and economy and also to outmaneuver them, both to give beyond economy and to give economy its chance [...] the idea is not utterly to demolish [cycles of exchange] but to interrupt them, to loosen them long enough to let something new happen, to let the gift be given" (171).

I want to suggest that we might conceive the work of commemoration in a similar manner. Instead of confining commemoration to specific knowable events that can be readily understood as historical injustices, this chapter seeks to explore commemoration as a critical practice that engages with the past in order to loosen and open it up to what has been repressed or buried—to the echo of silent voices, the sigh of remembered sighs, and wordless words. To that end, what follows are two brief "thought exercises" that are meant to interrupt our understanding of historical time by refiguring the present scene of Asian Canadian critical practice in light of commemoration.[8]

II

With the completion of the Canadian Pacific Railway (CPR) in 1885, the federal government lost its main justification for maintaining a steady and available supply of Chinese labourers.[9] Responding to considerable pressure from politicians and civic groups in British Columbia to exclude Chinese and other Asians from the nation, the government of Prime Minister John A. Macdonald imposed a head tax on all Chinese entering Canada. As the head tax was being debated and enacted, the House of Commons also considered a law that would regulate who could exercise the right of franchise.[10] On May 4, 1885, the House debated an amendment that, when it was ultimately passed, defined personhood in the following manner: "'Person' means a male person, including an Indian, and excluding a person of Mongolian or Chinese race" (Canada, *Official Report* 20). In effect, this amendment defined the significance of race and gender (as well as class, since owning of property was also a condition for exercising the franchise) to the political life of the nation. It is important to note that it simultaneously racialized Asians (the "Mongolian or Chinese race") and First Nations, although these two groups were treated very differently under the law: Asian immigrants were subject to various exclusion measures, while the *Indian Act* legally defined most Natives as dependants of the state. Although the amendment in question did enfranchise some male Natives, only those who owned a certain amount of property outright (as opposed to living on tribal lands, which were legally Crown property) were eligible to vote, a requirement that effectively disqualified most from the franchise.

In her study of the parliamentary debates on the franchise, Veronica Strong-Boag suggests that the Natives and the Chinese viewed the franchise quite differently: whereas many Natives considered exercising the franchise as tantamount to assimilation, many Chinese saw their lack of political rights as a sign of their inferior social and legal status.[11] Strong-Boag argues that with regard to the Chinese, the new *Franchise Act* was especially significant because it inscribed a clearly racial distinction between Asians and Europeans into Canadian law. Even though members of Parliament were generally hostile to the Chinese, the records of their debates reveal a range of views regarding the status of the Chinese in Canada (members from British Columbia were usually the most hostile).[12] Some opposed the amendment on the grounds of democratic principle, while others praised the "wonderful civilisation" (Canada, *Official Report* 1587) of the Chinese and expressed regret over their mistreatment even as they cited the inability of the Chinese to assimilate into Canadian society as ground for their exclusion from the franchise. The most rabid opponents of Asian immigration reiterated a myriad of racist stereotypes and insisted on the right of individual provinces to decide who can exercise the right of franchise.

I want to focus here on a particularly telling comment from Prime Minister Macdonald in which he spells out the logic of denying the franchise to the Chinese:

> [W]hile [the Chinese immigrant] gives us his labor and is paid for it, and is valuable, the same as a threshing machine or any other agricultural implement which we may borrow from the United States on hire and return it the owner on the south side of the line; a Chinaman gives us his labor and gets his money, but that money does not fructify in Canada; he does not invest it here, but takes it with him and returns to China; and if he cannot, his executors or his friends send his body back to the flowery land. But he has no British instincts or British feelings or aspirations, and therefore ought not to have a vote. (Canada, *Official Report* 1582)

Here, the operations of the gift find their way into the citizenship debates through a convoluted logic. Macdonald compares Chinese labourers to "threshing machines" and "agricultural implements" in order to underscore their utilitarian function. As borrowed tools, the "Chinaman" can be returned when no longer needed and easily removed from the body politic, which bears no responsibility toward his well-being.

According to the prime minister, the Chinese give their labour, but are then "paid for it." Here, giving is simply part of an exchange that is completed through the payment of wages. Macdonald goes on to fault the Chinese for taking their wages back to China instead of spending them in Canada, a claim that was simply not accurate: New Brunswick MP Arthur Hill Gillmor, who was more sympathetic to the Chinese, responded that trade conducted by Chinese in Canada generated $162,300 per year in additional tax revenue, and cites the following finding from the 1885 Royal Commission on Chinese Immigration: "the Chinese labourer earns about $300 a year, and that it costs him from $250 to $275 to live; so he could not take more than $30 or $40 away." Gillmor concludes, "They do not, therefore, take their money out of the country" (Canada, *Official Report* 1585).[13]

Macdonald's argument, however, is not really about economics, but rather about the cultural basis of national belonging. Although he seems to suggest that the Chinese could theoretically receive social and political belonging in return for their capital, he immediately forecloses this possibility by asserting a fundamental *cultural* difference by insisting on British "instincts," "feelings or aspirations" as the basis of political and civil rights. To underscore his point, he declares,

> The Chinese are not like Indians, sons of the soil. They come from a for-eign country, they have no intent, as a people of making a domicile of any portion of Canada; they come and work or trade, and when they are tired of it they go away, taking with them their profits. They are, besides, natives of a country where representative institutions are unknown, and I think we cannot safely give them the elective franchise. (Canada, *Official Report* 1582)

When asked whether Chinese from Hong Kong, who were British colonial subjects, were entitled to legal rights, Macdonald replies in the negative and insists, "I used the word Chinaman to designate a race" and goes on to approv-ingly note the Australian practice of excluding Hong Kong Chinese on racial grounds (Canada, *Official Report* 1582).

Reading Macdonald's words today from the perspective of Asian Canadian critical practice, we cannot help but be struck by what he neglects to mention: that the working conditions of Chinese labourers in Canada were thoroughly exploitative. According to historian Anthony Chan, Chinese labourers on the railway received a dollar a day in wages while White workers were paid between $1.50 to $2.50 a day. Chinese were also made to pay for overpriced provisions and supplies (60). In addition, Chan notes, they endured extremely dangerous work conditions: "failure to warn Chinese rail hands of imminent explosions, inadequate protection from falling boulders and rock slides, and the lack of safety precautions against cave-ins gave rise to the saying in Canada's China-towns that 'for every foot of railroad through the Fraser canyon, a Chinese worker died'" (66–67). The exploitation of Chinese labour was critical to the development of the province and the building of the CPR in particular, so much so that overt exclusion measures enacted by the BC legislature were often disqualified by the federal government in order to ensure the unabated impor-tation of Chinese labour. Yet insofar as he conceives national belonging as the gift of a (supposedly) benevolent state, Macdonald imposes a debt of gratitude that insidiously masks the exploitation sanctioned by the very same state.[14]

Macdonald's invocation of the gift can well be dismissed as an ideological cover for coercive domination. Nevertheless, I want to suggest that one way to read his words against their grain is to recover the logic of the gift in order to articulate our current responsibility vis-à-vis embedded histories of racism. To do so would take seriously our having received the results of exploited labour *as a gift*. My point is not to mythologize Chinese workers by incorporating their painful histories in sanitized, patriotic narratives of nation-building. Instead, I want to follow Derrida's lead and ask what kinds of responsibility this "gift" of labour demands from those of us who inhabit the Canadian nation today. This question cannot be answered within the confines of a politics that focuses on rendering restitution to victims of injustice: those who "gave" their labour, after all, are no longer with us and, unlike the case of the head tax in which set monetary amounts were transferred, the debt of exploitation is not measurable in concrete terms. What would it mean to give back a life that could have been lived differently? How can we, enjoying the comforts of a province and a country that were built through exploited labour, find ourselves as anything but the recipients of an unintended gift—a gift that was never meant to be given, but a gift nonetheless? Reading the historical facts of racism in light of the gift forces us to confront questions of responsibility—of *our* responsibility—to which the work of commemoration unfolds as a partial response. Our task requires nothing less than reimagining the temporality of citizenship in order to refuse narratives of progress and closure that reinforce the power of the nation and think instead at the moments in which the gift erupts in our time to reveal the kinds of forgetting and erasure that enable the nation to persist.

III

More than a century later, another conservative government, this time led by Brian Mulroney, finally negotiated a redress settlement with the National Association of Japanese Canadians (NAJC) regarding the internment and incarceration of Japanese Canadians during the Second World War. In *Redress: Inside the Japanese Canadian Call for Justice*, critic and poet Roy Miki writes at length about the moment in which the settlement was announced in the House of Commons on 22 September 1988. The figure of the gift plays an important role in his account and marks the ways in which an ethics of commemoration necessarily exceeds the concrete measures achieved in this landmark settlement. Miki, who observed the proceedings from the visitors' gallery as part of the NAJC delegation, describes the announcement as a moment of exchange in which "the 'Japanese Canadian' identity that was constituted by a history of injustices at the hands of the nation was given up as a gift to the nation and therefore ceased to exist in the conditions of its desire for a resolved future" (*Redress* 323). This exchange, in turn, fundamentally transformed what it meant to be Japanese Canadian:

> In receiving the gift of redress from a nation that had stripped them of their rights in the 1940s, [the NAJC delegates] also gave the gift of redress to a nation that had acknowledged the injustices they suffered as a consequence of that action. [...] When Japanese Canadians achieved their settlement—this "dream of justice," in the language of their movement—they gave their wartime experience as a gift to the official history of the nation. And in a reciprocal process, the "Japanese Canadian" identity that was forged in its negotiations with the Canadian nation, an un-redressed identity that was so intimately connected to the conditions of "enemy alien," was released from its historical boundaries. The 20th century history that had been carried in the living bodies of Japanese Canadians for over many decades had to be resolved—it was one of the givens in their negotiations with the nation—but in the singular event of redress, that history had to be surrendered. (Miki, *Redress* 325)

In the course of the settlement, the Canadian government offered symbolic acknowledgement, as well as monetary compensation, for a terrible injustice while Japanese Canadians "gave" a way to resolve a gaping hypocrisy in the history of Canadian democracy. Unlike the settlement itself, which included an official apology and spelled out in detail the financial terms of redress, the gift offered by Japanese Canadians is far more difficult to quantify. Miki breaks down this gift into two parts: first, Japanese Canadians gave up their "wartime experience as a gift to the official history of the nation" at which point the internment could be written into the official narratives of a liberal state. Although this gift was a necessary outcome of the settlement, it also enabled the nation to incorporate histories that would otherwise challenge its legitimacy. Second, a long-standing attachment to an "unredressed identity" formed from "the racialized national boundaries that had disenfranchised [Japanese Canadians]" was finally given up.

The irony of redress, according to Miki, is that it was both a moment of loss as well as gain. Shuttling between giving and giving up, he suggests that to give up an un-redressed identity is to lose an entire way of being in time, both in relation to a painful past and a future that may bring about a resolution of injustice. In this sense, redress is constituted by complex and uneven exchanges that collide in a temporal instant. Miki is not arguing that it would have been better had redress not been achieved. Rather, he problematizes the very structures of exchange that inevitably circumscribe redress as a concretely actualized project. By interrupting the time of redress (and, by extension, the historical narratives of internment it enables), Miki imagines an ethics of commemoration that exceeds the mechanisms of exchange, both symbolic and material. In this sense, he undertakes the work of the historical materialist who, according to Benjamin, writes in a present that is "not a transition," but rather a moment "in which time takes a stand and has come to a standstill"; it is precisely in this "messianic arrest of happening" that the historical materialist recognizes "a revolutionary chance in the fight for the oppressed past. He (sic) takes cognizance of it to blast a specific era out of the homogenous course of history" (396).

Conceived in this manner, commemoration is not a matter of putting forth a narrative that would just challenge dominant national histories that marginalize minorities and obscure realities of racism. Although narratives such as those put forth by projects such as Anniversaries are necessary and valuable, Miki's account of redress suggests another understanding of commemoration, one that interrupts our experience of temporality, arresting its movement in order to grasp how commemoration exceeds circuits of exchange. This concept of time stands in stark contrast with more conventional models of Asian Canadian critical practice. At various moments in the history of Asian Canadian organizing, activists have claimed that by knowing the past, we can understand the present, and that this knowledge would help secure what is, after all, an unpredictable future.[15] For example, the lead editorial of the inaugural issue of the *Powell Street Review* in 1972 declared, "there have been so many gaps in our own history here in Canada, that we are only now on the verge of comprehending who we really are in this society. [...] [W]hat is it that makes up the Japanese Canadian character? For that we must look into our experience—our past, present, future" ("A Reaffirmation" 1). Or, as activist and academic Anthony Chan bluntly puts it, "We have a history. And with a history, 'we damn well know where we've been so we damn well know where we're going'" (cited in Li 41).

I want to suggest, however, that projects such as Anniversaries of Change should be grasped as an occasion for something rather different: not the bold grasping of time in its entirety, but an openness to the messy debts of time, to

the possibility that the totality of Asian Canadian history, accessible and inac-
cessible, is sedimented at this very moment and demands our commemoration. Benjamin calls this understanding of temporality "now-time," a state in
which entire histories "appear in a tremendous abbreviation" (396). A century
after riots solidified a regime of racial terror, the urgent task of Asian Canadian
critical practice is to search for ways to inhabit our own "now-time" through
acts of commemoration, to recognize our debts, and invest them toward a
more just future.

NOTES

I thank Alice Ming Wai Jim for inviting me to present an early version of this chapter at the
symposium Redress Express: Current Directions in Asian Canadian Art and Culture, held
in Vancouver in August 2007. I am grateful to Mary Sui Yee Wong for her encouragement,
Maia Joseph for her research assistance, and to Rob Ho, Larissa Lai, Kirsten McAllister,
Hayne Wai, and Henry Yu for helping me formulate the ideas in this chapter. This chapter
is respectfully dedicated to the memory of Professor Edgar Wickberg.

1 A partial list of sources on the history of the 1907 riots include: E. Lee, Miki (*Redress*),
   Price, Roy, Sugimoto, and Ward. In the aftermath of the riots, the government held an
   inquiry (led by future Prime Minister William Lyon Mackenzie King) into the event
   and resulted in compensation for property damages. See both reports by King.
2 According to historian Patricia Roy, "In 1866 [five years before British Columbia joined
   Confederation], the governor estimated there were 3,070 whites and 1,705 Chinese in
   the mainland colony, but no one was sure of the exact figures. One fact was clear; both
   groups were minorities; the Mainland was also home to over 30,000 native Indians" (5).
3 For accounts of anti-Asian racism during this period, see Roy and Ward.
4 For discussions on the history and stakes of the term "Asian Canadian," see, for example, Goellnicht, Li, and Miki ("Can Asian Adian?").
5 For more information about Anniversaries of Change, see <http://www.history.ubc.ca/
   documents/faculty/yu/AofC_brochure_08_lores.pdf>. Also see C. Cho.
6 For a discussion on the implications and contexts of the term "redress," see McAllister
   and Miki (*Redress*).
7 Derrida's writings on the gift are part of a larger discourse on the relationship between
   the gift and exchange economies, which began with Marcel Mauss's anthropological
   study on the potlatch, published in the 1923. Since then, thinkers such as Claude Levi-
   Strauss, George Bataille, Lewis Hyde, and Pierre Bourdieu have responded critically to
   Mauss's findings. For his part, Derrida mobilizes the gift in texts such as *Given Time* and
   The Gift of Death as part of his larger deconstructive project vis-à-vis Western metaphysics and its humanist foundations. In addition to the sources on Derrida cited in the text
   of this chapter, see Osteen for a more general discussion of theories of the gift. For a
   particularly relevant use of the gift with regard to race and settler colonies, see the final
   chapter in Hage.
8 I borrow the notion of "thought exercise" from Hannah Arendt's *Between Past and
   Future: Eight Exercises in Political Thought*.

9   This shift is more a matter of political rhetoric than economic reality. As Lily Cho has shown, construction work on the CPR continued for years after its putative completion in 1885 ("Rereading").

10 The franchise had previously been determined at the provincial level.

11 It is also significant that during the debates over the Chinese, several members brought up the status of Black Canadians, who possessed legal rights even though they were considered by many to be members of an "inferior" race. In other words, what Strong-Boag labels the "citizenship debates" reveals how unstable racial hierarchies were being defined by what was, after all, a group of White men.

12 For a detailed discussion of the range of political views on Asian immigration around this period, see L. Cho ("Rereading").

13 It is important to note that Gillmor's valorization of the Chinese, which was at times rather patronizing in tone, was based on the claim that they compared favourably with Natives (even though he also claims to sympathize with the latter). In any case, his sentiments were immediately dismissed by those claiming that members from BC could provide more reliable knowledge than the Royal Commission Report.

14 We might also note that this logic persists, albeit in very different form, in our contemporary multicultural moment. Although the racist measures he advocated have been repealed for some time now, the notion of the citizenship as the gift of the nation still circulates widely. Then, as now, the figure of the gift covers up the economic as well as racialized bases of immigration through the lofty and idealized language of citizenship.

15 For a detailed account of Asian Canadian activism, see Li.

Diasporic Longings
(Re)Figurations of Home and Homelessness in Richard Wagamese's Work

Renate Eigenbrod

Being strangers in our own land is a sad story, but, if we can speak, we may turn this story around.

—Rita Joe, *Song of Rita Joe* (14)

We are what we imagine. Our very existence consists in our imagination of ourselves. Our best destiny is to imagine, at least, completely, who and what, and *that* we are. The greatest tragedy that can befall us is to go unimagined.

—N. Scott Momaday, "The Man Made of Words" (103)

IN THE FIRST VOLUME OF the *Diaspora* journal, William Safran refines Walker Connor's definition of diaspora as "that segment of a people living outside the homeland" and suggests that the term be a descriptor for different groups of peoples (qtd. in Safran 83). He lists six characteristics: the dispersal from an original "center"; "a collective memory … about their original homeland"; not being "fully accepted by their host society"; the view of "their ancestral homeland as their true, ideal home"; a commitment to the "original homeland," and a continued relationship with that homeland which defines the "ethnocommunal consciousness" (83–94). In his comparative discussion of various diasporas in the body of his article, Safran does not include Indigenous communities. This is not surprising as indigeneity and diaspora are, or should be, seen as the opposite sides of a people's expressions of belonging and home since "Indigenous" connotes a sense of home as living on the land you were born into, i.e., not displaced from, while the notion of diaspora originates in the description of the Jewish dispersion in Babylonian times and, as Ashcroft,

Griffiths, and Tiffin comment on the respective text in Deuteronomy 28, verse 25, means a scattering, an exile ("Introduction" 425). However, due to the colonial ideology of *terra nullius* at the time of contact, Indigenous peoples in settler states were pushed off their homelands as they were seen as less than human and as not truly inhabiting the land. In various stages and through different forms of dispossession, physical removal, and cultural alienation during colonization, Indigenous peoples in North America have become strangers in their own land, or, in other words, may also be seen as living in the diaspora— geographically, culturally, and ideologically away from home. In my understanding of diaspora I go beyond the postcolonial definition of "voluntary or forcible movements of peoples from their homelands into new regions" (Ashcroft, Griffiths, and Tiffin, *Key Concepts* 68) and, instead, align myself with Cree (Nêhiyaw) scholar Neal McLeod, who outlines two aspects of diaspora: spatial and ideological. "I define the removal of an Indigenous group, in this case the *Nêhiyawak,* from their land as *spatial diaspora....* I call the alienation from one's stories *ideological diaspora:* this alienation, the removal from the voices and echoes of the ancestors, is the attempt to destroy collective consciousness" (19). In the following, I analyze the work of Richard Wagamese in relation to the dual diaspora caused by colonialism while also considering diasporic theories related to immigrant diasporas.

Although diasporas like those formed by Asian Canadians and Afro-Canadians are different from Indigenous communities because the displaced peoples have another home to reconnect with, whereas Indigenous peoples' home is here and nowhere else, there are crossovers and similarities in their respective histories of oppression, displacement, racism, and marginalization. In recent years, authors like David Chariandy and Dionne Brand have integrated into their own narratives about immigrants, *Soucouyant* and *What We All Long For,* a recognition of Indigenous peoples as first peoples on this land; among the Indigenous authors in Canada, Wagamese is one of the few writers who acknowledges histories of displacement, other than those of his own peoples, in his work.[1] In his first (autobiographical) novel, *Keeper'n Me* (1994), it is a Black family in Toronto with whom the Anishinaabe character finds a home for the first time in his life; in his third novel, *Dream Wheels* (2006), cross-cultural support is reversed: here, the Native people (a cowboy family) help a Black family. In each case, Wagamese reimagines the notion of being Native through the relationship with another marginalized and racialized group. In his first novel, foster care and the urban environment should have "killed the Indian," according to the proponents of assimilation, but in

Wagamese's story, the mingling of cultures in a place like Toronto leads to the Native character's reconnection with his family. In the second case, reaching out to the Black youth enables the injured Native cowboy to reconnect with his source of strength, the stories of his family. In Wagamese's work, diaspora is portrayed in its genocidal force, but also as generating transformative possibilities by rebuilding Aboriginal communities and resistant individuals. In Wagamese's last novel, *Ragged Company*, the homeless characters suddenly come into a large amount of money. Published in 2008, one may read this plot device as an allusion to compensation paid to residential school survivors. In each case, the question arises whether sudden wealth (relatively speaking) changes traumatized lives, and in each case it becomes clear that financial compensation can restore, but it can also kill.[2] Echoing the symbolic connection between the bingo master and the trickster Nanabush in Tomson Highway's well-known play *The Rez Sisters*, one of the characters in this novel calls their win a trickster as well (*Ragged Company* 88). The plot of Wagamese's novel suggests that the fulfillment of diasporic longings not only requires economic change, but also the sharing of stories, of *all* stories. Through his choice of characters, both Native and non-Native, homeless and wealthy, he imagines a society in which each person recognizes his or her dislocation; however, he, the displaced Anishinaabe author, turns the story of being a stranger in his own land around, as Rita Joe says, and creates a different one. Resisting the diasporic discourse of cultural loss, he writes a novel from the perspective of an Anishinaabe world view as, in Scott Momaday's words, "our best destiny is to imagine, at least, completely, who and what, and *that* we are" (103).

In contemporary Aboriginal writing, "home" is sometimes identified as the reserve (while immigrant society frequently conflates the two); however, the reserve is already a consequence of dispossession: a small parcel of land allotted through treaties (or, as in British Columbia, outside of the treaties) without much consultation regarding size and location. McLeod observes: "Once *Nêhiyawak* were removed from their land and put on reserves, there was a gradual decay of the 'spatial anchor' (in which *Nêhiyawak* had grounded themselves)" (19). On the other hand, for better or for worse, reserves have become home for many Aboriginal peoples by necessity. For Okanagan writer Jeannette Armstrong, coming home to the reserve after a long time away is a healing process, reflected in both her novels, *Slash* (1985) and *Whispering in Shadows* (2000). This is not the case for many other Aboriginal writers, especially those who, like Anishinaabe Wagamese, left the reserve under traumatizing conditions and at a young age. For him, homecoming is problematic

not only because of his personal estrangement from the community but also
because the reserve does not fully meet the criteria of home. The history
of dispossession that created reserves in the first place, and is continued by
resource exploitation of the traditional land base surrounding the reserves,
taints the sense of home and makes it a diasporic place. *Keeper'n Me*, set in the
reserve of White Dog (Wabaseemoong First Nation) in northwestern Ontario,
opens with the elder Keeper describing the community in the following way:
"Get a lotta tourists this way now. Never used to be. When I was a boy this
here country was still Ojibway land. Anishanabe we called ourselves. Lottsa
huntin'and trappin', fishin' still good in the rivers. Not like now. Everywhere
there's big expensive fishin' and rich Americans huntin' lodges for rich Americans...." (1). The introductory description of the setting of the novel points
toward unsettling changes caused by displacement from the original territory
and from living off the land. These changes cause further displacements as
people move to urban diasporas for employment. The opening also shows that
the "diasporic dimension of contemporary tribal life," as Clifford points out,
is linked to a distinctive sense of themselves through their orientation toward
"a lost or alienated home defined as aboriginal" (303). The connection with
the lost home, or, in Safran's terms, the original or ancestral homeland, is a
pronounced presence in diaspora discourses; however, for tribal people, to stay
with Clifford's wording for now, this homeland is in the country where they
live, not on another continent; it is a proximity that produces an acute, tangible, and re-traumatizing daily reminder of their displacement ("When I was
a boy this here country was still Anishinabe land"; *Keeper* 1).

Wagamese was taken from the Wabaseemong First Nation reserve as a
young child, and moved around in the welfare system until he was adopted
at the age of eight or nine by a Caucasian family. He was taken without his
siblings because, as Suzanne Fournier and Ernie Crey point out, "a bizarre
holdover from the residential school days dictated that native children could
be better acculturated and assimilated if they grew up away from their brothers and sisters" (87). Although Wagamese reconnected with his birth family,
the relationship remains strained (Kirman 2). As he explains in his interview
with Paula E. Kirman, his first two novels, *Keeper'n Me* and *A Quality of Light*,
are only to some degree autobiographical with each containing "the skeleton"
of his life story (Kirman 4). It may be argued that one of the most brutal
"processes of diaspora" was the removal of children to both residential schools
and into foster care (Lawrence, *"Real" Indians* 203). Due to the traumatizing impacts of the experiences, "many children," as McLeod argues, "never

came 'home': instead they spent their lives ensnared in alcoholism and other destructive behaviours" (28). The experience and legacy of "cultural genocide and spiritual exile" shaped Wagamese's life and also his literary work (McLeod 28). In this chapter, I want to pursue a reading of his texts that analyzes them as aesthetic responses to a life in diaspora.

Understood as his most autobiographical text, *Keeper'n Me* tells the story of Garnet, a boy "scooped up" by child welfare workers at the age of three from the backyard of his home, who reunites with his family on the reserve at the age of twenty-five. However, in the description of the road that leads to the reserve, the reader is immediately drawn into a dialogic discourse that questions a simple interpretation of the homecoming theme. Leaving "civilization behind," Garnet explains, "it's an agonizing trip on this washboard road that's hard as dusted steel in summer, soupy as poor stew in autumn and slippery as the Department of Indian Affairs in winter time" (Wagamese, *Keeper* 4). The allusive description of the "uncivilized" world contains a scathing criticism of "slippery" politics and governmental neglect of First Nations' communities living in Third World conditions as suggested by the treacherous unpaved road and the allusion to poverty. Although thus undermining the colonial discourse of "the dichotomy of civilization versus savagery" (LaRocque, "The Métis" 87), the description still makes a point about the ghettoized diasporic space of the reserve as not only different from but also inferior to dominant society, especially as expressed by a character who returns home after being immersed all his life in racist discourses about the uncivilized Native. In this context the comparison between the Jewish diaspora experience and colonial displacements is relevant as "the exile of the Jews from their historic homeland" signified as well "the oppression and moral degradation ... *implied* by that dispersion" (Safran 19; emphasis added). In other words, diaspora is not only a matter of "ethnic affiliation and cultural movement but also of social position" (Ashcroft, Griffiths, Tiffin, "Introduction" 426), differing, for example, from my own *chosen* diasporic situation as a first-generation German immigrant in Canada. Ironically, as immigrants of Caucasian background, my family is accepted by our adopted country, whereas Safran's third characteristic of diaspora—of feeling not "fully accepted by their host society"—holds true for Aboriginal peoples' sense of relationship with the rest of Canada (19), peoples who were the original hosts on this land. Their alienation is perpetuated by stereotypes about them so that their spatial diaspora is heightened by an ideological diaspora that not only separates them from their own world views, but also marks them as inferior to the rest of society.

The many layers of dispossession of Aboriginal peoples make it difficult for them to return home and gain a sense of belonging in a non-conflicted way. The undoing of harm done on so many levels takes time, and Wagamese's first novel is only the beginning of a process (for Wagamese and for his audiences) of a "working-through" of a traumatic history (LaCapra, *Representing* 205). Nevertheless, the novel makes a strong case for the importance of storytelling as a way out of the ideological diaspora. In conversations between the elder Keeper and the homecoming Garnet, it becomes clear that stories "act as the vehicles of cultural transmission by linking one generation to the next" (McLeod 31). Through Keeper's stories, as Balzer points out, "Garnet is able to discover his culture and build his reality based not only on the few years of his life but also on the centuries of Anishanabe tradition" (230). For the homecoming Garnet, the "discovery of his culture" also means becoming a storyteller himself. Therefore, the book begins with Keeper's storytelling and ends with Garnet's. Read autobiographically, it is Garnet, alias Richard Wagamese, who is encouraged by the elder to be "a storyteller. Talk about the real Indyuns" (*Keeper* 214). In his own life, Wagamese takes on the task of using storytelling/writing as a teaching, offering to his son his book *For Joshua* as a means of fulfilling the traditional responsibilities of a father (9); as the creator of fiction, with his own life providing "the skeleton" of the story, he writes a second novel that exposes the challenges of asserting from an ideologically and spatially diasporic place, what it means to be "real Indyuns."

In *Keeper'n Me*, a Native character plays with identity construction by posing as Hawaiian, Chinese, and Mexican/Apache; these episodes are humorously told in spite of the pathos of wanting to be anything but "an Indian." In Wagamese's second novel, *A Quality of Light* (1997), the reserve as home plays only a marginal role, but the constructedness of identity is central to the story. The journey is the central theme and trope: home is a quest and cultural identity a becoming rather than something already in place, a returning "but 'by another route,'" to borrow Stuart Hall's description of diasporic homeward journeys in a different context (232). The cover image of *Keeper'n Me* shows two figures; as we find out in the text, they represent the two narrative voices of the elder and teacher, Keeper, and the homecoming Garnet. On the cover of his second novel, there are again two faces, this time picturing an adopted Anishinaabe youth and his Caucasian friend whose narrative voices are again intertwined. Besides the commonality of the twin images, the similarity of the colours used on each book cover also invites a comparative reading of the two texts. The first one suggests unambiguous differences between the

Caucasian and the Indigenous peoples as reflected in Keeper's comment on Garnet's childhood in non-Native foster care: "Got raised up all white but still carryin' brown skin. Hmmpfh. See us we know you can't make a beaver from a bear. Nature don't work that way. Always gotta be what the Creator made you to be" (37). However, in his second novel, this assertion of bio-logical identity is revised, as this story is about two friends "*becoming* Indians together, one because he wanted to and one because he had to. It's only now that I understand that those parts are interchangeable" (*A Quality* 9; emphasis added). The novel tells the stories of Joshua, an Anishinaabe boy adopted into a caring, Christian farmer's family in southern Ontario, and Johnny, a boy of Caucasian background who grows up in an abusive, dysfunctional fam-ily with an alcoholic father. It is his friend, and not his adoptive parents, who teaches him about what it means to be "Indian" by passing on what he learned in books that he read to escape from his own desolate childhood. The novel is ambivalent about whether it is Joshua who "had to" *become Indian* because of his appearance or if it is the non-Native boy who had to adopt another culture to survive, the noble savage image presenting a way out of his con-fined and troubled life. Ironically, it is Joshua's friend who makes him aware of his diasporic situation by telling him that his adopted family is not really his home, and that the land his adoptive father farms was taken away from Indigenous peoples and contains stories of dispossession. In other words, the voice of non-Native society tells him how to live his life as a "real Indyun" and further corroborates the adopted boy's diasporic situation because when "one is uprooted from ancestral lands, the next landscape under siege becomes the body and its identities," as Cherokee scholar Daniel Heath Justice explains ("'Go'" 160). Freedom of identity formation is a threat to the colonial ideol-ogy and therefore comes "under siege"; the *Indian Act*, which continues to rule Aboriginal peoples' lives, is all about control. Wagamese's character self-determines his identity as Anishinaabe in the sense McLeod describes when he comments on the so-called hybridization of one of his ancestors: "While he adopted a hybridized form of Christianity and adopted elements of modern technology such as the camera, he was still a Cree" (25). Joshua chooses not to participate in Indigenous activism (like his friend), but to become a spiritual warrior instead. On the other hand, the novel does not dismiss the reasons for political activism as it is framed within the events at Oka and therefore illustrates that Indigenous peoples were "forced into diaspora in two *overlap-ping* senses, spatial and ideological" (McLeod 19; emphasis added). The first two novels by Wagamese about two youth "put away in both an ideological and spatial sense" (McLeod 28) in the mainstream child welfare system open with the description of loss of land and livelihood on an Anishinaabe reserve (*Keeper*) and allusions to the dispossession of land in Mohawk territory (*A Quality*). Together the two novels demonstrate the intertwined connections among colonial processes of diaspora and their impact on individuals.

In *A Quality of Light*, the story's reminder of unresolved land claims, through reference to Oka, is more than a backdrop;[3] it shows that the personal turmoil of the Native character—attacked by some members of the domi-nant society because of his racialized body and expected by others "to play the part"—is linked to the primary deprivation of his people and their removal from ancestral lands. That the dispersal from land and community is followed by assaults on body and identity shows the genocidal underpinning of colonial ideology; the Native person is in a no-win situation as he is attacked for being both Native and not Native enough. As Wagamese explains at the end of *For Joshua*, responses to the primary loss may result in a deeply felt sadness, which is acted out, like in recoveries from trauma, in different ways:

> Our neighbours in this country ... [n]eed to hear that there is so much unrest among their Native brothers and sisters because of grief and long-ing.... [W]e're not angry. We're sad. They need to know this. They need to know that for us, for tribal people who carry the memories of drums on distant hills, the land itself haunts us. It reminds us of what we have lost every time we look upon it. It reminds us how far away from those tribal fires we have moved, of how incredibly things have changed, of how with every fibre of our beings we seek a return to the things that kept us vital, dynamic, spiritual, and alive forever. They need to know that every land claim, treaty negotiation, blockade, and court case is born out of that desire. They are born out of a spiritual hunger, not of a physical greed. They are actions created by a profound sadness and longing for the flames of those tribal fires. (222–23)

This sadness may be read as Nativist nostalgia for "an essentialized past" (Hall 225), contradicting postcolonial theories that challenge such essentializing and contest the assumption that decolonization can be affected by a recovery of pre-colonial societies. However, Wagamese does not want to go back to an imagined past; he wants to explain the long-lasting impacts of the trauma of dispossession and Aboriginal peoples' search for the source of their strength.

Although assimilation seems to become an issue in the second novel because Joshua's move to the reserve joins "sweetgrass, sage and the teachings of the Gospel" (322), his way of life is shaped, as mentioned above, by his own choice and may therefore be seen as adaptation rather than assimilation. Wagamese's third and fourth novels are even further removed from "the tribal fires." However, I want to argue that each narrative looks back to a precolonial society in the sense that "the experiences of the present can be understood as a function of the past" (McLeod 33). In this way, coming home from the diaspora is "a hermeneutical act" (McLeod 33); it interprets the social and natural environment through the relationship with the homeland without restoring the homeland in a literal sense. This does not negate the necessity of reclaiming a land base; on the contrary, "an ideological home needs to have a spatial, temporal home as well" (McLeod 19). Wagamese explains repeatedly in his journalistic writings and in his fictional allusions to unresolved land issues that the interpretative act based on being Anishinaabe is possible only as long as there is land to practise being Anishinaabe.

Wagamese does not dwell on dispossession or victimization in his novels; even his first narrative contains only a short section about the foster home experience. Jo-Ann Thom explains this literary strategy (different from a novel like *In Search of April Raintree*, for example) as the choice of an author who has "become cognizant of readers' low tolerance for seeing Aboriginal people portrayed as victims and white people as victimizers" (304). Building on her analysis of Wagamese's first novel and my knowledge of his work published after Thom's article, I would add that Wagamese draws his "neighbours" in by explaining the spiritual ways of being Native so that they understand and support the reasons behind land claims. Non-Aboriginal Canadians, for the most part, choose to ignore Aboriginal land claims, not wanting to change the settler story of the two founding nations to acknowledge "underlying Aboriginal title" as Ted Chamberlin demands (230). Changing the story the Canadian settler nation has lived by for so long will take time, and Wagamese seems to want to make a contribution to a renewed understanding of Aboriginal peoples by including "the others" into his stories, creating new communities or, as Daniel Heath Justice would say, honouring kinship obligations. Although his work starts out with fictionalizing cross-cultural adoption in a colonial context evoking an "adoption origin fantasy" (Wasyliw 31) and creating "imaginary homelands" in Salman Rushdie's sense (10), he continues his novel writing by embracing the theme of adoption more broadly. In his third book, *Dream Wheels* (2006), adoption as an action performed by the Child Welfare Agency is replaced by a non-institutional adoption that echoes adoption practices in traditional Aboriginal societies. Wagamese challenges the impact of colonialism as totalizing by going outside the white/Native binary and imagining relationships informed by Indigenous-centred values.

At the end of his memoir *For Joshua*, Wagamese writes: "Seek me out when you are ready. I won't be too hard to find. I'll be on the land somewhere, feeling its heartbeat on the soles of my feet, knowing with each breath that it is home, that I am home, wherever I might be" (225). His memoir talks about his restless wanderings. In 2005, he finds a home in British Columbia, in cowboy and ranching country, and it is from this home base that he writes his award-winning novel, *Dream Wheels* (2006). This story is inspired by the life of an Indian cowboy and his family whom he befriended (as he states in the "Acknowledgments"). The plot is about the coming together of a Native cowboy family and a Black woman with her troubled teenaged son. Community and a revisioned idea of family are created through the storyline and also, as Eric Miller points out in his review of the book, through the stylistic device of "subtle juxtaposition" (6). The text parallels, for example, the fate of Joe Willie, a badly injured bull rider, and that of Claire Hartley, an abused Black woman, "implying kinship without asserting it" (Miller 6). In this novel, pain and loss experienced by the Native characters are not caused by governmental intrusion or an oppressive and racist society but by fate. The first sentence of the novel introduces fate as something not controllable by humans: "The Old Ones say that fate has a smell, a feel, a presence, a tactile heft in the air" (Wagamese, *Dream Wheels* 1). Racism and sexism, however, do hurt the Black woman and her mixed-race son.

Dream Wheels has the themes of diasporic literature: disconnection, displacement, loss and a longing for home, belonging, tradition, and reconnecting. But the story shifts the diaspora theme from the Native characters to the Afro-Canadian woman and her son. Although the Ojibway grandfather, Lionnel, starts out as disconnected from "the old ways" because he has been raised in mission schools (27), he is being reconnected with the help of his non-Native wife and "an old man" (28). Together they start a family and develop a successful rodeo business; their son and Sioux daughter-in-law are portrayed as strong characters that gain their strength from their relationship with the land. These three generations of Indian cowboys help those whose dispossession is foregrounded in this novel: Claire, the single Black mother traumatized by a life of sexual abuse, raised by a mother who was a drug addict, and her teenage son Aiden, who ends up involved with gangs and eventually in prison. Although the Native family has to cope with the tragedy of a horrific accident that seriously disables their bull riding and award-winning son and grandson, their teachings become stronger. Their resources are the land, their spirituality, and their stories, or their dream wheel—"the sum total of a people's story" (320).

An old story-carrying truck can be the site of such a dream wheel as traditions and teachings are not static but adaptable or relational. "'Nin-din-away-mah-john-ee-dog,' Joe Willie said.... 'My father's talk. Ojibway.... It means ... all my relations'" (357–58). He uses this often repeated phrase in a moment of danger. To understand oneself as part of everything creates a fluid notion of identity, a way of "being Indian," which Justice sees as crucial for survival: "[w]e exist today as indigenous nations, as peoples, and the foundation of any continuity as such is our relationship to one another—in other words, our kinship with other humans and the rest of creation. Such kinship isn't a static thing; it's dynamic, ever in motion" ("'Go'" 150). One might argue that Wagamese advocates for adaptation—not to be confused with assimilation—as a means of surviving as an Indigenous person. In those imagined and reimagined kinships "with other humans and the rest of creation," he reconciles identity and exile.

Wagamese's writing comes from a place of traumatic displacement, both from his ancestral homeland and from his community and biological family; this preoccupation with diasporic experience gives his novels a thematic cohesiveness despite the texts' differences. His novels reimagine family and home through different versions of adoption and relationships with the land. In each, dispossession is seen as not only affecting Native peoples but other groups in Canadian society as well; in each story, "being Native" is constructed as an ideological position not dependent on signifiers like living on a reserve or speaking the language. For Wagamese it means above all to be teachers to the newcomers to this land, a responsibility he finds expressed in Anishinaabe oral traditions, which he retells in his memoir *For Joshua*. This memoir relates the fictional story of *Dream Wheels*, in which the Native family guides the Afro-Canadians, to Anishinaabe oral traditions. The stories Wagamese draws on tell how the animals taught the first humans how to live on this Earth, and how the Indigenous peoples, as the original peoples on this continent, have a responsibility to pass on these teachings and already did so by being the hosts to the newcomers: "We are the original people. We are the ones who emerged from the forest to welcome the strangers when they arrived here so long ago.... We taught them to be at home here.... It was our role to do those things. It was our responsibility.... It is still our role. It is still our responsibility" (*For Joshua* 217–18). Indeed, the First Peoples helped the Europeans to create a home, but they are the ones who are homeless now. Wagamese's fourth novel, *Ragged Company* (2008), is about homeless people, but it is through references to the story of the Animal People as the original teachers that one of the characters identifies himself as "Indian" (287). Writing about an extreme diasporic situation, the novel makes a strong point that Native peoples may be physically homeless, but spiritually they are not.

Each one of Wagamese's novels has an autobiographical strand, if only because it is set in a place where he has lived: his family's reserve, the adoptive home in southern Ontario, his present home in British Columbia, and his life on the streets of Canadian cities. Ironically, the displaced author writes with a sense of place, out of his relationship with a place, including those sections of "the geography of our city" that we never really know "until we are forced to look," as the middle-class character, who lives in a condo home, a "Square John" in the slang of the homeless people, comments (*Ragged Company* 161–62). We never know, he continues, "the holes where the lonely go, the lost, the displaced, the forgotten. The holes that lives disappear into" (162).

The Ojibway character Amelia finds a sense of belonging when her feet touch the pavement and she leaves behind the confines of walls. She identifies with the street: "I knew that the part of me that was born and the part of me that died on those streets would be joined with it always; my spine concrete, my blood rain, my heart unrestrained walls" (*Ragged Company* 155). Her identification with the street recalls Bonita Lawrence's observation about the diaspora of urban Native peoples that "it is inevitable that the bulk of cultural practices related to living on the land are simply unavailable to urban Indians. Nevertheless, the fact remains that the strength of Indigenous spirituality lies precisely in its rootedness to the physical world we live in" (*"Real" Indians* 166). Amelia links her rootedness with her traumatic history; the street becomes a part of her because it is her "mourning ground": "Everyone has a mourning ground, a place where the course of life turned, changed, altered, or disappeared forever" (*Ragged Company* 17). Residing in this place of memory and mourning, where parts of her were born and died, is important for her healing, and she knows that the three homeless men she befriends and takes care of as an elder all carry the street with them in a similar way. Wagamese writes that "[t]hey carried the story of their street life, the story of how they got there, the story of how they had survived" (192). The story of Amelia's diasporic experiences opens Book One of the novel with the statement "IT WAS IRWIN THAT STARTED all the dying" (5). A sequence of deaths follows the drowning of her brother Irwin in a river on the Ojibway reserve where she was raised: she loses both parents in a fire in one of those "cheap government houses" (8); her youngest brother freezes to death when he attempts to run away from the residential school; her older brother John dies in a fight after he leaves school; her brother Frank kills two men in an act of revenge and later hangs himself in a prison cell; and after her boyfriend's death from an overdose of morphine, she herself starts to drink and live on the streets. Her story at the opening of the novel condenses the history of colonial "processes of diaspora," which Lawrence considers genocide (*"Real" Indians* 203), into a few traumatic events and uses them to explain her homelessness. Although the series of tragedies may seem exaggerated, they speak to the legacy of government policies, which include inadequate funding, institutionalization with its various forms of abuse, and the racism-induced violence that shapes the lives of many Aboriginal peoples in Canada today.

The histories of the two Métis members of the "ragged company" also start out with stories of dispossession. Digger, the toughest of the four street people, alludes to the history of the landless Métis, the Road Allowance people, after the 1885 resistance and their "squatting" on "low-lying, marshy, mosquito filled" land (115). He disowns his Métis heritage as "the half-breed label" had been good for nothing (115); he describes his Métis ancestry as "a thinned-out fraction of rebel blood" (115). "Kinda like Digger" (288), the second Métis character, Double Dick, is more traumatized than his friend and, in his story, reveals more details about his Native background. He also refers to the dispossession of the Métis: "we hadta leave the reserve on accounta there was no work an' there was a big buncha us that set up shacks on land no one wanted near the sawmill. Swampy kinda land" (288). He was not formally educated as the family was not "real Indian" and only white kids went to school in town.[4] So he worked with his dad, who "wasn't even half" Indian, but "he looked like it" and he told him stories about the Animal People (288). In order to make a living, these "sawmill savages," as they were called (288), made their own home brew, "moose milk" (288); it was the influence of alcohol since childhood that brought forth the tragedy that made him "carry the street," a trauma to which he succumbs eventually (52). However, it is his voice as a spirit traveller that frames the whole novel and takes it beyond the reality of colonialism. A conversation between the elder Amelia and the spirit Double Dick prefaces Book One with the promise of telling their story, and the novel concludes with their conciliatory view:

Quite the story.
Quite the journey.
Quite the life.
Yes.
I wouldn't change a single part of it.
Me neither. (376)

A challenge for people living in the diaspora is to recreate a new community, sometimes a new family, to work against the fragmentation and "the scattering" produced by the disconnection from the homeland. The Ojibway character Amelia in *Ragged Company* could have been written as one of those many people who "never came 'home'" from their spatial and ideological exile (McLeod 28), but Wagamese creates a different story for her. As she no longer has a biological family, she creates a new one. Her adoption recalls the adoption fantasy in *A Quality of Light* and the formation of a new, intercultural family in *Dream Wheels*. In each case, adoption is seen as a form of community building, an overcoming of loss, and a healing from diasporic experience. These positive representations of adoption contrast starkly with the better known discourse of the devastating effects of adoption of Aboriginal children. The emphasis on community in Amelia's story echoes the reality of initiatives taken by Native women in the diasporic environment of urban centres.[5] Her story ends with her creation of "a special place for women" (*Ragged Company* 375), but she herself goes back to the streets as she is "one of them" (375). Her way of coping, or rather healing, involves leaving her own diaspora behind and creating a new family. Her character shapes the tone and themes of this novel as she is not only an older person but an elder in a traditional sense, a guide and teacher, and the founder of the "ragged company."

The title of the novel alludes to the material condition of homelessness without reductively ascribing a social problem to a certain group of people. In tune with the epigraph by John Steinbeck that "whores, pimps, gamblers" may also be seen as "saints, angels, and martyrs and holy men" if "looked through another peephole" (n.p.), Wagamese writes a story that emphasizes perspective and positioning in social relations. Homelessness becomes an inclusive term. Granite, the fifth character, first an outsider but then increasingly becoming a part of the "ragged company," is a wealthy person who suffers from the loss of family due to a fatal car accident. After he tells his story, Digger says: "'Wow,' ... 'You're as friggin' homeless as I was'" (213). Still, Digger, the most outspoken and proud of the four about being a "rounder," tries to play that "tidy little 'us and them' game" and sees the non-homeless person, the "Square John" Granite, as "the other" (348). It is made clear that, for Digger, to reconcile with events in his own life, he must let go of the binary of home and homelessness (which functions as an analogy with the Native/non-Native divide that is also eschewed in this novel). The multi-vocality of this novel, in which chapters are titled after characters and give voice to different perspectives, emphasizes the novel's focus on inclusiveness. The fourth member of the group, a homeless non-Native character, suffers from guilty feelings after leaving a wife who did not seem to recover from a coma. His grief is given as much attention as the traumas caused by social injustice. In the face of diasporic disruptions, Wagamese fictionalizes the importance of crossing racial and social class borders and creating new communities.

In order to change relationships among different social groups, hierarchical structures that regulate how we "help the deprived" need to be replaced by the realization that we are *all* tourists and are *all* in need of a guide as the elder character in Keeper'n Me states. This insight forms the basis for the character development of "the outsider" Granite. For the longest time, Granite sees himself as distinctly different from those "chronically homeless" people who, as he explains to an audience from his own social class, are socio-economically "displaced" in a way they could not imagine (133). The character's observation that "the displaced and the dislocated ones are not simply the inhabitants of shelters and missions, of the cardboard boxes and empty doorways" forms the prerequisite for an understanding between partners instead of helper/victim relationships (96). In the terms of the novel, "Square John" Granite learns from the "half-breed" Double Dick Dumont, the uneducated "sawmill savage" from a people most displaced by colonial policies of diaspora, that "home is a truth you carry within yourself. It's belonging, regardless" (358). The education of this one "outsider" character about the meaning of home comes from those who seem to be most homeless. Writing against the common understanding that homelessness is an economic issue, Wagamese creates a novel that is primarily about homecoming as a spiritual journey: "a returning to yourself. Reconnecting. Getting whole again" (214). Framed within the ultimate displacement of death—the novel opens and ends with death—Wagamese's story is closely connected with the spirit world and the presence of "the shadowed ones" (16).

Wagamese's fictional work is written out of the diasporic experiences of an Anishinaabe person responding to his personal displacements, as well as those experienced by his people systemically; it expresses in various plots and through different literary devices a longing to return, not to a specific home or the past, but to a connectedness with values and beliefs that emanate from an ancestral homeland and a pre-colonial past. Instead of dwelling on experiences of dispossession, his work is about transformation as it adapts stories that carry Indigenous values to new situations and translates them into new contexts. Wagamese articulates many ways of being Anishinaabe in the face of diaspora and against the discourse of cultural loss. His imagination transcends boundaries of dogmatic constructions of indigeneity, but is grounded in what Safran terms "ethnocommunal consciousness" (84); by creating new communities he is able to leave the diaspora and no longer live "on reserve." This last point about Aboriginal authors leaving the reserve, the reserve in their minds, is made by Daniel David Moses in the preface to his co-edited third edition of *An Anthology of Canadian Native Literature in English* (2005). "Some of our new writers," he continues, "are articulating that 'same old story' but with fascinating new vocabularies" (ix). Wagamese is not a new writer, but his work is part of a new phase of Aboriginal literature in Canada with "less need for resistance" that instead concentrates on "consolidation and healing," as Terry Goldie says in his response to Moses (Moses x). Wagamese contributes to the social process of reconciliation through his inclusiveness by reaching out to different groups of people while at the same time asserting Anishinaabe land-based values and beliefs as fundamental to our society. As immigrants, we can only appreciate this latter theme if we are willing to admit with "Square John" Granite that we are the displaced ones, and that it is important for us to see, know, understand, and correct our own dislocation.

NOTES

1   There is a need for more scholarship on the relationship between Aboriginal peoples in Canada and non-European immigrants. Some work has been done by Sneja Gunew, particularly in her book *Haunted Nations: The Colonial Dimensions of Multiculturalism*. The election of Barack Obama as president of the United States, very much applauded by Aboriginal peoples in Canada as a change in the US government that all so-called minorities will benefit from, may inspire a discourse that recognizes interconnected histories and goes beyond a celebration of cultural diversity.

2   Recently, stories have come out about suicide and other forms of violence as a consequence of compensation payments for residential school attendance; however, there are also people who put the money to good use. Depending on individual circumstances and severity of trauma, the stories range from getting more deeply into alcohol and drug addiction (like the character Double Dick in *Ragged Company*) to saving it for the future use of grandchildren or to make a donation to a charity (like the character Amelia in the same novel).

3 Here I take my cue for reading Wagamese's novel from Wagamese himself. In a recent book review of David Bergen's *The Retreat*, he criticizes the author for using the events at Anicinabe Park in 1974 (which Wagamese alludes to in his own novel) merely as backdrop and for presenting "little of the racial tension that could be smelled in the air like cordite" ("Cross-racial Tragedy" 19). The reading of *A Quality of Light* may be easily depoliticized if one emphasizes the Native character's path as a spiritual warrior. However, the non-Native friend is his twin, representing the other side of the struggle of "becoming Indian" and his serious activist engagement in the fictionalized Oka crisis (pointed out as historical truth in the "Author's Note" prefacing the novel) is the main character's story too; in fact, at the end, Joshua "disappears" into Johnny's words (*A Quality* 317).

4 Education is not a treaty right for the Métis, and until the 1940s, they also did not have access to provincial schools. After their dispersal in 1885, many of them became "Road Allowance people," i.e., they did not own property and therefore did not pay taxes, which would have allowed them to go to school.

5 As Sylvia Maracle observes, Aboriginal women often "were forced to leave their communities but they took their identities with them as women, as clans, as Nations. And so, even though so many had no choice but to become urban, and some endured terrible experiences in the process, the creativity of these women turned hardship into opportunity" (72).

Afro-Caribbean Writing in Canada and the Politics of Migrant Labour Mobility

Jody Mason

So far as the economy of the metropolitan country is concerned, migrant workers
are immortal: immortal because continually interchangeable. They are not born:
they are not brought up: they do not age: they do not get tired: they do not die.
They have a single function—to work. All other functions of their lives are the
responsibility of the country they come from.
—John Berger, A Seventh Man (64)

THE "METROPOLITAN COUNTRY" BERGER SPEAKS of in his 1975 documentary study specifically refers to those European countries—such as Germany
and Switzerland—that depended on labour migration schemes in the postwar
period. Although Canada's role as an importer of migrant labour is often rendered invisible in contemporary state discourses of tolerance and multiculturalism, Berger's comments apply equally to Canada. Analysis of cultural forms
in Canada should therefore account for the growing use of temporary migrant
labour that took root in the postwar period but which has flourished since the
mid-1960s.[1]

Yet many critical discussions of diaspora and globalization treat transnational forms of mobility as if they were untethered, seeking tropes of de-ter-
ritorialization without also looking for the ways that these tropes are implicated in the re-territorializing politics of, for example, the Canadian state,
which in the late twentieth century has refined and strengthened its ability to
police the mobility of migrant workers.[2] Other critics simply fail to acknowledge that migrant labour constitutes a central aspect of Canadian immigration
and labour policy. Indeed, in his 1998 discussion of the relevance of diasporic
perspectives to Canadian studies, Alan Anderson argues that "cheap migrant

labour" diasporas, composed of labour "imported into industrialized states to supplement a labour shortage and thereby maintain capitalist economic expansion," are characteristic of countries like Germany, not Canada (24). Anderson's contention is simply false: there have been labour importation schemes in this country since its inception. Moreover, since the 1973 introduction of the Non-Immigrant Employment Authorization Program (NIEAP), more than three-quarters of immigrants entering Canada as workers have been temporary migrant labourers (Sharma 110).[3] A central contention of sociologist Nandita Sharma's 2006 study *Home Economics*, and one that influences my thinking here, is that temporary labour migration is now outpacing immigration for permanent residence in Canada. While the bulk labour schemes of the immediate postwar period in Canada were meant to ease temporary labour shortages, non-immigrant labour migration programs have remained in place, and have indeed grown in size, since the postwar years. Sharma argues that the introduction of the purportedly "non-discriminatory" immigration policy in Canada in the 1960s coincided with the curtailment of certain immigrant rights. By 1972, for example, workers who fell under the category of "visitors" could no longer change their status to "landed immigrants" (now permanent residents) from within Canada (Sharma 90). Not coincidentally, once this right to change status was removed, the limited and scattered postwar policy of admitting temporary agricultural and domestic workers was expanded in 1973 into the broader and more permanent NIEAP, which remains in place today. A federal domestic worker program has been in place in Canada since the introduction of the Domestic Scheme in 1955. This program has operated since 1973 under the guidelines of the NIEAP and since 1992 has been called the Live-in Caregiver Program (Silvera 7; Bakan and Stasiulus 121). The state-managed program of agricultural labour migration, which targets male rather than female migrants, began in 1966. The recruitment of temporary agricultural workers is currently administered through the NIEAP as the Seasonal Agricultural Workers' Program (SAWP), which brings workers from Mexico and a number of Caribbean nations to Canada on seasonal contracts that last eight months or less.[4] Sociologist Vic Satzewich contends that racialization has played a key role in the Canadian state's differential incorporation of immigrants and migrant workers (47–51), and immigration statistics support his claim: between 1973 and 2004, the largest proportion of non-professional temporary workers in Canada came from the Caribbean region (Sharma 127).

Although they contribute to state programs that were developed in the context of ideas about the social rights of citizenship in the postwar period, migrant workers cannot be citizens of Canada.[5] If the nation-state's restriction of citizenship rights to those who are deemed worthy of incorporation into the nation means that citizenship is always actively produced in relation to non-citizens—those who are deliberately *not* incorporated, such as migrant workers (Bakan and Stasiulus 118)—then maintaining a permanently marginalized population *within* the nation is important to the value that Canadian citizenship currently bears. The exclusion of migrant workers therefore occurs *within* Canada's borders, a key point that Sharma emphasizes in her discussion of the Canadian state's practices of "differential inclusion" (18). This suggests that the freedom to move between states (or across borders) is not necessarily in peril. Sharma's study of migrant workers in Canada alleges that federal immigration policies and their infrastructure are not actually intended to restrict migration; instead, the state's power resides in its ability to restrict the freedom of migrants *once they have entered the national labour market* (24–25).

Given these facts, those who seek to understand how diasporic formations exist in relation—and tension—with Canada as nation and state must consider the politics of migrant-labour mobility. I use the term "politics of mobility" here to suggest my interest in a particularly grounded, materialist study of diasporic formations. In the 1990s, Doreen Massey coined the phrase "politics of mobility" to refer to the systems of power that divide and distribute mobility. Mark Simpson develops a useful explanation of the phrase in his more recent study of mobility in the nineteenth-century US: he theorizes the "politics of mobility" as "the contestatory processes that produce different forms of movement, and that invest these forms with social value, cultural purchase, and discriminatory power" (xiii–iv). What is at stake in Simpson's theorization is a resistance to travel as a ubiquitous—and often metaphorical, ahistorical—way of describing human movement. Significantly, however, the politics of mobility, as Simpson employs it, is not exclusively concerned with reading through metaphor to discover what "actually happened"; its concern with what Maria Margaroni and Effie Yiannopoulou theorize as the dialectics of materiality and discursivity aims to "restore, at the forefront of critique, the materiality of mobility alongside its differential production and reproduction" (Simpson xix).

Despite the twentieth-century salience of what anthropologist Liisa Malkki calls "sedentarist" thought in Canadian literary and critical debates—I am thinking in particular of the ascendance of romantic nationalism in the late

nineteenth and early twentieth centuries and the influence of regionalism in
the latter half of the twentieth century—in the last thirty years critical discourses such as postmodernism, postcolonialism, globalization, and diaspora
studies have challenged assumptions about human mobility and the negative
values assigned to it; however, scholars in these fields have tended to view
discursive or metaphorical mobilities as inherently liberatory. Celebratory uses
of the trope of travel characterize, for instance, what Diana Brydon disdain-
fully refers to as "the 'Globalit' story," which has championed nomadism and
border crossing as triumphant narratives of globalization ("Metamorphoses"
10–11). The trope of travel has also beleaguered postcolonial theory more
generally; as Pheng Cheah observes, the desire to rethink sedentarist tenden-
cies in postcolonial thought has resulted in the "dematerialization" of culture,
insofar as scholars like Homi Bhabha theorize "a transnational realm of cultural hybridization unmoored and exhibiting a subversive freedom from the
weighty constraints of political and economic determinations" (324).[6] However, scholars such as Diana Brydon and Inderpal Grewal and Caren Kaplan
have suggested that only a working through of the interrelation of postcolo-
nialisms and global capitalism will invigorate the field of postcolonial studies.
Such a working through will certainly involve attention to the nation-state's
rapidly expanding institutionalization of migrant-labour practices, which is
embedded in Canada's colonial history and its legacy of exclusionary immigration and labour-market policies.

Thinking through nomadism and challenging "sedentarist" paradigms
requires a historically attentive methodology that recognizes how the politics
of migrant-labour mobility is produced through the entanglement of state policy—the state's management of migrant-worker programs and citizenship, for
example—and emergent cultural forms that seek to participate in mobility's
meaning. The literary texts that have emerged from the diverse communities
of the Afro-Caribbean diaspora since migration to Canada began in the late
1950s are rich examples of such cultural forms. This chapter will now turn to
close readings of fiction by two writers—Austin Clarke and Cecil Foster—
who now live in Canada but who were born in Barbados, and whose writing
is embedded in the institutionalization of migrant-worker programs within
Canada. Clarke's Toronto trilogy and his short-story collections *When He Was
Free and Young and He Used to Wear Silks* (1971) and *Nine Men Who Laughed*
(1986) explore the lives of the Barbadian women who came to Toronto in the
late 1950s and 1960s under the auspices of the Domestic Scheme. Influenced
by Clarke's fiction, Foster's novel about migrant farm workers in southwestern

Ontario, *Slammin' Tar* (1998), offers the other side of the migrant-work experience in late-twentieth-century Canada: its setting is rural and its characters are almost exclusively male. Both writers meditate on the meanings of space and place, exploring the effects of state-imposed restrictions on the migrant workers' movement within Canadian society, the politics of mobility that attend the material practice of writing, and the transformative thinking about space that can challenge the re-territorializing effects of migrant-labour schemes.

DEPARTURE AND ARRIVAL

Writers such as Clarke and Foster recognize the vexed legacies of Euro-American (including Canadian) modernity and its naturalized national subjects. Their writing points to the ways that these legacies—embodied in migrant-worker programs, for example—circumscribe the mobility of specifically raced and gendered subjects. Clarke and Foster shape their narratives around scenes of departure and arrival, urging the reader to notice the critical role that movement through space plays in the life of the migrant worker. Clarke's *The Meeting Point* (1967)—the first novel in his Toronto trilogy, which also includes *Storm of Fortune* (1971) and *The Bigger Light* (1975)—is structured so that a scene at Toronto's Pearson International Airport plays a pivotal role in the plot; indeed, one-quarter of the novel is devoted to the arrival of Estelle, the sister of a Barbadian domestic named Bernice. Foster's *Slammin' Tar* similarly literalizes this anxiety about mobility by extending the opening airport scene, in which the trickster-narrator Anancy describes the departure from Barbados of a group of male migrant workers, across the first third of the novel's space. Both novels juxtapose the open-ended promise of travel with moments of closure—circumscribed spaces, bodies under surveillance—that undermine the way that travel often functions as a metaphorical shorthand for all mobilities.

The perceived threat embodied in racialized female sexuality makes the experience of arrival particularly precarious for Clarke's female characters. In *The Meeting Point*, Estelle's uneasy arrival teaches her what her sister Bernice already knows—that meaningful participation in Canadian society cannot be guaranteed by official documents. Although Estelle has a passport, she, like Bernice, is vulnerable to the racism that makes a farce of the "regulations" governing entrance into the country and the conditions of temporary work. Standing in line at Customs, Estelle is equally aware that her racialized body is sexualized by the prying eyes of the White Canadians around her. Bernice's long and anxious wait for her sister, who is held up at Customs, culminates in a reunion that marks "a victory over the experience of arrival" (58). Such a victory "over" arrival reinforces the fact that "social relations of space are experienced differently" (Massey 3): while the White man who sat beside Estelle disappeared after the plane landed as if "he was going to a different world altogether" (59), Black women do not arrive so easily. Moreover, a "victory over the experience of arrival" suggests that Estelle does not actually arrive but rather momentarily eludes the potential entrapments of arrival. Boysie, one of the few Barbadian male characters in the trilogy, later testifies to the entrapment of arrival by comparing their situation in Canada to the practice of slavery: "We were not born here. We in captivity here" (60).

Indeed, in the late 1950s, migrant domestics were legally indentured to their employers. They were granted landed status upon arrival in Canada, but were obliged to remain in the household of one employer for a year before they were permitted to seek employment elsewhere (Silvera 8).[7] Clarke explores such rigidly bounded spaces—figured as a "triangle of life" (95) in *The Meeting Point*—and employs them as spatial tropes for the invisible processes of state power and institutionalized racism that domestics confront. They may work and live in the homes of the affluent but, as potential contaminants, racialized others, and sexual threats, they are uneasily housed.[8] Moreover, Bernice is not an active participant in her social world, but rather observes what she can from the tiny window of her top-floor quarters in her employer's house. From the limited perspective accorded to the female migrant worker, Bernice fails to anticipate the danger threatening Estelle, who is having an ill-fated affair with Sam Burrmann, her employer. The one afternoon of unadulterated joy Bernice experiences occurs in the public space of the city, which she and Estelle traverse with ease and awe as they sample clothes they cannot buy, and indulge in daiquiris and curried chicken at the West Indies Federated Club. Yet Bernice's reprieve from the drudgery of domestic work and the strictly limited space of her life in Forest Hill is marred by two incidents that demonstrate the tenuous footing of her joy in the city: they encounter a group of Black men and women marching to "END RACE PREJUDICE NOW," and, subsequently, Estelle's secret efforts to induce an abortion cause her to be violently ill. Bernice's brief experience as *flâneuse* therefore comes to a violent halt, and, as the summer sun disappears from view, she must face the shameful cause of her unmarried sister's illness in the refuge of a friend's rented room.[9]

Foster's *Slammin' Tar*, published more than three decades after *The Meeting Point* and clearly influenced by Clarke, similarly queries the relations among gender, class, race, and spatial mobility.[10] As Anancy tells the reader in the first pages of the novel, the airport is the "most important building" in Barbados:

> All roads lead to it. Even nature crowns it as such. The heat waves form a halo above it and even the clouds have parted to pay homage. Unimpeded at this moment, the sun makes a point by surgically spotting a concen-trated beam on the only possible refuge from its daily attacks. (7)

While the triumph of technology over nature that the airport symbolizes "promises escape" to the Barbadian migrant workers, hundreds of Canadian tourists seek the island each year, "anxious to begin worshipping the god [the sun] everyone else is fleeing and fighting" (12, 21). Ironically, although the migrant workers and the tourists pursue different trajectories and have deeply divergent experiences of mobility, they use the same technology to arrive at their respective destinations, which suggests that these groups exist in very unequal relation to the technologies of modernity.[11]

The narrative of deliverance suggested by the airport's promise of escape does not materialize. The men arrive in Toronto and are bused to a farm in the southwest corner of the province, but this nighttime journey along the 403 lacks all the hallmarks of the literary road trip. The men are like "prisoner[s] heading down some highway to an undisclosed rendezvous" (73). They are isolated individuals despite the predicament they share, and each of them, even the most experienced workers, such as Johnny, who has come to work seasonally in Canada for twenty-four years, lacks the ability to read the spatial and temporal markers of southern Ontario: "We just don't know the lay of the land, the hidden minefields, no Brer Dove to counsel us. In this country, there is nobody, nothing really, to tell the future" (73). Both space—the "lay of the land"—and time—"the future"—are unrecognizable.

WRITING MOBILITY

These departures and arrivals attest to what Kaplan calls the "uneven opera-tions" of mobility (155). Yet Clarke and Foster are not only interested in how such operations involve migrant workers; in different ways, they thematize the troubled role of the writer in relation to his subjects—migrant workers whose experiences crossing borders and inhabiting national space reveal the differentiating processes that give mobility meaning. Treating the unequal distribution of mobility's meanings as one of the most determining aspects of human experience, Clarke and Foster refuse to render invisible their own participation in such operations.

Clarke's arrival in Canada in 1955 coincided with the commencement of the Canadian state's recruitment of female domestic workers from the anglophone Caribbean. His early fiction, which emerges from this historical coincidence, has been called "the earliest and fullest literary account of post–Second World War Caribbean experience published by a Canadian" (Coleman, "Austin Clarke" 208).[12] Despite the poverty in which he was raised, Clarke came to Canada not to care for the children of a wealthy Forest Hill family but to study political science and economics on a student visa at the University of Toronto. Clarke's biographer describes how he and his West Indian friends from the university eventually "overcame their reservations" about consorting with the domestics with whom they shared the very White urban space of postwar Toronto, and made regular visits to a social centre established for the benefit of the domestics a "normal part of their lives" (Algoo-Baksh 36). In a 1962 CBC Radio talk, however, Clarke admitted that "free West Indians are not too eager to go out with domestics. This is a harsh fact of colonial-indoctrinated social bigotry" ("The West Indian" 5). Indeed, it was Clarke's marriage in 1957 to Betty Reynolds, the Canadian-born daughter of Jamaican parents, that allowed him to remain in Canada (Algoo-Baksh 38). The short stories "If Only: Only If ...," and "Coll. SS. Trins. Ap. Toron—A Fable," which appear in *Nine Men Who Laughed*, thematize the "social bigotry" Clarke describes above. Like Clarke in the 1950s, the male protagonist of "If Only: Only If ..." is a West Indian student at Trinity College in the decade after the Second World War—the "Middle Ages o' Immigration!" (98). Despite his desire for a domestic named Doreen, a "fellow-countrywoman" in a land "o' pure winter whiteness," he ultimately snubs her when his fellow West Indian friends at Trinity object to the pairing: "We does call them servants back home. And we does foop them. Not date them nor walk-'bout with them" (113).

If Clarke's arrival in Canada was shaped by the class privilege that distinguished him from the female domestics who were his somewhat unlikely contemporaries, his fiction employs indiscriminate satire as a means of suggesting that the author and third-person narrator are implicated in the predicaments his characters face—having their mobility policed and regulated, feeling threatened by Toronto's strangeness and hostility, being unsure of how to "read" the city and its people, and, consequently, performing various identities in the difficult process of making the city familiar.[13] Samuel-Sonny, the West Indian student at Trinity College who is the protagonist of "Coll. SS. Trins. Ap. Toron—a Fable," can be read as a metafictional proxy for Clarke, and the story reveals the irony of the protagonist's belief that he has come up in the world: he and the former domestic he disdains as an unwed mother "on welfare" are both stopped by a police officer who apprehends only their suspicious blackness (202–3). The Toronto trilogy also makes the writer and the intellectual perpetual objects of its satirical barbs, using, for example, a metafictional reference to Clarke himself—"this big writer like that fellow from Barbados" (*Storm of Fortune* 284)—as a means of critiquing the elevation of cultural work over service work. Indeed, the reference to Clarke as a "big writer" may be derisive, but it also acknowledges how educated immigrants like Clarke were able to capitalize on the emerging cultural industries in Canada in the late 1960s and early 1970s. As his work during this period for the CBC on racial politics and pan-American Black cultures proves, Clarke's cross-border mobility was both enabled by and constitutive of his affiliation with Canada's public broadcaster.[14]

Similarly, Foster uses metafictional and thematic devices to attend to the material practice of authorship. *Slammin' Tar* employs the convention of the narrator-as-author in order to call attention to the work of writing and to the conditions of mobility that enable it. Although Anancy is an unreliable, self-conscious narrator who is at a distance from the author because of his inflexible commitment to an "unbiased" reporting of "the true history" (140), he is also Foster's double because both are "chroniclers"—Anancy as a storyteller for Mother Nyame's network and Foster as a journalist/author who engages the issue of what it means to be Black in Canada. Like Foster, who came to Canada in 1979 to work as a journalist and who did not arrive under the auspices of the NIEAP, Anancy moves across borders more easily than the migrant workers he is documenting.[15] Yet Foster narrows the gap between the narrator-author and the migrant worker by thematizing the idea of the writer-as-worker; like any other worker, the writer can do a job badly and is vulnerable to the processes of social change that will render him redundant. Like the migrant labourers he is following, Anancy must reject the segregationist thinking of Marcus Garvey and grasp the "new spirit of openness" (261) that Mother Nyame, the "great warrior mother" who "owns all the stories" (2), advocates. His failure to do this, and his inability to anticipate that Johnny and Winston, the youngest worker in Johnny's crew, will choose to "slam tar" (flee the program illegally), effectively leads to his unemployment at the end of the novel. Anancy's ultimate failure therefore thematizes the uncertainty of Foster's own writing project, which is echoed again in the novel's open-ended conclusion.

UTOPIAN ENDS, NEGOTIATED CITIZENSHIPS, PLACE AS PROCESS

Through such metafictional devices, Slammin' Tar suggests that the writer and public intellectual have crucial roles to play in evaluating the relations between discursive and material mobilities. Failing to examine the material conditions in which Johnny and the other migrant workers live, Anancy is devoted to the Afrocentric politics of Marcus Garvey and, consequently, views the ambivalent experience of the migrant workers' departure from Barbados and arrival in Canada as one that can be resolved only in the telos of return to Africa—a return that promises the restoration of the Black patriarch. He is aligned with a mode of narrative that depends on a discourse of racial purity; the irony of this lies in the fact that the Anancy figure is more often employed as a reading trope for the "patterned web of connections and interrelationships" that shape Caribbean writing (Jonas 2). Yet the narrative of Slammin' Tar develops this latter sense of the Anancy figure by sampling from a broad range of Black diasporic cultural forms produced within and transformed through the "unforeseen detours and circuits" of the Black Atlantic (Gilroy, Black Atlantic 86), what Wilson Harris calls the "limbo gateway"—the Anancy-like, shape-shifting process of cultural transformation that merges past and present experience into hybrid forms (157). Forms that embody such spatial and temporal criss-crossing abound in this novel—the ideas of Black intellectuals such as Garvey and Du Bois, narratives of Old Testament Christianity, and West African folk traditions transmitted through the Caribbean all attest to the complex heritage that the novel explores, and explicitly subvert Anancy's idea that space—the African continent—can remain untouched by time.

Slammin' Tar also deploys practices of mobility that challenge Anancy's notion of space as something that can be partitioned into discrete, bounded units for culturally distinct peoples. If the politics of re-territorialization that Foster explores include both Anancy's Garveyism and the Canadian state's policing of migrant workers' movement in space, the novel's conclusion resists these ways of conceptualizing space. In choosing to "slam tar" instead of returning to Barbados at the end of the harvest, Winston and Johnny embrace a very uncertain fate as undocumented workers. Although Johnny initially rejects the possibility of "burnin' up the road, smoking it down, slammin' tar" because there "ain't no future in that" (237), he ultimately decides to join Winston, whom Mother Nyame has decided is a latter-day W.E.B. Du Bois. Like the interwar narratives of transience that this open-ended conclusion alludes to—one might think of John Steinbeck's *The Grapes of Wrath*—*Slammin' Tar* concludes with figures on the road that indicate the dissolution of the "knowable communities and settled social relations that provide the underpinning for realist narrative" (Denning 119). The road that Winston and Johnny embark on lies outside the narrative's grasp and well beyond the kinds of "face to face" encounters that Raymond Williams associates with realism's "knowable community." This space is also host to an alternative form of mobility that contrasts Anancy's failed politics and aesthetics, which leave him "literally pinned to my bed, my legs kicking in the air" (427). In one sense, the conclusion reinforces the nation-state's exclusion of the migrant worker, who must take to the liminal space of the road—what Michel Foucault would call a "heterotopia of deviation." Yet it simultaneously ventures outside the plot's departure-arrival-departure trajectory to gesture to Du Bois's ideal of integration, materialized and individualized in the potential union between Winston and his employer's White daughter, Jessica. In this sense, the road is a utopian non-place rather than a heterotopian counter-site because it is never directly represented in the narrative and bears an almost exclusively temporal meaning at the end of the novel, as the bounded limits of Edgecliff Farm are traded in for Mother Nyame's future-oriented vision: "Let's move on and show this new spirit of openness, of looking forward with eagerness to what's ahead, to a brand-new future" (261).[16]

Clarke's early fiction is less utopian and future-oriented than Foster's, and is more committed to remaining within the space of the city that the migrant domestics cannot themselves escape, as both the title *The Meeting Point* and the sustained form of the trilogy suggest. While Winston and Johnny leave rural Ontario and "slam tar" in the direction of Toronto, where they hope to slip unnoticed into the urban social fabric, Clarke's workers are already in the city, and, in any case, as the poems of Dionne Brand's *Land to Light on* (1997) make clear, rural Ontario offers few utopian hopes for Black women. To be sure, however, the conditions of possibility that governed Clarke's writing were quite different than those Foster confronted in the late 1990s. The West Indian community that Clarke was representing belonged to the first wave of domestics who came to Canada in the late 1950s and early 1960s— women who could apply for landed immigrant status after one year of employment as live-in domestics, and who could then apply to bring their families to Canada to join them (Silvera 7). The drawn-out narrative of Clarke's trilogy casts an unflinching eye on the fragile community that results from these circumstances.

Remaining static in space, Clarke's characters push at the limits of this space with the tools of language—what Lloyd W. Brown calls Clarke's "dramatic sense of verbal performance" (4). Clarke's early writing thus undertakes the work that Silvera tackles in *Silenced*—the work of reconceiving citizenship as a process that individuals and groups negotiate and shape. Challenging the "differential inclusion" entailed in citizenship, the voices that Clarke makes heard destabilize the nation-state's power to define citizenship as "a linear, static, thing-like status which is earned by or bestowed upon individuals or groups" (Bakan and Stasiulus 119). In "Waiting for the Postman to Knock," which appeared in *When He Was Free and Young and He Used to Wear Silks*, Clarke represents a domestic named Enid, who is living in her own cramped apartment, but who gleans no independence from this situation. Ill and alone, she finds herself fighting eviction.[17] No human beings knock on her door, but in the form of bills, eviction notices from her rental company, and a telephone solicitor, she confronts the metonymic forms of capital, which, abetted by the state, seem to determine her existence. Yet Enid volubly protests her situation. Ironically, her bombastic rhetoric is pointed at no actual interlocutor, which only emphasizes its bathetic quality; however, she does succeed in addressing the reader, who is uncomfortably slotted into the role of the faceless corporate and state forces that govern her life.

Moreover, like Silvera's *Silenced*, Clarke creates a community of readers that must bear witness to the grievances of isolated domestics, while representing the power that might accrue to voices that are not isolated from one another. Significantly, both Clarke and Silvera (and Foster) also choose to represent Creole vernaculars; as Silvera acknowledges, this abrogation is "an act of empowerment, particularly for these women who work as live-in domestics and for the most part have not been able to speak their own language on a daily basis" (viii–ix). In other words, the choice recognizes the politics of space and the way that certain knowledges cannot be heard in certain spaces.[18]

Admittedly, however, language has limits in a racist society, and this is made clear in the conclusion of *The Meeting Point*, when, from the tiny window of her employers' house, Bernice witnesses White police officers assault a Black man she thinks is Boysie, but fails to intervene: "Bernice saw it happen, all of it, and she didn't have the courage to lift a finger, to move, to scream, to call for help. She didn't whisper any advice, as she had done earlier" (246). Lacking the wherewithal to "whisper" help to the unhearing victim and knowing that an appeal to the police is impossible, Bernice is utterly silent and silenced. The following morning, Bernice's friend Dots summons language to describe the beating, but the phone call from Dots, which concludes the novel, only reinforces the spatial insularity and circularity of the domestic's world: "'Jesus God! This is a savage world....' Dots went on talking and talking" (250).

Indeed, Clarke's trilogy keeps coming back on itself. The centripetal narrative, which refuses to leave the space of the city, resists the utopian impulse in favour of a more ambivalent conclusion. The final section of *The Bigger Light* juxtaposes a scene in Dot's and Boysie's apartment—in which Dots and Bernice are preparing food for a party that no one will attend—with Boysie's renunciation of his material possessions and his decision to use his newly acquired automobile to take to the road. In the apartment, which is figured as a "prison" (27) and a "coffin" (29) throughout the novel despite the fact that it is a material sign of Dots and Boysie's class mobility, Bernice indulges a nostalgia for Barbados that offers a thematic parallel to the closed space of the apartment: "I going back home I tell you. There must be some man down there willing to have an old woman like me" (282). Dots rejects the circular dead end of Bernice's logic, saying, "But look at we two! You and me. Right where we started from" (282). Contrasting the women's confinement is Boysie's trip "towards Hamilton, on the 401 Highway West, which was the highway that led anywhere" (285). He has finally escaped the city, and he has no map and no destination. Initially, the highway is a trope for freedom, but when he reaches the US border in the final lines of the novel, the narrator makes it clear that his journey is less about liberation and the "spatial freedom" of the US American road narrative (Sherrill 210) than about exchanging "one kind of space for another one" (288). As in Clarke's 1971 story "The Motor-Car," the automobile represents a deeply compromised performance of masculinity and power. Moreover, as Clarke's extensive treatment of African American cultures in both his fictional and non-fictional writing suggests, the United States offers no place of refuge for West Indian Blacks.[19]

"Precisely" at the moment of Boysie's arrival at the border, Bernice observes that "it will soon be light" (288). Referring to the literal coming of the dawn and the figurative dawning of a transformed urban existence, the conclusion of *The Bigger Light* refuses to let its titular trope stray too far from the city. As I have shown, the trilogy charts the ways in which Bernice and her Barbadian friends negotiate the meanings of citizenship in Canada, but it also shows how immigration from the West Indies alters the meanings of Toronto's urban space from the mid-1950s to the mid-1970s. A product of both spatial and temporal relations, Toronto in these novels is more accurately conceived as

what Massey calls a "process" or "practice" than as a static entity or inert backdrop (3). Although in *The Bigger Light* Boysie wishes to distinguish himself
from the "conspicuousness" of the brash, young West Indians who form the
new generation of Toronto's Caribbean diaspora, their presence "on the streets
everywhere in Toronto" and in professions like law attests to the fact that
Toronto is a process that is altered by those who participate in it (15, 234).
Clarke's fictional Toronto thus suggests the broader ways that the categories
of ethnic, minority, and diasporic literatures in Canada will be altered by the
state's embrace of temporary worker programs.[20]

A politics of migrant-labour mobility urges us to look to the imbrication
of mobile practices and their representations. Such a theoretical strategy, I
argue, offers a means of thinking through one of the pervasive binaries of
twentieth- and twenty-first-century thought—that of "sedentarist" and what
Tim Cresswell calls "nomadic" metaphysics. We are living in a time when the
"common neoliberal imagined geography of the globe as a smooth, de-centred,
borderless, level playing field" (Roberts et al. 894) offers a particularly seductive obfuscation of the way that nation-states use their borders to enable the
functioning of the labour market under global capitalism. Working against
such obfuscation, my readings of Clarke and Foster have attempted to demonstrate that laying bare the social processes through which space is given meaning is a crucial part of the work that a politics of mobility can do.

NOTES

1   While sojourning and other forms of labour mobility were common in Canada prior
    to the Second World War (see Donald Avery, Anthony Chan, Judith Fingard, Robert
    Harney, and James Struthers), migrant-labour schemes introduce new legal restrictions.
2   Theorists of globalization, such as Michael Hardt and Antonio Negri, have made much
    use of Gilles Deleuze and Félix Guattari's concept of de-territorialization. As Stuart
    Elden notes, Hardt and Negri diminish Deleuze and Guattari's insistence that de-terri-
    torialized and re-territorialized spaces overlap. This overlap occurs when, for example,
    nation-states attempt to "cling to their sovereignty and territorial integrity in an age of
    globalizing markets and culture and emergent global modes of governance" (56).
3   Sharma is comparing the number of immigrants who come as temporary migrant work-
    ers with the number who come as "destined" permanent residents (i.e., immigrants who
    apply for permanent resident status through any of the various categories, and who
    indicate that they are destined to seek work in Canada) (110).
4   For a full account of the terms that govern the SAWP, see "Temporary Foreign Worker
    Program: Hiring Foreign Agricultural Workers in Canada" on the Human Resources
    and Development Canada website. Migrant labourers are poised to assume a rapidly
    expanding role in the Canadian labour force. Indeed, Canada's Temporary Foreign
    Worker Program (TFWP) now allows employers to hire migrant workers in a multitude

of sectors, depending on assessed "need" within the province in question, and since 2001 the TFWP for Occupations Requiring Lower Levels of Formal Training has enabled the expansion of migrant labour in the agricultural sector by admitting workers from nations not included in or governed by the standards of the SAWP (Hanley 16). As Sandra Elgersma's 2007 parliamentary report reveals, the demand for migrant workers has increased throughout Canada, but this growth is most pronounced in the province of Alberta, where there was a 41 percent increase in demand between 2005 and 2006.

5 Migrant agricultural workers contribute to Employment Insurance and the Canada Pension Plan, and they also pay income tax. Although the situation varies from province to province, some agricultural migrant workers are denied the right to form job unions and bargain collectively, and employment standards and occupational health-and-safety legislation provide uneven protection because they are not always applied to migrant workers (Hanley 4).

6 See also: Brydon, "Postcolonialism Now," Keya Ganguly, and Andrew Smith. Not surprisingly, immigration and labour historians have also argued for the necessity of careful distinctions among practices and effects of mobility. See, for example, Rose Baaba Folson and Dirk Hoerder.

7 Until April 2010, the Live-in Caregiver Program compelled migrant domestics to live in the homes of their employers for two years of a three-year contract (Bakan and Stasiulus 121). Currently, caregivers have up to four years to complete 3,900 hours or twenty-four months of full-time employment in a live-in context before they can apply for permanent residence. See "Temporary Foreign Worker Program: Live-in Caregiver Program" on the Human Resources and Development Canada website. As Makeda Silvera's interviews with domestics in her 1983 book *Silenced* demonstrate, the isolated working conditions of the live-in program make domestics vulnerable to exploitation because labour law is difficult to enforce in such contexts.

8 For an interesting class-based analysis of domestics and their relationship to space in Canadian writing, see Roxanne Rimstead.

9 Clarke describes how White Toronto was transformed on Thursday afternoons in the early 1960s, the one day that domestics were not working. Yet he observes that the liberty of free time was seriously curtailed by the "self-conscious uneasiness so common to black immigrants to this country" ("West Indian Domestics").

10 Foster is unabashed in his description of Clarke as a literary mentor and calls his Toronto trilogy a "seminal work on the immigrant experience" ("A Long Sojourn" 19).

11 I am influenced here by Paul Gilroy's reading of W.E.B. Du Bois's Pullman porter, who "benefits from the enhanced mobility provided by modern technologies," but "does so in a subordinate role, managing the travel experiences of others and servicing their needs at the expense of those of his own family" (*The Black Atlantic* 133).

12 The original manuscript of *The Meeting Point* was written in 1962 (Algoo-Baksh 49); during this period, Clarke explored the lives of West Indian domestics in other pieces that are less well known—a play for the Caribana festival called "Children of the Scheme" and the short story "I Hang on, Praise God!" (published in the Barbadian literary magazine *Bim* in 1963) (Algoo-Baksh 55, 60).

13 Fredric V. Bogel suggests that the satiric act *must* begin with a "partial identification" between the satirist and the satiric object because otherwise the assertion of difference

between the two would not be necessary (46). See Coleman, *Masculine Migrations* for an excellent discussion of the performance of masculinity in Clarke's fiction.

14   Clarke began his affiliation with the CBC in the late 1950s, when he worked there as a stagehand after quitting his university studies. Despite his recognition that the CBC bureaucracy could be racist, he worked in various capacities as a freelance journalist and broadcaster for the CBC during the 1960s and early 1970s, writing radio documentaries and other pieces on the Black civil rights movement in the US, on West Indian writers and writing, and on West Indians in England, among other topics. As was the case for many other writers in Canada in this period, Robert Weaver's CBC radio show "Anthology" also provided a consistent source of support for his ventures in short fiction (Algoo-Baksh 57–93).

15   After 1967, when Canadian immigration policy was purportedly made non-discriminatory, there was a wider variety of potential ways for immigrants from the Caribbean to enter Canada.

16   In *A Place Called Heaven*, Foster aligns this temporal ideal with Du Bois's notion of integration, which Foster grounds in the Canadian nation and turns to the liberal ideal of multiculturalism. He argues that Blacks will "arrive" in Canada when they form "an integral part of the Canadian mosaic" (320).

17   This story was written in 1961, during one of Clarke's first sustained efforts at writing short fiction (Algoo-Baksh 47).

18   Silvera cites Clarke's fiction as an influence on her own activism and writing, particularly because he insisted on using the Barbadian English that the domestics around him actually spoke and that certainly had not yet played any significant role in what was then becoming known as Canadian literature (viii).

19   In chapters 3 and 4 of her biography, Algoo-Baksh discusses this aspect of Clarke's work in great detail.

20   I have already discussed the fact that the numbers of people entering Canada as migrant workers have increased since the 1973 introduction of the NIEAP. In 1973, 69,901 temporary employment authorizations were issued; in 2004, the figure was 228,677 (Sharma 113). Moreover, the Canadian state is increasingly sourcing its temporary workers from less economically developed countries (LEACs) in Africa, Asia (excluding Japan), North and Central America (excluding the United States), the Caribbean, South America, and Oceania (Sharma 129–30).

III Future Imperfect

Racialized Diasporas, Entangled Postmemories, and Kyo Maclear's The Letter Opener

Christine Kim

KYO MACLEAR'S *THE LETTER OPENER* (2007) begins with the disappearance of Andrei, a recent Jewish refugee to Canada from Romania, and the sense of loss felt by his friend and colleague Naiko, the Canadian narrator of Japanese and Scottish ancestry. Andrei and Naiko met as co-workers in the Undeliverable Mail Office (UMO) in Toronto, a setting that introduces the notion of vulnerable circulation and movement of memory that is woven throughout the text.[1] The fragility of memory is taken up most explicitly in two of the novel's narrative threads: the first reconstructs Andrei's story, which includes his flight from Ceausescu's Romania and the loss of his lover Nicolae, and the second explores Japanese Canadian social memory through Naiko's mother, Ayumi, and her struggle with Alzheimer's, and through the personal connections Ayumi's neighbours have to Japanese Canadian internment during the Second World War. The UMO workers use their detection skills to return lost packages, often sorting through piles of vaguely labelled correspondence and tracking down addressees in order to deliver long-lost messages and objects. As the employees sift through items such as a package of cake mix and birthday candles sent by a young child to his father, it becomes clear that their true task is to restore misplaced attachments. The irony that neither she nor any of her colleagues can locate one of their missing co-workers is not lost on Naiko. And it is while repatriating objects to lost owners that Naiko becomes a collector herself, unable to relinquish the memories and narratives invoked by an object long after she has either returned or given up on returning it to the intended recipient.

Andrei's disappearance sets into motion the central dynamic of the novel, a dialectical play between the memorializing of loss and an unravelling of the process of loss itself. Naiko's uneasy and, from the perspective of her colleagues and boyfriend, obsessive attachment to Andrei's disappearance eventually drives her lover, Paolo, to ask why she can't be like "Other people. The ones who stick to their own business." He continues by noting, "It's strange. It's almost as though you take pleasure from it" (161). He points out that Andrei abandoned her without a word of explanation and suggests that what she considers loyalty is actually a degree of attachment bordering on lunacy (160–61). This moment in the novel is provocative not least because of how it approaches relations between multiple diasporas—represented through, for instance, Paolo, who grew up in Argentina and moved to Canada as a young man; Baba, a Lebanese Canadian co-worker at the UMO; the senior citizens who populate Sakura (the Japanese Canadian retirement home where Ayumi lives); the group of men with whom Andrei shares a settlement house when he first immigrates to Canada; and, of course, Naiko and Andrei—and imagines both the difficulties and possibilities produced through social intimacy. Paolo's comments echo views promulgated by Naiko's co-workers and her sister, Kana, all of whom seem to advocate placing strict temporal and emotional parameters around mourning in an attempt to suture together wounds in the most expedient fashion possible. Anger, acceptance, and disavowal are held up as appropriate responses to loss and abandonment, whereas the seemingly unending morass of grieving that Naiko enters into is perceived as pure folly.[2]

Naiko's refusal to relinquish her attachment to this loss, one that, to paraphrase Paolo, is tedious and much too intense, simultaneously gestures toward the significance of this friendship and signals resistance to the belief that people should limit their entanglements in each other's lives (14). Mourning occurs most obviously for Andrei, the missing confidant, but is also undertaken in response to the apparent ease with which people are able to let go of those around them and move into a space of indifference. But this self-imposed emotional burden is complicated by the fact that Naiko is mourning the loss of a friend who seems not to want to be remembered or found. The desire to remember Andrei and understand the subsequent wound she is left bearing are irrational and perhaps even intrusive tasks, but nonetheless ones that drive both Naiko and the narrative. For much of the novel, Naiko is unable to let go of Andrei; indeed, doing so would constitute another kind of psychic loss. The process of mourning here needs to be read as an integral part of Naiko's own subjectivity and as central to how she understands her ethical and historical position in the world. Her unshakeable attachment to this loss far exceeds her relationships with other individuals and, I would argue, gestures toward certain potential intimacies between diasporas that are not immediately visible to those involved.

In this depiction of memory, history, and loss, Maclear touches upon concerns that are strikingly similar to those invoked by critic Anne Anlin Cheng in her psychoanalytic explorations of racial dynamics in the American context. In *The Melancholy of Race*, Cheng uses African American and Asian American literature to explore questions of identity and racialization, asking how best to understand race as a product of both material and psychic processes. She suggests that much of the critical work on race tends to focus on the social injury caused by race, positing it in terms of a "vocabulary of grievance (and its implied logic of comparability and compensation)" and notes that there has been comparatively little scholarship produced about "the more immaterial, unquantifiable repository of public and private grief that has gone into the making of the so-called minority subject and that sustains the notion of 'one nation'" (6). Cheng frames race relations as a form of wounding to allow for movement between the conventional association of race as the source of social and legal grievances and the need to grieve the kinds of subjectivities produced through the process of racialization. One of the central tenets of Cheng's important theoretical work is that a shift in discussions about race and American national identity needs to occur; she asserts that "[r]ather than prescribing how we as a nation might go about 'getting over' that history, it is useful to ask what it means, for social, political, and subjective beings *to grieve*" (7). This profoundly important manoeuvre, pairing racial affect and emotion with the recognition of race in social and political terms, underscores the need to both broaden and deepen our collective understanding of racialization and make that a key part of larger projects of social and cultural transformation.

Drawing on Freud's work on mourning and melancholia, Cheng argues that the ongoing negotiation of desire and repulsion at work in racial melancholia affects the formulation of both white and racialized identities in the US. Whiteness is produced "through the melancholic introjection of racial others that it can neither fully relinquish nor accommodate and whose ghostly presence nonetheless guarantees its centrality," whereas racialized subjects are marked by a sense of loss, a "never-possible perfection," as they will never be able to conform to the dominant ideal (xi). This partial digestion of racialized subjects by the nation situates race, whiteness, and identity in a set of difficult and slippery relations. The perpetual negotiation of loss and desire,

longing and mourning, that characterizes race relations in the US is eerily
similar to the tumultuous emotions experienced by Maclear's protagonist who
has introjected Andrei's narrative. Although the object of mourning in *The
Letter Opener* is not visibly racially marked, Andrei, nonetheless as an individual who fled Romania under Ceausescu because of his sexual orientation
and whose Jewish mother survived the Holocaust, is positioned precariously
in relation to multiple nation-states, much like the kinds of visibly racialized subjects Cheng describes. By thinking through the implications of this
intersection of race and diaspora, this investigation considers what it might
mean for Maclear to invoke a common set of concerns and images among her
characters in order to work through both diasporic relationality and the politics of race, citizenship, and nation-states. This overlap is especially intriguing
because, while Maclear's text reworks the acts of circulating story, history, and
memory,[3] familiar tasks within the larger project of diasporic writing, it does
so in order to generate a host of pressing new questions about diasporic ethics,
racial affect, and relationality, such as what causes us to be moved by certain
narratives of diaspora and not others? How might we understand psychic and
social investments in another's pain? And how are various diasporic populations affectively bound together?

CONTEMPORARY POSTMEMORY

In her work on visual representation and the Holocaust, Marianne Hirsch critically examines the way that trauma shapes both immediate survivors and subsequent generations, focusing in particular on how those who did not directly
experience events are affected by cultural memory. To explain these representations of historical trauma, Hirsch develops the concept of postmemory,
which she defines in "The Generation of Postmemory" (2008) as a term that

> describes the relationship that the generation after those who witnessed
> cultural or collective trauma bears to the experiences of those who came
> before, experiences that they "remember" only by means of the stories,
> images, and behaviors among which they grew up. But these experiences
> were transmitted to them so deeply and affectively as to *seem* to constitute
> memories in their own right. Postmemory's connection to the past is thus
> not actually mediated by recall but by imaginative investment, projection,
> and creation. (106–7)

Postmemory provides a means of understanding the connections between generations and underscores the complicated ways in which the past continues to seep into and influence the present. "Remembering" through postmemory carries considerable ethical implications because this binding together of generations extends the work of witnessing. Hirsch calls this form of witnessing "retrospective" and lauds its ability to address the temporality of trauma itself:

> If indeed one of the signs of trauma is its delayed recognition, if trauma is recognizable only through its after-effects, then it is not surprising that it is transmitted across generations. Perhaps it is *only* in subsequent generations that trauma can be witnessed and worked through, by those who were not there to live it but who received its effects, belatedly, through the narrative, actions and symptoms of the previous generation. ("Surviving Images" 12)

Postmemory and its reliance upon representations of a traumatic past offers a way of engaging with painful experiences and understanding the ethical obligations and affective connections that exist between generations, but one that is always mediated by the work of memory, imagination, and symbolic systems. As a creative act that bridges personal and collective memory, postmemory is a practice that produces new narratives of social belonging as it sifts through representations of memory. By actively engaging with difficult pasts, the collector inserts herself into assemblages of memory.

Hirsch repeatedly refines this term and explores the theoretical potential of postmemory in various critical works, such as *Family Frames* (1997), "Surviving Images" (2001), and "The Generation of Postmemory" (2008), thereby demonstrating how postmemory itself has accumulated its own history and memory, a point that corresponds to the reworking of diaspora definitions and affective buildup that I will return to later. The transmission of trauma and the inheritance of memory are preoccupations that occur in *The Letter Opener*, but deviate in at least one crucial way from Hirsch's discussion of postmemory. In Maclear's novel, Naiko takes up the role of witness to Andrei's trauma and performs this obligation by telling stories about him and constantly remembering his memories on his behalf. While Naiko is indelibly imprinted by these inherited memories and engages in an imaginative relationship with the past, she is obviously not saturated by the memories in the same way and over the kind of prolonged period of time that Hirsch observes in the Holocaust postmemory generation. Instead, Maclear's novel fashions a willing listener who takes up another's memory, plunging herself into the task rather than having it thrust upon her. The dynamic that *The Letter Opener* describes is the movement of memory and postmemory between contemporaries rather than over generations, and the creative forensics involved is expressed most clearly when Naiko wonders to herself: "How can I truthfully know the lives of people I have never met? I reassure myself I am as good a detective as any. After all, it has become a life work reconstructing other people's stories. I spend each day before my mountain of scraps, and imagine" (36). Although postmemory does not permit Naiko to "know" these people's lives, it does move her tentatively toward the project of understanding them. And in the same way that Hirsch states that "[p]ostmemory is not identical to memory: it is 'post,' but at the same time, it approximates memory in its affective force," I would suggest that the kind of revised postmemory relationship that Naiko enters into is not identical to the original definition, but is affectively similar (Hirsch, "The Generation" 109). What makes the affective charge remain as strong as the postmemory invoked by Hirsch, even though Naiko voluntarily reconstructs Andrei's memory instead of having it bequeathed to her, is that something of Andrei's forgotten story echoes her own. When Andrei confides to Naiko that he has been battling what he calls a "memory flu" by rehearsing the names of places and people that he used to know and Romanian words for everyday objects, Naiko speculates that this is Andrei's "way of not forgetting the world of Nicolae" (112). While loss of home, family, and sense of social location are common to both figures, it is Andrei's fear that all of these things are becoming part of a static past and his realization that he is capable of forgetting them that triggers a desire to remember in Naiko.

The transmission of pain between diasporic subjects repositions Hirsch's formulation somewhat and, in so doing, asks who can take up the task of postmemory and what might drive them to do so. And yet, I believe that the concept of postmemory is elastic enough to accommodate this kind of interdiasporic exchange between contemporaries. In *Family Frames*, Hirsch targets the children of trauma survivors as the logical inheritors of postmemory, but suggests toward the end of the book that those are not the only people she hopes to address in these terms:

> As such, they can also remind us of the distance, the absence, the unbridgeable gap that, in postmodernity, makes us who we are. In this "we" I do not include only Jews or those whose families were directly affected by the Holocaust either as victims, as perpetrators, or as bystanders: I include the much vaster community of postmemory that will, ideally, be forged by the

aesthetics of the Tower of Faces, or of Boltanski's and Attie's installations. This aesthetics is based on the identifications forged by familial looking. (267)

In subsequent publications, Hirsch returns again to the identificatory potential of postmemory, suggesting that the work of postmemory as a "form of remembrance need not be restricted to the family, or even to a group that shares an ethnic or national identity marking: through particular forms of identification, adoption, and projection, it can be more broadly available" ("Surviving" 9–10). That postmemory might not only connect generations of survivors and their descendants, but also reach beyond this demographic and touch those with little or no immediate connection to the trauma itself is crucial in terms of its ethical and affective potential. The work of postmemory "strives to *reactivate* and *reembody* more distant social/national and archival/cultural memorial structures by reinvesting them with resonant individual and familial forms of mediation and aesthetic expression," thus creating a multitude that might engage with these memories in the future ("The Generation" 111).

The relationship between Naiko and Andrei, as well as the one Naiko has to her sense of loss, offers a site for working through memory, postmemory, and identification. Naiko's taking up of Andrei's narrative should not be read simply as an act of appropriation, given the direction these memories lead Naiko and the potential conversations they open up for and between various diasporas. The process of mourning—both the figure of Andrei as well as the wounds he leaves on Naiko's psyche—becomes a route that returns the Asian diaspora in Canada to its own losses, but one that simultaneously decentres and expands the ethical and political potential of this community. When Naiko takes up the task of maintaining and interrogating memory for Andrei, she not only expands the parameters of postmemory, but also those of diasporic obligation. Her loyalty toward a non-Asian diasporic memory suggests a movement away from identity politics and immediate self-interest, and thus demands that the costs of foregrounding the particular narratives attached to Jewish and Romanian experiences over Asian Canadian ones be calculated. In underscoring this tension between the perceived obligations diasporans have to their "own" diasporas and the ethics of caring for other diasporas unmotivated by immediate self-interest, my intention is not to suggest that identity politics must or should necessarily determine which narratives should be prioritized. Rather, my interest lies in why particular diasporic configurations appeal so strongly to others and what kinds of insights might be gleaned from this instance of interdiasporic loyalty.

OLD AND NEW DIASPORAS

The multiple representations of diasporic experiences in *The Letter Opener*
are, individually and collectively, suggestive for the way they bring together
classical and postcolonial paradigms of diaspora and push our understandings
of how their everyday experiences intersect in a Canadian context. At the
same time, these figures also remind us that, historically, the reconfiguration
of national citizens into racialized citizens or diasporans has produced disturbing consequences (as is well illustrated by the spate of recent Canadian redress
agreements and government apologies for racially motivated injustices that
include the internment of Japanese Canadians, the Chinese Canadian head
tax, and Aboriginal residential schools). And even as the language of apology and compensatory payments dominates the contemporary Canadian landscape, it seems that the wounds of racialization not only, to borrow Cheng's
language about racial divides in an American context, cannot be "gotten
over" but continue to be inflicted. The ongoing symbolic and material violence levied on supposedly terrifying diasporic bodies as part of the "War on
Terror" testifies in a very real way to the impossibility of dislodging the process of racial wounding from discourses of Canadian citizenship. As Davina
Bhandar demonstrates in her reading of two cases of racialized border cross-
ings, the 1907 Anti-Asiatic riots and the 2002–3 imprisonment and torture
of Syrian-born Canadian Maher Arar, recent changes to national security and
border policing have produced different yet familiar forms of racism that dehu-
manize racialized bodies.[4] That events spanning nearly a century continue to
sound the same refrain suggests that before we can distance ourselves from the
sorts of racial violence inflicted by nation and state and view these wounds as
healed, we need to first begin a process of racial grieving in Canada.

While the risk of becoming trapped within an endless and emotionally
taxing cycle of melancholia is certainly real, it is not necessarily an unproductive site to occupy. Drawing on Walter Benjamin's "Theses on the Philosophy
of History," David Eng and David Kazanjian make this point eloquently, arguing for the generative work enabled by mourning "as that creative process
mediating a hopeful or hopeless relationship between loss and history" (2).
Part of the way that Eng and Kazanjian recuperate mourning is by expanding
our understanding of loss to also include the traces and remnants that survive
and showing that an ongoing relationship with the past "generates sites for
memory and history, for the rewriting of the past as well as the reimagining
of the future" (4). Incorporating an "attention to remains generates a politics

of mourning that might be active rather than reactive, prescient rather than nostalgic, abundant rather than lacking, social rather than solipsistic, militant rather than reactionary" (2). As Judith Butler writes in "Violence, Mourning, Politics," successful grieving is transformative as it leads to a reconceptualization of the mourning subject, social relations, and even the category of the human itself. It is by negotiating the process of loss that the surviving subject, "the human[,] comes into being, again and again, as that which we have yet to know" (49).

The complex task of memory work in relation to Japanese Canadian history in *The Letter Opener* largely depends upon Naiko's tenuous connections to other diasporas. Naiko's deep fixation with Andrei's narrative contrasts sharply with what appears to be a comparatively minimal investment in stories of Japanese Canadian internment, a dynamic that needs to be understood both in terms of how specific diasporas are located within particular nation-states, as well as within the scholarly field of diaspora studies. In terms of the latter, multiple critical discussions have taken place about the changes to the term "diaspora," with many interlocutors weighing in on the inclusion of "ethnic or immigrant communities" within the category and the subsequent repositioning of the classical Jewish, Armenian, and Greek diasporas. In the inaugural issue of the journal *Diaspora*, for example, William Safran argues for a strict definition of diaspora that envisions very specific relations between members, homelands, and collective memories. Safran holds up the Jewish diaspora as an "ideal type," cites others such as the Armenian, Chinese, and Turkish diasporas as legitimate but not conforming fully to the definition, and seems to view other ethnic communities that use the term "diaspora" "as [a] metaphoric designatio[n]" as troubling (84).

While Safran's position is perhaps a bit extreme, other critics have also articulated a similar sense of unease with the recent critical transformations to diaspora studies. For instance, Khachig Tölölyan's important article, "Rethinking Diaspora(s): Stateless Power in the Transnational Moment" (1996), warns that changes to "diaspora" need to be considered quite carefully and within the broader context of global political and economic change because "re-naming is usually accompanied by an attempt to overthrow the older understanding of a category and to make the new term and refashioned category the focus of a new intellectual order" (4–5). The establishment of Israel, for example, was seen as a diasporic victory; a by-product of this Jewish success was the new positive set of connotations for diaspora, which other ethnic communities were able to harness. Drawing on his own personal intellectual and biographical history, Tölölyan writes about the complicated negotiations between diaspora, nation-state, and identity that have been undertaken for centuries. By tracing the meaning of diaspora back to ancient Greece and then connecting it to the classical examples of the Jewish and Armenian diasporas, Tölölyan suggests that pain, suffering, and lost homelands have long since formed the heart of diaspora. While there are certain affinities shared by ethnic communities and diaspora, namely a commitment to "a collective identity other than the hegemonic one that dominates the hostland," a significant point of departure is that for ethnic communities, the "commitment to maintain connections with its homeland and its kin communities in other states is absent, weak, at best intermittent, and manifested by individuals rather than the community as a whole" (16). In contrast with his discussions of ethnic communities with limited investments in earlier homelands, Tölölyan cites the examples of the Jewish and Armenian diasporas for their continued efforts to maintain strong bonds between diaspora and homeland. As he maps out the intellectual history of diaspora and identifies what he views as the crucial ethical and political work of diaspora, Tölölyan discusses the tension between demonstrating diasporic solidarity and identifying as a diasporan. Tölölyan uses his own example to explain that while simply identifying as part of a diaspora, and specifically as Armenian, renders him vulnerable in certain parts of the globe, the dominant view espoused while he was growing up "was that just as being the citizen of a nation-state had a cost (taxes, the draft, obedience to laws), so also membership in a diasporic branch of the transnation must have a cost, a demonstration of loyalty that undertook the responsibility of sacrifice" (15). At the same time, diasporic identity is largely subjective and the question of how a diaspora "feels about itself and 'represents' itself to itself and others" is one that Tölölyan acknowledges as important (16).

Without dismissing the significance of Tölölyan's argument and particularly his insight into the nature of diasporic citizenship, I want to note that the work of other scholars has posed certain challenges to parts of his argument. Robin Cohen, for instance, limits the possibility of reading the Jewish diaspora purely as a victim diaspora by noting that trade and finance were also reasons for migration, and Daniel Boyarin and Jonathan Boyarin complicate the meanings attached to Zionism for particular segments of the Jewish diaspora. The Boyarins insert a measure of discord into Tölölyan's reading of Israel as diasporic achievement by discussing dissenting positions, including their own, that "peoples and lands are not naturally and organically connected," which contradicts Tölölyan's simpler connection between diaspora and homeland

(723). A different sort of challenge is raised by David Chariandy's reading of the expansion of diaspora to include a broader range of people and issues of social justice as a positive and enabling shift. The inclusion of what he calls postcolonial diasporas (such as African and Asian diasporas) into the broader field of diaspora studies does not necessarily demand a turn away from classical diasporas or the history of diasporic scholarship ("Postcolonial"). On the contrary, earlier traditions of diasporic thought need to be engaged with, but he notes that this is different from "privileging one particular historical conception of diaspora" which runs the risk of "mak[ing] all other conceptualizations of diaspora derivative or secondary, or illegitimate" ("Postcolonial"). Chariandy proposes a way of engaging with diaspora that differs from the more literal reading practices of critics such as Tölölyan and Safran and advocates moving instead toward, without eschewing the importance of those literal dimensions, the metaphoric aspects of diaspora and striving to "understand diaspora not as a reality to be empirically analyzed, but as something self-consciously figurative or metaphorical and thus a special agent for social change." Far from diluting the meaning of diaspora, Chariandy argues that it is precisely in the opening up of diaspora to other sorts of approaches and questions that diaspora studies can find new meaning and "make inventive demands on existing political, institutional, and epistemological constraints."

Despite the many well-expressed concerns about the displacing consequences that the arrival of postcolonial diasporas would have for classical diasporas, I am not entirely convinced that the critical shift has occurred in as abrupt or absolute a fashion as had been predicted by some diaspora critics. On the contrary, the affective dimensions of these classical paradigms seem to continue to exert considerable, albeit less easily discernible, force on newer and postcolonial conceptions of diaspora. The complicated dynamics between classical and postcolonial diasporas is rendered visible in *The Letter Opener* through the relationship between Andrei and Naiko as figures who represent these communities. Specifically, the text uses Andrei, as a romanticized figure of multiple diasporas and migrations to embody loss and trauma in catastrophic terms. This is made abundantly clear in Andrei's narrative of flight from Romania with his lover Nicolae and their travels across the Black Sea by ship and subsequent swim across the Bosporus. Nicolae, however, does not make it to shore, and Andrei is traumatized by the loss of his love object, which is never recovered to prove it was gone. His narrative enables Naiko to return to Japanese Canadian histories, but only after she has been immersed within the paradigm of what Cohen calls "victim diasporas." In this

manner, Naiko's memory work becomes an introduction to a particular form
of diasporic grammar, not just diaspora writ large, but according to a model of
trauma and pain that is reinstalled as paradigmatic. Viewing Japanese Canadian matters through this lens does, as Chariandy warns of idealizing the Jewish diaspora, pose the dangers of delegitimizing Asian diasporic concerns and,
I would argue, of privileging only those experiential dimensions that are common to classical and postcolonial diasporas. This hierarchy manifests itself
in the novel, for instance, through a sense of temporality attached to narratives of diaspora. While Andrei's survivor story is marked by a strong note of
urgency, given the pressing political conditions in Romania and his ardent
desire to literally return to his homeland, the text presents Japanese Canadian
history largely as a matter of postmemory, replacing the pressure to act with
the struggle to remember. This particular agenda is underscored by the loss
of memory suffered by Ayumi, a change that causes Naiko to envision her
mother's "mind as a Jackson Pollock painting: repetitive, overlapping loops,
bundling and broken lines, all searching vigorously for a beginning," and the
devastating consequences a return to cultural memory has for Gloria, another
resident of Sakura (106). Positioning these narratives in this way runs the risk
of viewing Japanese Canadian struggles as enacting a different and therefore
lesser demand than classical victim diasporas. The text hazards these dangers
and, in so doing, renders visible the stakes of performing Japanese Canadian
memory work and demonstrates the ways in which diaspora and racialized
citizenship intersect in this particular instance.

DIASPORIC DEMANDS, RACIALIZED CITIZENSHIP

Locating Japanese Canadian history within the Asian diaspora and diaspora
studies more broadly allows us to perceive the sometimes difficult and contradictory demands that literal readings of diaspora can make upon its subjects.
This is demonstrated by the tension between the kinds of lists of defining
criteria provided by seminal critics such as Tölölyan, Safran, and Cohen, and
the particular situation of diasporic groups such as Japanese Canadians. In
Global Diasporas, Cohen outlines nine common features of diaspora, which
include allegiance to a community or homeland and "strong ethnic group consciousness sustained over a long time and based on a sense of distinctiveness,
a common history, the transmission of a common cultural and religious heritage and the belief in a common fate" (17). While these criteria are familiar
ones to diaspora studies, for Japanese Canadians, they have been historically

undermined by another common diaspora feature, namely "a troubled relationship with host societies, suggesting a lack of acceptance or the possibility that another calamity might befall the group" (Cohen 17). The difficult social location of Japanese Canadians within Canada has historically worked against the maintenance of a "strong ethnic group consciousness" and firm ties to Japan, and the evacuation of Japanese Canadians from the West Coast during the Second World War and the government's subsequent refusal to allow them to return to their homes even after the end of the war is perhaps the clearest expression of this problem.[5] The disruption of existing community structures and push toward assimilation by the dominant society is explained in Roy Miki's important account of the Japanese Canadian dispersal and later redress movements. Here he describes the white liberal groups' social pressure on Japanese Canadians, and the Nisei in particular, "to remake themselves as "Japanese *Canadian*," with the emphasis falling on their role in Canada as citizens" (*Redress* 106). Social and political invisibility was encouraged and even seen as a way of helping Japanese Canadians across the racial line that divided Canadian citizens and enemy aliens. However, *Redress* also reminds us that this is a false dilemma as the evacuation of this community from British Columbia was always already tied to "[t]heir racialization as the 'enemy' within the nation" and not, as was argued at the time by the government and politicians, to any matter of national security (94–95).[6] The representation of Japanese Canadians as Japanese rather than as Canadian citizens—in other words, racializing them—was an effective strategy for deflecting attention away from their citizenship rights and rendering them vulnerable in social, political, and economic terms. It also made the government's option for Japanese Canadians to "return" to Japan seem logical as it positioned them as part of an Asian diaspora and the move then as a return home.

The residue of this social memory of racially and economically motivated forced dispersal clings to Maclear's narrative and shapes how various forms of diasporic memory interact with each other. Naiko's initial preoccupation with Andrei as a refugee early on in their friendship can be seen as one such instance. In her struggle to define the category of refugee and locate Andrei within it, Naiko inadvertently identifies herself as a figurative refugee, one who is emotionally bereft and historically uncertain:

What made Andrei a refugee? Was it his bony chest? No, that was too obvious. His second-hand wardrobe? Perhaps, but that could also be attributed to general thriftiness. (I, for one, regularly shopped at Goodwill.) The reality was that there was no single outstanding characteristic—and why should there have been? Andrei frequently saved half his sandwich and kept the remaining Saran Wrap to use later, but to a different degree, I, too, was frugal. He appeared to own few personal belongings, but so did I. As to his deference to the manager, which seemed then the classic surviv-alism of the refugee, well now so much later I look more closely at myself, at my own often deferential demeanour. There were layers and layers to Andrei, I would discover, and refugee was but the latest, and thinnest. (25)

Naiko's consideration of displacement as it occurs in a variety of forms and in inter- and intranational terms highlights the obvious similarities between concentration, internment, and refugee camps in Europe and Canada during various points in history. Andrei explains that "people don't generally like to be called 'refugees.' That's a file word. Like 'asylum-seeker.' Or 'displaced person.' People have their prejudices about refugees" (25). His observations about the language of displacement remind us that the politics of this pro-cess depends heavily on euphemism. The importance of remembering that people are located within social narratives and memories about displacement is powerfully illustrated by the case of Japanese Canadians who internalized the language of "evacuation" to understand and speak of not just "the event itself, but also to identify the weight of all its phases—dispossession, deporta-tion, dispersal and assimilation" (Miki, *Redress* 50). Language was instrumen-tal in the Canadian government's ability to render palatable its actions to the majority of its citizens. By renaming the forced dispersal of certain Canadian citizens as the evacuation of Japanese enemy aliens, the government was able to "translate the inherent racism of its policies for Japanese Canadians into the language of bureaucratic efficiency. This way of neutralizing the abuse of power generated a complex of terms that rendered 'normal'—in the eyes of the Canadian public—its brutal implications" (Miki, *Redress* 51). Andrei's resis-tance to the bureaucratic language of asylum seekers and refugees, and Naiko's interest in the machinery of euphemism reminds us of the role that language plays in dispossessing individuals of memory. The unyoking of politics from the representation of events and processes makes the task of understanding the connection between historical pain and the contemporary condition that much more difficult.

The challenge of finding one's way to social memories whose meanings have been obfuscated is represented by Naiko's own tenuous connections to Japanese Canadian internment history. The novel never reveals whether the government's wartime practices had any direct impact on Naiko's family as the only stories told about her family history focus on her parents' divorce or the deterioration of her mother's memory. Experiences of mass uprooting and internment are connected to other Sakura residents, such as Roy Ishii whose "harmless hobby" of predicting the weather at Tashme based on cloud formations was prohibited by the government during the war as a dangerous activity for an enemy alien to undertake (119). Her mother's friend Gloria, however, becomes perhaps the most visible, and certainly most extended, representation of Japanese Canadian social memory when Naiko, via the UMO, gives Gloria a quilt that originally had been intended as a gift for her aunt and uncle. As John and Margaret Kimura had chosen to be "repatriated" to Japan instead of being sent to an internment camp, they never received this quilt. Upon inheriting this memory object, Gloria sets herself the task of restoring the quilt to its previous state and undoing the outward traces of physical damage. But once the object of memory is restored to its former condition, the work of remembering begins and Gloria is left to work through painful historical wounds; consequently, she finds herself getting "out of bed and wrapp[ing] herself in it [the quilt], and then a woman whose days and nights had no centre walked down the hall and set fire to a wastepaper bin in the women's washroom" (125). Unable to overcome the pain inflicted by a history of racialized citizenship, Gloria acts out criminally and consequently is sent upstairs to the "restricted ward—living under lock and key with full-time attendants" (226). Sequestering Gloria can be read as a moment of reinterning the lingering effects of wartime injustices and the administration of sedatives to her as a sign that her condition has been pathologized, both moves that are perhaps not surprising given the significant challenges posed by these less visible wounds.

Andrei is also a figure that is presented as having difficulties overcoming the past, but his struggles are treated much more sympathetically by the novel as he is given a receptive listener in Naiko, one willing to engage in the arduous task of memory work. As the bearer of stories about surviving Ceausescu's repressive dictatorship and a link to his mother and grandmother's narratives of Ravensbrück and Birkenau, Andrei is connected to social memories that are simultaneously older and newer than those of Japanese Canadian internment. And yet, the particular ways in which the novel has fashioned these two different diasporas—representing one through the figure of an older, visibly racialized woman whose attachment to the past produces pathological and criminal behaviour, and the other as a romantic and non-visibly racialized young man who has lost his lover, family, and country—suggests that there seems to be a certain degree of exhaustion, or at least fear of exhaustion,

associated with Japanese Canadian internment that is absent from responses
to narratives of the Holocaust and eastern European communism. The novel
explores a fear that the public's limits of sympathy with respect to Japanese
Canadian internment narratives have been reached by representing Japanese
Canadians not as a cohesive community pushing for social change or a return
to any homeland outside of Canada, but instead largely as an aged population
living in the shared space of a nursing home.[7] The current rhetoric of social
injury and apology at work in Canada suggests a strong desire to believe that
the work of public acknowledgement and taking of responsibility are singular
acts rather than ongoing processes. The novel returns to the residual emotions
and affects of Japanese Canadian history via the figure of the non-racialized
victim diaspora, a move that legitimizes certain forms of pain and loss while
presenting them within an unmarked subjectivity. Andrei's story possesses a
level of masculine authority that Naiko's own tentative narrative lacks, while
still addressing key forms of social difference.

The binding together of diasporas posits a different return to the intranational displacement and ongoing process of racialized citizenship experienced
by Japanese Canadians, and demonstrates that while the Japanese Canadian
community might not meet all of the criteria used to define diasporas in more
literal terms, there is still much value in continuing to think of them as a
diaspora. That Japanese Canadians have historically been made conscious of
a sense of non-belonging within the host country despite the generations that
have lived in it suggests an ongoing need to use diaspora as a way of unravelling the nexus of race and citizenship. While anthropologist and diaspora critic
James Clifford poses the question of "When does a group become indigenous?"
in his landmark article (309), I think that in this instance, the question needs
to be revised into "*How* does a group become indigenous?" Race as a marker of
difference makes it impossible within the current logic of national identity for
certain individuals and communities to be read in these terms. While Clifford
frames indigenous belonging as a matter of temporality, the history of Asian
Canadians suggests that it might instead be viewed as a matter of positioning;
race, as a constant reminder of histories of social difference and the histories of
diaspora, whether consciously or subconsciously acknowledged, renders that
positioning visible.

The novel's somewhat romantic turn to Romanian and Jewish experiences suggests a desire to exist differently in both nation and diaspora, and
signals a move toward that transformation through the forging of a new set of
identifications. Near the conclusion of *The Letter Opener*, Naiko speaks about

beginning to let go of Andrei's story, not out of a desire to forget or repress it, but as "simply loosen[ing] the grip of my need to possess and comprehend it. More difficult to release was the feeling of purpose his need and despair had given me" (298). The postmemory relationship between Naiko and Andrei eventually makes her conscious of her own racialized diasporic grief, and thus leaves her able to feel and imagine more intensely. Indeed, the various futures that the novel leaves open for Andrei become ways for Naiko to expand her affective capacity, a key transformation if, as Brian Massumi suggests, "[o]ur degree of freedom at any one time corresponds to how much of our experiential 'depth' we can access towards a next step—how intensely we are living and moving" (214). The return to Romania that Naiko presumes Andrei has undertaken provides closure to this diasporic narrative, and is a utopic script that, like the creation of Israel according to some critics, other diasporas might strive toward. At the same time, there still exists a possibility that Andrei continues to dwell somewhere in Canada as, given the diligence with which he learned Canadian social behaviours and his absence of visible racial markers, an ideal citizen. And while the possibilities of escaping elsewhere or assimilating seamlessly into dominant Canadian society are more threatening than attractive for the Asian diaspora given the events of the past, they nonetheless present a particular affective lure as fantasies of escaping certain difficulties attached to diaspora and racialized citizenship. These narratives of other diasporas, however, ultimately lead Naiko back to Japanese Canadian social memory and enable her to creatively mourn a range of past and ongoing losses. It is, after all, by working through Andrei's narrative that Naiko is able to claim and comfort Gloria as she is in the throes of a breakdown, and affirm to her own mother that the option of leaving the nursing home is always available.

Interdiasporic connection offers a means of returning the diasporan to those social histories she is most directly connected to, but also of engaging deeply with other forms of diaspora and, in so doing, working through the common politics of feeling and remembering. By probing Naiko's attachment to Andrei's narrative of loss and dislocation, as well as her comparable detachment from Japanese Canadian narratives, the novel encourages us to think about the precise ways in which we are touched by certain diasporic stories and how our own personal and collective histories shape our emotional and political responses. The moving narratives of Communist Romania and the Holocaust let Naiko enter into a generative relationship with loss, and this allows her to finally begin grieving Japanese Canadian social memory. His narrative, in other words, becomes a site for re-injecting the affective urgency of mourning within a field rendered static by a melancholic dynamic of incorporation of an unknown loss. By creating different sets of social identifications and introducing new emotional investments, interdiasporic relations foster transformations within the self, as well as within multiple wider communities. Diasporic intimacy, then, is critically important as it repositions individuals and communities in relation to various forms of diasporic and racialized loss, helps us finds more hopeful ways of interpreting such stories, and encourages the formation of new social and psychic attachments.

NOTES

1 My thanks to Elena Basile, Sophie McCall, and Melina Baum Singer for their thought-provoking feedback.

2 In their responses to loss, Naiko and her loved ones demonstrate the difference between Freud's categories of mourning and melancholia, the former referring to a finite expression of grief, and the latter to an interminable and pathological one. While much of "Mourning and Melancholia" (1917) is spent drawing a sharp distinction between the two states, Freud reconsiders this position toward the end of his essay and suggests that perhaps melancholia seems pathological only because we are not familiar enough with it. Freud further develops this idea in his later writings and eventually understands mourning and melancholia as deeply intertwined; David Eng and David Kazanjian paraphrase Freud as suggesting that "the work of mourning is not possible without melancholia ... [because] the ego is constituted through the remains of abandoned object-cathexes" (4).

3 Maclear's theoretical work, Beclouded Visions (1999), also engages with questions of memory, witnessing, and trauma. Beclouded Visions looks specifically at Hiroshima and Nagasaki in order to call for new modes of visual representation to both image and imagine cultural trauma.

4 It is important to note that the language of victims and security threats used in redress agreements and apologies, and as part of the "War on Terror," are two different processes of racialization that occur within the nation. The first refers to melancholic incorporation, and the second to psychotic foreclosure. The first produces an "inferior" human (worthy of pity as long as it remains grateful); the second produces a "non-human" human, an absolute other with whom no "civilized" mediation is possible. The two processes are complementary in helping reinforce the outer and inner boundaries of the nation. My thanks to Elena Basile for this insight.

5 The desire to disperse Japanese Canadians throughout Canada and prevent them from reorganizing as a community in British Columbia continued after the end of the Second World War. In a speech given at the House of Commons on 4 August 1944, Prime Minister Mackenzie King spoke about the need to redistribute and assimilate Japanese Canadians. He argued that it was best if the "Japanese" were not allowed to return to British Columbia because their high concentration had caused unpleasant feelings on the part of White British Columbians: "Rather than exclusion and expulsion, the

desired mode of resolving the 'Japanese problem' in B.C. before the war, King proposed the absorption of Japanese Canadians in small doses across the country so that they would disappear as a group" (Miki, *Redress* 40).

6   *Redress* also shows that the injustices committed against Japanese Canadians during the Second World War were part of a longer historical process of racialization and national exclusion. An early example of Asian Canadians being located outside of the parameters of the nation is Tomekichi Homma's failed attempt to obtain the franchise in British Columbia. Miki highlights the tension between race and citizenship that Homma's 1900 challenge made visible. He notes that while the Provincial *Election Act* clearly states that people of Asian heritage are ineligible for the franchise, Homma argued that as a naturalized citizen, he should not be read in those terms:

> Homma was able to turn this regulation back on itself. Although "Japanese" was defined as "any person of the Japanese race, naturalized or not," in the language of citizenship, as "naturalized" person, he was no longer the "Japanese" named in the Act. Naturalization had made him a "British subject," a status that was under the jurisdiction of the federal government. In this way, Homma sought to displace the racialized language of the Act by drawing on the broader (British and European) understanding of naturalization as a process through which he had been transformed from one status ("Japanese") to another ("British subject"). (Miki, *Redress* 26)

Even though Chief Justice Angus John McColl, the judge presiding over the case, sided with Homma and the Supreme Court of Canada upheld this decision when it was appealed, the vote was still withheld from Homma and other Asian Canadian citizens. The Privy Council struck down these rulings and allowed the BC government to continue to withhold the vote from certain populations by "resort[ing] to 'race'—rather than citizenship—as a basis for enfranchisement" (Miki, *Redress* 27).

7   Sakura might be read as modelled upon the retirement home of the same name (New Sakura-so) in Burnaby, British Columbia, which was established in part through funding from the redress agreement. It is the only depiction of a Japanese Canadian community in the text, and it should be noted that it is an institutionally sanctioned space for an older population. By locating the past in limited terms without providing a similar measure of space for a younger generation or wider community, the suggestion is that the Japanese Canadian community is dwindling instead of expanding. The reduction of community to a collection of individuals as exemplified by Naiko is also a way of transforming a diaspora into a group of ethnic individuals. It is also worth noting that in Miki's discussion of the long process of redress, he mentions that one of the earlier and unaccepted redress packages, which envisioned group rather than individual and group compensation, included a provision to take care of the needs of the elderly through a "nursing home," for the most part the "issei," [which] struck a compassionate note and showed respect for the elderly. The foundation, in gesturing toward Japanese Canadians more in terms of social "needs" than of "rights," would have accommodated mainstream (read "white") liberal values and given the impression that Japanese Canadians were good citizens—even when seeking redress for the violation for their rights (*Redress* 175).

Underwater Signposts
Richard Fung's Islands *and Enabling Nostalgia*

Lily Cho

PARTWAY THROUGH RICHARD FUNG'S 2002 video, *Islands*, there is an extravagant death scene. The figure on the screen collapses, clasping his hand to his chest, flailing. There are explosions going off around him. Dirt flies everywhere. It is a death repeated again and again. The inter-title explains: "When the explosions go off he does not react.... The director yells at him.... He is asked to fall in the mud over and over ..." (*Islands*). The man is Fung's Uncle Clive. He is an extra on the set of John Huston's 1956 film *Heaven Knows, Mr. Allison*. The video's repetition of the footage from this death scene poses this death as a recurring problem that hovers between the singularity of a performance and the blurred collectivity of Clive's role in the film. In Huston's film, this one death will stand in for the fall of an army. This Chinese man in Trinidad will stand in for a Japanese soldier in the South Pacific. In raising the problem of substitution, *Islands* poses the problem of the desire for a specificity that escapes the trap of exceptionality. That is, how can we understand the specificity of Chineseness and, more specifically still, Chineseness in Trinidad through the lens of a filmmaker in Canada, without taking refuge in arguments for the unique experiences of Chinese diasporic subjects? This question of exceptionality attends to Canadian multiculturalism's attempts to resolve the paradox of celebrating difference while still containing it within a particular national frame—the paradox of encouraging the singular without sacrificing the universal. Citing documents from Multiculturalism and Citizenship Canada, Eva Mackey observes that official multiculturalism is meant to function as a "'great national bandage'" that "allows the state to highlight and manage diversity without endangering the project of national-building"

(81). The bandaging of difference regards the claims to exceptionality (think "special interest") as deeply suspect. In arguing for the specific (for example, Chineseness in Trinidad refracted through Canada), diaspora has also tried to sidestep the claim for the exceptional in order to make powerful connections across minoritized communities. As Melina Baum Singer suggests in her chapter for this volume, the study of diaspora has moved from its focus on Jews and Jewish experience and become much more closely allied with critical race theory—arguably a move from the claim to the exceptional to that of specificity within the context of a multiplicity of specificities. This shift suggests that the study of diaspora in Canada must grapple with the problem of the specificity of race without losing sight of the connections between racial formations and the political possibilities of sustaining diasporic connections that extend beyond the nation. This chapter proposes that Fung's *Islands* offers a way of understanding specificity through what Edouard Glissant has called the poetics of relation.

For Glissant, the question of the specific, of the relation between one death and that of many others, emerges as one of relation and thus also of history. In *The Poetics of Relation*, he writes:

> For though this experience made you, original victim floating toward the sea's abysses, an exception, it became something shared and made us, the descendants, one people among others. People do not live on in exception. Relation is not made up of things that are foreign but of shared knowledge. This experience of the abyss can now be said to be the best element of exchange. (8)

As Ian Baucom notes in his meditation on this passage, Glissant discovers in the scene of slaves being thrown overboard "not an injunction to melancholy but the double promise of relation, the promise of an inherited solidarity and the promise of the connective, rhizomic identity of the nonidentical" (71). In attempting to find a relationship between one death and that of many, between Black and Asian diasporic experiences, between one ocean and another, I am arguing not for a subsumption of the particular or the singular into a universal, but for the relation of the specific and the singular to a constellation that includes other singularities without reducing them to synecdochic moments of the same.

In a historicizing move, Baucom reveals that the scene of Glissant's "original victim" is not a reference to just any scene of death at sea, but rather to the case of the massacre that occurs on the *Zong* ship and the horrors of that

specific history. A slave ship loses its course and the captain, Luke Colling-
wood, decides that there were not enough supplies to ensure that the whole
of his "cargo" would not perish prior to arrival. He decides that the only way
to turn a profit on this run is to jettison 132 "sickly" slaves and then collect
the insurance on their loss once he returns to London. It is a history that has
survived in the colonial archive not because a white man ordered the murder of 132 Black people, but because the insurance company refused to pay
and thus initiated a legal battle that entered the public record. However, as
Glissant proposes, there is another history, one that is anchored in the abyss
of the sea and which lives on in and through relation. Thus, the drowning
of one slave does not live on in exception, but through the relation of this
death to 131 others; and the scene of the massacre on this one ship survives
not only because it becomes exceptional in its entry into the colonial archive
through the cold logic of actuarial value, but because this story of the Zong has
become a repository of shared knowledge in Black Atlantic culture. It is the
Zong, as Baucom recognizes, that lies behind not only Glissant's theory of the
poetics of relation, but also Paul Gilroy's now paradigmatic metaphor of the
slave ship, Wilberforce's abolitionist appeal, J.M.W. Turner's 1840 painting
Slavers Throwing Overboard the Dead and Dying—Typhoon Coming, and Fred
D'Aguiar's novel Feeding the Ghosts. Out of this one story, many have followed;
out of one massacre, many others call out for justice; and out of one death,
many more demand to be recalled.

I begin this chapter on Fung's Islands, Asianness, and the specificity of
Chineseness in the Caribbean through the lens of Chineseness in Canada,
by detouring through a story that is so foundational to Black Atlantic history
and culture, because the problem of relation that Glissant poses is one that I
hope to extend across the Atlantic and into the histories of the Pacific. Thus,
in my meditations upon Islands, I want to think through the relations between
Black Atlantic and Asian diasporic culture, between slavery and indentureship, between forms of Asianness, between Chinese actors and Japanese soldiers, and between tropical islands. And in thinking through the possibility
of relation, of what lives on in that which is shared, I hope to arrive at an
understanding of specificity that does not sabotage the possibility of collectivities. How can we argue for the potentiality of some shared knowledge of
death and loss between Black and Asian diasporic histories without losing
sight of that which has made the Black diaspora, in Khachig Tölölyan's words,
"exceptional" (23)? Given the vexed and antagonistic history of Sino-Japa-
nese relations, can we take from the atrocious irony of asking Chinese actors

to play the role of Japanese soldiers something more than an insistence upon the immutability of difference, something that might attend to that which is shared in Asian diasporic culture?

For Baucom, the circulation of the story of the *Zong* and Glissant's poetics of relation raises the problem of exchange, the exchangeability of one story for another, one slave for another, and the need for a postcolonial theory of value. Baucom is concerned with

> the logic by which that body of writing "relates" the body it writes ... the logic which marks the former as a cenotaph to the latter, the logic which marks the body of writing as both the burial ground and the resurrection of the written body, the logic which thus codes this poetics as not only a form of memorializing the body but also a mode of allegorizing it. (69)

Within this logic, "*exception* ... is Glissant's word for the moment of drowning" and "exceptionality is not merely anterior to relation but is that which blocks relation" (71). As Baucom so aptly recognizes, in the interests of justice and memory, our impulse is to sacrifice the specific for the universal, to see how we can read for the history of many out of the story of one. The problem with this impulse is that it

> constantly runs the risk of articulating itself as a form of insurance, either by substituting for the singularity of any given experience of loss an actuarial knowledge of that loss's systemic value and meaning or by offering itself as a mode of compensation in which systematic understanding and ... a global theory of relationality, creolization, or hybridity promise to reverse damage by conferring a conceptual exchange value on all those things whose loss it at once inventories and absolutizes. (73)

If the impulse to address the losses resulting from the ways in which European colonialism has divided Black and Asian peoples, between slaves and indentured labourers, between Chinese and Japanese, by looking for that which is shared among these communities, then the risk of this impulse lies in the suggestion of their exchangeability. Let me recall the generosity of Glissant's poetics: "People do not live on in exception. Relation is not made up of things that are foreign but of shared knowledge. This experience of the abyss can now be said to be the best element of exchange" (8). And yet, this element of exchange threatens exceptionality. It makes of the specific moment of the slave drowning in the sea, of the death that will not live on in exception, that which blocks relation. Its uniqueness must be smoothed away in order for it to work within this impulse to justice and memory. In another context, this move might be called a flattening out of difference. It is what postcolonial and minority discourse critics so often accuse dominant culture of doing. It is, in many ways, what Fung's *Islands* stages.

Fung's video plays with a 1957 Hollywood movie, *Heaven Knows, Mr. Allison*. Directed by John Huston, starring Robert Mitchum and Deborah Kerr, it is set in 1944, ostensibly "somewhere" in the Pacific Islands. The film is about a US marine, Mr. Allison, who is shipwrecked on an island in the Pacific during the Second World War. The only other person on the island is a nun, who is stranded there after the conscription of the natives by the Japanese and the death of the local vicar. They eventually fall in love, but the film ends with their love unrequited. *Islands* pulls out of Huston's film the story of Fung's Uncle Clive, who was an extra on the set when the film was made in Tobago. Fung's video is made up almost entirely of footage from the Huston film. It is recut, re-edited, and linked with inter-titles that are full of Fung's signature humour and sharpness.

It is tempting to read *Islands* as a "writing back," in the postcolonial sense, of Hollywood cinema's deployment of Asianness and stereotypes of the tropical. Indeed, I would not want to lose sight of this reading of the film. Fung's rescripting of Huston's film through the figure of Uncle Clive offers an urgent postcolonial critique that asks its viewers to think about the production of Asianness and its circulation within the popular Western imaginary. In the moments when Fung tells us of the way the audience responds to the call of the kookaburra or the mischievousness of the ajouti and the manicou, he asserts an understanding of the specifics of locality, which takes up Huston's effacement of specificity in using Chinese Trinidadians to stand in for Japanese soldiers, using Trinidad and Tobago to stand in for the South Pacific. Through the logic of the "extra," Huston's film inserts Uncle Clive within a logic of substitution that erases the particularities of race, history, and geography. *Islands* asks its audience to see in the fuzzy, pixelated figure of Uncle Clive something more than the facelessness of an extra. If my reading were to end here, then *Islands* could be understood as a critique of the kind of sloppy exoticization that dominant cultural mechanisms such as the Hollywood studio system seem to generate so endlessly. In many ways, *Islands* can be understood as a call for specificity.

And yet, if we follow Glissant's call for relation, this reading of *Islands* would situate Fung's video as an obstacle to the poetics of relation. This reading would, ironically, function as a denial of alternative histories even as it asserts an alternative history that is buried within the glossiness of *Heaven Knows, Mr. Allison*. The logical end of such an argument would be that Huston should have known better than to cast Chinese actors to play Japanese soldiers, that Trinidad and Tobago are not just any islands, and that the Caribbean is simply not the South Pacific. Put another way, these are arguments for authenticity. Put into play as a reading practice, insisting upon specificity emerges as what might be a much more familiar, and fraught, insistence upon the authentic. As postcolonial and diasporic critics know all too well, the perils of such a positivist critique lie in reconsecrating the idea of "real" culture and history over and against that which is less pure. *Islands* is not a cultural nationalist work, nor does it assert a form of diasporic Chineseness that is authorized by Eurocentric classifications of race and ethnicity.

However, dispensing with the call for specificity in its entirety also seems unsatisfactory. To do so would seem to be to side with the kind of logic that allows Huston to proceed in the first place. What is the difference between Chinese and Japanese? Why not shoot the movie in the Caribbean? Isn't one tropical island pretty much like another? Clearly, *Islands* suggests otherwise. Localities matter. Differences do register.

I suggest another possibility, another layer to this critique. Let me return once again to the extravagant death scene with which I began this chapter. It is the merest of moments in Huston's film. Set against the camera's constant caressing of the faces of Mitchum and Kerr, Uncle Clive's death scene passes all too quickly. We can barely make out the contours of his body as it falls into mud. In pulling this moment out, in arresting, pausing upon, and returning to this scene of death, Fung's video asks its viewers to engage in an act of remembering. Excavating this scene of death from Huston's film, the rewinding and replaying of Uncle Clive's performance inserts a different temporality into the movement of *Heaven Knows, Mr. Allison*. It asserts a temporality that moves backward even as it moves forward. It suggests that this death does not simply happen once, but rather that it recurs: "He is asked to fall in the mud over and over" (*Islands*). I have been referring to this death scene as "extravagant" because it is in the excesses of this performance of death, in the ways in which Uncle Clive must extend and exaggerate his body so that this dying might register onscreen, that I want to locate the synchronicity of this death with that of others. Uncle Clive fulfills his role as an extra in the fullest sense. In the excesses of this dying, I want to locate synchronicity within the diachronic movement of the video, the film, and histories of relation.

In looking for the synchronicity of one death with that of others and trying to situate that synchronicity within the diachronic, I suggest that Uncle
Clive's death scene in *Islands* functions as a cue toward the kind of "temporal
double consciousness" that Baucom proposes with respect to the *Zong* massacre. He writes:

> To "witness" this event is to regard something that appears both in the
> guise of the event and in the form of a series, to see what we see as if we
> are seeing again what we are seeing for the first time, to encounter history
> as déjà vu. (77)

Fung exhumes the dying body of Uncle Clive and, in so doing, makes his
death both strange in its excess and eerily familiar in its recurrence. The body
of Uncle Clive rehearses the singularity of death even as it recalls other deaths
in other times and other places. That is, I want to read this scene not as a
witnessing but as a call for relation. It is not that Uncle Clive's performance of
death translates as a specific recollection of the *Zong* massacre, or even of the
deaths of indentured Asian labourers. Rather, it is that this scene of death, as
it has been recut and re-edited by Fung, asks its viewers to see twice. And in
seeing twice, it asks its viewers "to encounter history as déjà vu." It asks us to
dwell in the sense that we have seen something like this scene before, that we
might see this scene again. Baucom argues "that to speak of the *Zong*, or the
case of the *Zong*, is already to speak of the identity of the non-identical" (77).
In the case of *Islands*, to dwell in the déjà vu of Uncle Clive's death scene is to
see in its singularity the possibility of its relationality.

I suggest that seeing twice enables an encounter with diasporic Asianness,
with the underwater signposts that stretch across the Atlantic and into the
Pacific. To see this scene once would be to register its specificity. To see it twice
makes possible the question of where it is that we may have encountered this
scene before, where we might see it again. Where before have we seen White
men asking non-White people to die? Where before have we seen White men
asking non-White people to die once, twice, again and again? The formal seri-
ality that Fung inserts into Uncle Clive's rehearsal of death through the visu-
ality of the scene slowed down, paused, and replayed, allows, if we open our
eyes to these histories that haunt, for the possibility of synchronicity, of "being
unable to decide whether the thing has or has not been seen before, whether it
is exceptional or serial, whether it belongs to a 'now' or a 'then'" (Baucom 78).
This experience of déjà vu also questions not only the progressivist historical

narratives that seek to separate the past from the present, but the divisions
between Black and Asian, slave and indentured.

In questioning these divisions, I am not suggesting that Black and Asian
diasporic subjectivities are the same, nor do I want to lose sight of the exceptionality of the history and experience of slavery and its distinctions from that
of indentureship. However, as subaltern historiography has shown, there is
also important work to be done in seeing the relation between these forms of
oppression and these oppressed subjectivities.

In attending to the specificity of Asian Caribbean formations within the
frame of diasporic connections to Canada and beyond, I want to turn now to
Stuart Hall's groundbreaking essay, "Cultural Identity and Diaspora." As Hall
makes clear, diasporic criticism offers important ways of getting to this problem
of specificity and universalism with which I began my chapter. Understanding
that cultural identity as more than simply "an already accomplished fact," Hall
emphasizes the ways in which identity functions as a constant process of production "which is never complete, always in process, and always constituted
within, not outside, representation" (222). Thus, for Hall, cultural identities
do not emerge in isolation but must rather come out of their articulation with
otherness. Working with Jacques Derrida's concept of *difference*, Hall suggests
that Caribbean cultural identity can be understood as being in relation to the
continual positioning and repositioning of three "presences": *Présence Afric-
aine*, *Présence Européenne*, and *Présence Americaine*. The first functions as the
site of the repressed memory of slavery and Africa; the second as a dialogue
with European colonialism, which is to be refused and recognized; and the
third as "the juncture-point where many cultural tributaries meet" (Hall 234),
the space of diaspora. Hall brings together a tradition of deconstructive thinking but also argues that cultural difference is not purely abstract and random.
He is not writing of pure signifiers but of how blackness emerges out of its
articulation with non-blackness in ways that are historically specific.

Within Hall's powerful and foundational call for an understanding of diasporic identity as unfixed and unfolding, Asian Caribbean identity emerges in
curious stops and pauses. Introducing the idea of the three presences, and the
idea of *Présence Americaine* specifically, Hall writes:

> Of course, I am collapsing, for the moment, the many culture "presences"
> which constitute the complexity of Caribbean identity (Indian, Chinese,
> Lebanese, etc.). I mean America here, not in its "first-world" sense—the
> big cousin to the North whose "rim" we occupy, but in the second, broader
> sense: America, the "New World," *Terra Incognita*. (230)

Eschewing the First World understanding of America, Hall explains the collapsing of other cultural presences by retrieving America from the United States and reinstating it as a site of possibility, of the forming and unforming of cultural identities. And yet, the frame of this collapsing does not entirely hold and there is a strange way in which the legacies of Asia and indenture impinge upon Hall's argument. And thus, caught in a parenthesis in a section when Hall discusses the traumatic rupture of slavery, we suddenly come upon the "truth" of Columbus. Referring to the use of indentured labour after the "abolition" of slavery, Hall writes:

> This neglected fact explains why, when you visit Guyana or Trinidad, you see, symbolically inscribed in the faces of their peoples, the paradoxical "truth" of Christopher Columbus' mistake: you *can* find "Asia" by sailing west, if you know where to look! (227)

The Asian presence in the Caribbean fits a little uneasily in Hall's writing here. It is parenthetical to the ruptures of dislocation from Africa. It is supplemental and yet embedded.

My point here is not that Hall does not attend to Asian Caribbean identity. Rather, I am hoping to draw, from looking at the spaces where Asianness fits uneasily into Caribbeanness, a sense of the difficulty of understanding the specificity of Asian Caribbean identity. In situating Asian Caribbean identity within the site of the *Présence Americaine*, Hall's thinking illuminates the problem of recognizing the relation between indentureship and slavery. Moreover, this situating of Asian Caribbeanness outside of the traumatic ruptures of incarceration and bondage divorces the diasporic from these histories of labour exploitation. Asia in the Caribbean becomes just one of many newly arrived cultures that will flow in the tributary of the Caribbean in order to make up the *Terra Incognita* of diasporic culture:

> None of the people who now occupy the islands—black, brown, white, African, European, American, Spanish, French, East Indian, Chinese, Portuguese, Jew, Dutch—originally "belonged" there…. The New World is the third term—the primal scene—where the fateful/fatal encounter was staged between Africa and the West. (Hall 234)

In situating Asian Caribbean identities within the third term, the primal scene, of the encounter of Black and White, Hall sheds light on the difficulty of recognizing the relation between indenture and slavery. The Asian presence has been relegated as a backdrop, a stage, for the meeting of Africa and the West.

It is telling that an article that does so much for unfixing identity from notions of authenticity and ossified notions of history struggles to situate Asianness and indenture in its conceptualizations. Of course, Hall does not set out to think through the place of Asianness in the Caribbean. The importance of Hall's article lies in its mapping out of an understanding of cultural identity outside of the ossification of claims to purity and authenticity. And yet, the article's situating of Asian Caribbean identity and histories within the context of the new, the *Présence Americaine*, signals the problem of aligning the figure of Asia with Africa, of relating the seemingly disparate histories of indenture and slavery.

Fung's *Islands* suggests that the space of diaspora functions not so much as a *Terra Incognita* where multiple cultures will mix and blend, but as one in which diaspora emerges as an inimitable space of relation. In emphasizing the necessity of relation, I want to extend the generosity of Hall's vision of diasporic culture as "defined not by essence or purity, but by the recognition of a necessary heterogeneity and diversity; by a conception of 'identity' which lives with and through, not despite, difference" (234). Differences are not random and the specificity of historical difference calls for a way of living *with* specificity *through* relation. *Islands* proposes a way of seeing in one extravagant, repeated death scene a way of living with the specificity of Chinese Trinidadian experience, even as it highlights the ways in which that specificity emerges in relation to other deaths, other histories. For Hall, a new Caribbean and Black British cinema enables a theorizing of

> identity as constituted, not outside but within representation; and hence of cinema, not as a second-order mirror held up to reflect what already exists, but as that form of representation which is able to constitute us as new kinds of subjects, and thereby enable us to discover new places from which to speak. (234)

Islands discovers within the tradition of dominant Hollywood cinema a new place from which to articulate Asian diasporic identity as both specific and related.

As I have noted, for Glissant, the poetics of relation is about a shared knowledge of the abyss, of an understanding of the underwater signposts that lead to an understanding of relation, of the doubleness of exception and relation. But it remains less clear how critical work might actually get to this shared knowledge, and what might be the modes and modalities through which this knowledge can be accessed, excavated. At the close of his article, Hall offers a glimpse of the possibility of a route to these underwater signposts. He writes:

> Who can ever forget, when once seen rising up out of the blue-green Caribbean, those islands of enchantment. Who has not known, at this moment, the surge of an overwhelming nostalgia for lost origins, for "times past"? And yet, this "return to the beginning" is like the imaginary in Lacan—it can neither be fulfilled nor requited, and hence is the beginning of the symbolic, of representation, the infinitely renewable source of desire, memory, myth, search, discovery—in short, the reservoir of our cinematic narratives. (236–37)

Who can ever forget those islands of enchantment? Hall's question is both a challenge and an invocation. It is a challenge to forget that which refuses to be forgotten. It is an invitation to fall into nostalgia, to embrace the longings and cravings for origins and for a time that has passed. Hall's question offers the possibility of finding the underwater signposts of relation through the work of nostalgia. It is the process of returning to the abyss, of returning to the sea, of embracing the desire for lost origins without also being swallowed by the abyss, the sea, desire. Nostalgia tethers its subject to the present even as it unrolls a line toward the past.

Nostalgia's relation to history is neither easy, nor is it innocent. Indeed, as observers such as Susan Stewart have noted, nostalgia can be understood as not only divorced from history, but also hostile to it (23). And yet, I want to hang on to the challenge and the invocation of Hall's question. In recuperating nostalgia for my reading of Fung's video, I want to turn to the one piece of footage from *Islands* that is not taken from Huston's film: the shots of the palm trees at sunset that frame Fung's video. *Islands* opens with these palm trees, silhouetted against a brilliant tropic sunset, and it closes with them. In this turn, I hope to illustrate the possibilities of understanding Fung's call for specificity as one that emerges *through* relation and through nostalgia.

There is a curious iconicity of the palm tree—its peculiar singularity *and* universality. It is tempting to assume that these shots are of the "real" Trinidad, of the Trinidad that Huston effaces. But what exactly singles out these palm trees from the ones you might see on a boulevard in Los Angeles, or down along the main drag of Waikiki, or in Barbados or Malaysia or any number of palm-treed places? The image of the palm tree is curiously non-specific, hard to place, even though, within the context of the video, it would seem to make sense to place these shots in Trinidad. Nevertheless, there is very little to separate this row of palm trees in *Islands* from any other row of palm trees in any other tropical place.

Within the Western imaginary, the image of the palm trees against a tropical sky unleashes a set of particularly powerful desires. Writing about the motivations for travel, about the disjunction between the destinations that many First World inhabitants might have in mind when they decide to go somewhere, and the later-discovered reality of those destinations, Alain de Botton writes of the "primordial innocence and optimism" embodied in those images of palm trees on tourism brochures for tropical vacations (8–9).

However, this innocence and optimism is not so much "primordial" as it is inextricably bound to histories of colonialism and imperialism, to the "innocence and optimism" of explorers and navigators like Captain Cook. de Botton draws the connection between the travel brochure, with its bewitchingly beckoning palm tree, and the iconography of British imperialism, noting that the images reminded him of the paintings of Tahiti that William Hodges brought back from his travels with Cook. They were first exhibited at the Royal Academy in 1776. These images from Cook's voyage point to the etymological origins of nostalgia itself.

As I have noted elsewhere, nostalgia has a colonial history.[1] In 1770, the crew on Captain James Cook's ship became so homesick that the ship's doctor named it as a pathology: nostalgia. The *Oxford English Dictionary* marks the first use of "nostalgia" in Cook's journal: "The greatest part of them [sic the ship's company] were now pretty far gone with the longing for home which the Physicians have gone so far as to esteem a disease under the name of Nostalgia." Nostalgia emerges in English as a pathology, as a homesickness brought about by the work of colonial expansion.[2] It makes sense then that nostalgia must be cast as a disabling pathology. Colonial expansion depends upon the ability to be cured of homesickness, so that the ships can continue to sail and so that crews will continue to follow their captains across oceans and territories. Thus, nostalgia has been relegated to the realm of sentiment. It is weak. It is ahistorical. It is a sickness that must be cured.

However, in the context of diaspora and the displacements of diaspora, Fung embeds another possibility, a recuperation of nostalgia from its colonial history and from mere sentiment that builds on the kinds of interventions made by Svetlana Boym and John Su by attending more closely to the possibilities of nostalgia for queer and diasporic communities. I want to attend

to this other possibility, this recuperation of nostalgia, through Gayatri Gopinath's concept of an *enabling* nostalgia.

Reading Shyam Selvadurai's *Funny Boy*, Gopinath develops the possibility
of "a generative or enabling nostalgia" (*Impossible* 176–77).[3] In the final section of *Funny Boy*, Arjie, the text's central character, must leave Sri Lanka for
Canada in the wake of the horrors of the 1983 massacre of Tamils by Sinha-
lese. Just before leaving, he sees his lover Shehan for one last time. Returning
from this visit, Arjie pauses over the smell of Shehan's body lingering on his
own. Gopinath observes:

> The moment in the narrative where Arjie remembers home through the
> smell of his lover's body encapsulates the text's deployment of what I would
> call a generative or enabling nostalgia and homesickness. Here the home
> that is evoked signifies multiply: as both national and domestic space, it is
> the site of homoerotic desire and cross-gender identification and pleasure,
> of intense gender conformity and horrific violence, as well as of multiple
> leave-takings and exiles. (*Impossible* 176–77)

Gopinath's recuperation of nostalgia and homesickness for queer diasporic
subjects makes possible forms of remembering and longing that are not simply
pathological and not entirely healing. Gopinath focuses on the intersection of
the deeply personal desire and the inextricably public longings figured within
national space. In Gopinath's formulation, nostalgia enables an understanding
of the past that is both private and public, domestic and national, pleasurable
and violent. Unlike Su or Boym, her recuperation of nostalgia functions as a
double-edged knife that inevitably cuts even as it opens up alternative histories and spaces.

Islands is not an overt meditation on the circuits of queer subjectivity in
the Caribbean. But this video is as much a love letter to a place that is at once
home and not home—a place that is not home partly because of the complexities of queer desire and its intersection with the politics of colonialism. In
the sense of Gopinath's reading, Fung's portrayal of Trinidad is neither merely
sentimental nor ahistorical, but an understanding that the sickness for home
enables a recognition of its multiple contradictions.

Fung gestures toward the pains and pleasures of representation, of the
shock of seeing one's home, one's family, both in the frame and not in the
frame, of looking for home in unhomeliness, of looking for familial history
in a fuzzy constellation of pixels. He illuminates the disjunction between the
destination of the mind and the destination of arrival by connecting it to the

disjunction between fantasy and memory. In his use of the palm trees and the
re-editing of Huston's footage, Fung does not valorize fantasy over memory.
Rather, the video asserts the complexity of the relation between fantasy and
memory—the ways in which the work of memory can be a kind of fantasy and
fantasy its own truth.

In allowing for the possibility of memory through the seemingly ahistorical
route of nostalgia and fantasy, Fung gives room for pleasure, guilty or otherwise, in this engagement with Huston's film. He gives room for more complex
and contradictory desires that allow us to linger over the ruggedness of Mitchum's masculinity and the luminousness of Deborah Kerr's face even as we
are all too aware of those whom this economy of gazes excludes. Fung gives us
room for the pleasures of fantasy and its role in the homesickness, in nostalgia.
By inserting these shots of the palm trees, Fung drops into his critique the
possibility of a longing for a home that exists as both a repository of fantasy
and memory.

Through this lingering over palm trees, *Islands* gestures toward an understanding of specificity through relation. In raising the dilemma of the interchangeability between Chinese and Japanese, Fung also gestures toward
another moment of interchangeability that haunts the Caribbean: the substitution of slave labour for indentured labour. *Islands* intimates an articulation of indentureship and Asian diasporic identity. Fung points to this longer
history of indentureship and slavery in *Islands*, these islands that are both the
name and the substance of a meditation on Asian diasporic presences. There
are underwater signposts across the Pacific as well as the Atlantic, and Fung's
video suggests a way to map this history within the circulation of desire and
nostalgia. *Islands* suggests that the study of diaspora in Canada is both grounded
in the specificity of racial formations, and inextricably tied to the connections
across communities and national spaces. It suggests that race in Canada is not
so much a project of bandaging difference as it is one of understanding the
ways in which those differences extend beyond and across national boundaries—that Chineseness in Trinidad is also about Chineseness in Canada, and
that the specificity of those differences is neither minor nor outside the scope
of Canadianness itself.

In this sense, *Islands* is not so much a call for specificity as it is an invitation—and here I am borrowing again from Baucom—to understand this way
of situating Trinidad, this tropical place, this paradise, as both a lament for
the effacement of the specific, the local, *and* a celebration of the relations
that connect one island space to another, one form of Asianness to another,

and one form of national belonging with another. It is appropriate, then, that *Heaven Knows, Mr. Allison* is a film about unrequited love. For longing and yearning are as much about the quest for love as for relation, for the relation between the Atlantic and the Pacific, between indentureship and slavery, between the past and the present, between one tropical palm tree and another, which sways in quite a different breeze.

NOTES

1 I discuss the relation between nostalgia and colonialism at greater length in my article, "'How Taste Remembers Life': Diasporic Memory and Community in Fred Wah's Poetry."

2 Although she does not explicitly discuss the relationship between nostalgia and colonialism, Svetlana Boym does suggest that the pathologizing of nostalgia in Europe took on patriotic overtones in the nineteenth century: "The symptom of sickness came to be regarded as a sign of sensibility or an expression of a new patriotic feeling. The epidemic of nostalgia was no longer to be cured but to be spread as widely as possible" (11). Extending Boym's suggestion into the realm of colonialism and the work of empire, it can be argued that from its inception as an eighteenth-century disease to be cured to a nineteenth-century epidemic to be spread, nostalgia's pathologization moves from the sphere of externalized empire building to an internalized one of nationalism and the maintaining of colonial possessions.

3 Previous versions of Gopinath's chapter on *Funny Boy* emphasize the concept of enabling nostalgia more than the version that has been published in *Impossible Desires*. I have nonetheless found this concept to be provocative and compelling and hope to draw out some of its possibilities for thinking about queer diasporic subjects.

"Phoenicia ≠ Lebanon"
Transsexual Poetics as Poetics of the Body within and across the Nation

Alessandra Capperdoni

"Of course I don't speak Arabic. It is
no guarantee, however I mine genetic memory"
—Trish Salah, *Wanting in Arabic* (12)

OVER THE PAST TWO DECADES, the signifier "trans" has gained increasing currency in social and academic discourse. Its most pervasive use has addressed concerns about the movements of people across the world, and especially the challenges to state boundaries of transnational migrants who, to different degrees, disrupt border regulations—a process not extricable from the movement of commodities and financial capital in the wake of economic globalization. The language of the nation, which has dominated cultural and political thought since the age of nation formation and subsequent nationalisms, seems to have shifted to a paradigm of transgression and fluidity whereby older political and social structures have given way to more flexible patterns of identification—patterns also contingent on the different degrees of "seamless" border crossing—and to have disrupted the naturalized relation of the national subject to cultural belonging. This shift has probably been best articulated by Homi Bhabha through the notion of the "transnational and translational" aspect of culture—that is, migrancy as a process that individuals and cultures undergo as an effect of the global movements of populations (172). In this context, recent diasporic theories of identity and cultural belonging have further investigated the relation of "origin" and "displacement" to the rearticulation of social identity in the diasporic subject, thus attempting to de-link the identifications produced by the nexus of ethnicity, culture, and nation from naturalized, and essentialized, notions of identity.[1]

The risk in highlighting these relations lies in a mapping that also rein-
scribes a linear trajectory reaffirming the centrality of the nation model to
the study of social and cultural identity (i.e., nationalism, nation-based studies, postcoloniality, cultural translation, diaspora, and, finally, transnationalism). The outlining of a stage theory is not what I am interested in doing
here. Instead, it is a different "trans" that I want to address—one that is also
implicated, in different ways, in the modes of existence and material practices
with which the above-mentioned discourses engage. Indeed, *transsexuality* and
transgenderism have been consistently erased in cultural and critical engagements with the nation and the notion of belonging, and, more often than not,
have been relegated to the recently constituted area of studies in gender and
sexuality—an outgrowth of women's studies departments in academia—and
questions of embodiment and identity. This erasure has operated on three levels: (1) representation in media and cultural practices in mainstream domains;
(2) academic work on the formation and representation of social identities;
and (3) the invisibility of alternative cultural practices specifically addressing the life conditions of trans people and problematizing the relation of culture and nation to gender and sexuality at large. As is often the case, the
recent visibility of transsexuality and transgenderism is the product of grassroots activism within the highly marginalized communities of transgender and
transsexual people, and, more often than not, sex workers. Real-life conditions, nonetheless, are still by and large unaddressed. As Canadian academic,
theoretician, and activist Viviane Namaste notes, transsexual and transgender
lives are often regulated through the "autobiographic imperative" or silenced
anew through a politics of identity that reads "trans" as "crossing" and subversion of gender and sexual categories.

Namaste's critique is the starting point of my investigation. The autobiographic imperative that she addresses opens the question of cultural representation, and self-representation, in relation to narrative modes of identity
and belonging ("Who are you?" and "What is your community?"), as well as
the pitfalls of critical theory when this is de-linked from material practices
and the urgency of "life." Indeed, Namaste's critique pushes the boundaries
of the self to ask: Why has critical analysis, especially in academic circles,
fastened upon theories of performativity and gender-crossing that delegitimize
the language of "man" and "woman," which is central to transsexuals' modes
of existence? Why has it neglected questions of labour, prostitution, and ethnicity, which articulate the positionalities of transsexuals and transgender
people to the structures of transnational capitalism, labour exploitation, and

imperialism? Why has much of the discussion revolved around the discourse of rights? These questions beg for urgent engagement and research in ways that exceed the limits of one article. In this chapter, I am interested in taking up Namaste's questions in relation to the cultural with respect to invisibility, identity politics in queer studies, ethnicity, and labour, and, specifically, the way in which these relate to the nation discourse within the current global order, in the hope that questions of sexuality and gender are opened anew in current critical discourse around the nation, transnationalism, and the diasporic in a productive way.

This urgency is apparent in Trish Salah's poetic sequence *Wanting in Arabic* (2002), which will ground my discussion in this chapter. Poet, academic, and cultural activist located in Toronto and Montreal, Salah writes the transsexual body as body of desire—a transsexual poetics that articulates trans subjectivity as subjectivity in language at the junction of the individual, the social, and the political. If, for Lacan, desire is always desire of the Other, the transsexual body is *literally* a body of desire materializing the workings of the imaginary and the symbolic (i.e., the signs of "woman" and "man"). Not surprisingly, then, it is also a body that signifies the notion of absence lying irremediably at the core of our identity, an identity we strive to achieve yet we cannot fully inhabit: it is in this sense that the trans figure always calls forth the notion of truth (of the self), the relation between the sign and signification in the gender-sex system. This irreducible absence is Otherness in language and central to the notion of desire. In the poems, the loss of language of the diasporic subject (concretized in her Lebanese father's migration to Canada and his daughter's inarticulate, and Other, language of origins) is not reducible to place: Lebanon does not equate Phoenicia, the object being always already absent from the name. As she unravels the traces of diasporic flows that situate her subject position in language ("Beirut" and "Belfast," the Lebanese and Irish points of departure of her father's and mother's ancestries), the poetic "i" re-inflects the diasporic by unhinging it from signifying structures of space and time as identificatory practices (i.e., ethnic and sexual nationalisms), and rereading it as ironic performance through difference in language. In the poem, "Phoenicia" is a sign bearing the trace of the material history of the ancient country carved up between southwest Asia and the eastern Mediterranean—land of maritime traders and navigators, in-betweenness (East and West), and cultural hybridization. But the trace does not saturate the meaning of the sign, which is irreducible to origin and historical development (the modern-day Lebanon):

> *i stole this poem from Robert Kroetsch*
> *but don't feel sad about it, he wasn't*
> *Phoenician & even at sea, even trading*
> *in words, in the past, in love, in the middle passage*
> in the in between
> *i'm not either*
> *but am i Lebanese?*
> *not like that dyke comic,*
> *do you remember her? playing coy,*
> *Ellen? the TV lesbian?*
> *who, coming out on Rosie O'Donnell*
> *was either Lebanese or lesbian, on TV or off*
> *(lesbian≠Lebanese≠TV)*

("Phoenicia ≠ Lebanon," *Wanting in Arabic* 5)

Indeed, "trading / in words" and "middle passage," as signs of the racialization of diasporas and cultures (i.e., Phoenicians as the traders of the ancient Mediterranean world, including the spreading of the alphabet, and the current trades in politics in the Near East), playfully recast "Lebanese" and "lesbian" (playful *différance*) as signs and social constructions, lived realities that are inextricable from the representations constituting them ("lesbian≠Lebanese≠TV") and, at the same time, multiple and non-mutually exclusive positions. In the text, the loss of the father's language can thus be rearticulated as *poesis*, language of "a body becoming its own" (23), rather than a claim to origins. As "*inhabitation* of desire" (30) and "hyperbole of desire" (14), this poetic act gestures toward the coming-into-being, and into writing, of the self against structures of erasure and the containment of representation:

> *horsexe/whore sexed*
>   *—hardly a fit subject for desire*
>   *speaking the whole story of a sex (k)not spoken*

("Phoenicia ≠ Lebanon" 31)

In doing so, it makes visible the tension brought forth by a sex and sexuality exceeding the dichotomous structures of the sex-gender system. Neither fitting within the normative paradigm that links gender to sex ("horsexe" echoes with *hors de sexe*, which suggests expulsion from and the simultaneous troubling of this paradigm) nor reducible to the institutional and economic imperatives on sexuality ("whore sexed" as the ambivalent position of transsexuality between the reality of prostitution in many trans lives and the social regulation of the economy of sex), trans sex is cast outside the legibility of language. It is precisely this unrepresentability that speaks the entanglement ("knot") of the linguistic and material conditions of trans desire, unspoken yet written.[2] But "language keeps its secrets" (23), and the poem remains suspicious of notions of recognition and identity, which can hide strategies of social exclusion ("'What do they want? Why are they here?'" 15).

The poems' preoccupation with subjectivity and language, therefore, is not a flight from the political. History and geography do not saturate the meaning of existing conflicts (origins of truth or land) and, rather, fully engage with the contingencies and complexities of the present:

> the Phoenicians were the ranging traders of another world
> on the news tonight shelling in this Lebanon,
> a trampled marketplace
> a strategic site
>
> occupied by the French, the Americans, the Syrians, the Israelis
> and Beirut is a hole in the ground through which the past comes up

("Phoenicia ≠ Lebanon" 5)

In this context, Salah performs a double gesture. Her transsexual poetics questions the constructed boundaries underlying identificatory practices between trans and non-trans people, national and foreign, as well as boundaries amid gendered, sexual, ethnic, and religious groups (and nationalisms), but it also recognizes the importance of community making in order to challenge state violence (military, judicial, economic, and discursive) and social discrimination (e.g., poverty, homelessness, health, and prostitution). On the other hand, her literary thefts/flights (vols), in the mode of Hélène Cixous's écriture féminine, traverse generic boundaries and established binaries—poetry and theory, national and foreign literatures, mainstream and experimental, psychoanalysis and politics—thus opening the possibility of unthought of textual communities of "poetic politics."[3] Central to the poems is the lyric mode of the ghazal, both in the tradition of Faiz Ahmad Faiz and Mirza Ghalib and modern writers like Agha Shahid Ali and Phyllis Webb. But Wanting in Arabic is also contaminated (creolized) by the hybrid and polyphonic forms of the postmodern Canadian long poem, echoed specifically in the reference to Robert Kroetsch ("i stole this poem from Robert Kroetsch" 5) and perform-ing a *pas-de-deux* with his poem "The Sad Phoenician."[4] The body of desire is, therefore, also a textual body of writers, theoreticians, and artists whose preoccupations and (Other) language speak together with, and through, this lyric "i."

To my knowledge, Salah's poetic sequence is the only literary work engag-ing with transsexuality and transgenderism in relation to the discourse of the nation while challenging simultaneously generic expectations and questions of national authenticity; a text, furthermore, circulating as cultural work beyond the boundaries of a gay scene or an underground and marginalized trans culture. The diasporic sensitivity of the poems weaves together a medita-tion on home, departure, and common destination with the situatedness and materiality of the body of desire (love, sex, and surgery). Indeed, her trans-sexual poetics re-inflects the grammar of the nation by illuminating (trans) sexuality and embodiment as nodal points of the nexus of body, subjectivity, and ideological state apparati, thus opening up to new possibilities of culture and social relations in ways that resonate with Namaste's preoccupations.

PERFORMATIVITY AS STRATEGY OF ERASURE

In the last two decades, the transgender and transsexual body has gained momentum in cultural and critical theory. From Judith Butler's publication of *Gender Trouble: Feminism and the Subversion of Identity* in 1990, followed by *Bodies That Matter: On the Discursive Limits of "Sex"* in 1993, the "trans" has become the privileged figure for the disruption (the "troubling") of identity categories of gender, sex, and sexuality. As Jay Prosser notes in *Second Skins: The Body Narratives of Transsexuality* (1998), the discussion of transgender and transsexual identities as actually existing bodies is limited to a few paragraphs in *Gender Trouble*,[5] and yet it is the figural status of the transgender body that has elicited enthusiastic responses among scholars, students, and critics at large, and has enabled the "arrogation" of transgenderism by queer studies. The canonical status of *Gender Trouble* in the constitution and institutional-ization of queer studies in academia has hardly gone unnoticed. Only a few years later, Eve Kosofsky Sedgwick commented on the "productive impact this dense and even imposing work has had on the recent development of queer theory and reading" (qtd. in Prosser 24). In many ways, Prosser notes, Butler's theory of gender performativity attempts to problematize the conflation of

homosexuality and gender-crossing underlying Sedgwick's own work. Nonetheless, it is in *Gender Trouble* that transgenderism is first fastened by the paradigm of queer theory and, in turn, transsexuality is assimilated to transgenderism. In addition, the 1990 release of the documentary film *Paris Is Burning*,
by filmmaker Jennie Livingston, which Butler discusses in her work, seemed
to secure the ground of theoretical investigation by foregrounding the theatricality of New York's drag balls of the 1980s and the gender "performance"
of drags. In the minds of most readers, as well as in Butler's own discussion,
and her disclaimers notwithstanding, the "drag" is the sign of gender instability. It is also telling that the documentary exploration of the imbrications of
homophobia, transphobia, and racism with issues of poverty, sex work, social
marginality, and the process of sex reassignment is barely addressed by Butler
in what is perhaps the best-known article of her book.

The critical success of Butler's theory of gender performativity owes much
to the ongoing social and political struggles of marginalized sexualities since,
at least, 1960s gay activism in the United States and the subsequent politici-
zation of gender and sexuality in the public sphere, which was written into
the social by turning a disparaging term ("queer") into a camp of identification and a base for political struggle. But the simultaneity of the appearance of the "trans" subject and the coming into being of "queer" studies cannot be coincidental. Prosser shows that the transgender subject is not only
part of but constitutive to the articulation of gender performativity, to the
point that transgenderism becomes the sign of gender as socially constructed,
rather than produced by the biological categories of sex. The "trans," therefore, is read as a sign of gender performativity marking the disappearance of
the referential, literal sexed body bounded by biology, and exposing gender
identity as always already incomplete and *différant*. As Sedgwick, and Butler
herself, also note, the enthusiasm generated by *Gender Trouble* slipped into
a notion of gender performance as theatricality, or a willing "act" produced
by an intentional subject, in ways that echo Erving Goffman's discussion of
identity and self-presentation through the metaphor of theatrical performance
(*The Presentation of Self in Everyday Life* [1959]). Indeed, the publication of
Bodies That Matter was meant to intervene into this discourse by clarifying,
in no uncertain terms, that "the notion of gender performativity introduced
in *Gender Trouble*" did not argue for a notion of gender as an act of choice by
an "instrumental subject" who would put it on and off at will in accordance
with his whims and desires (x). Instead, the emphasis on discursive construction in *Bodies That Matter* grounds Butler's deconstructive analysis in speech

act theory and Foucault's and Derrida's notions of discourse and citationality, while taking into account the phantasmatic identifications and disavowals of sexuality, desire, and gender identity explored by psychoanalysis. The notion of performativity is thus brought back to the materiality of the sexed body— a body that is not reducible to either "simple fact" or "static condition" but is the product of a "materialization through a forcible reiteration of [those] norms" (2). Performativity, then,

> must be understood not as a singular or deliberate "act," but, rather, as the reiterative and citational practice by which discourse produces the effects that it names. What will, I hope, become clear in what follows is that the regulatory norms of "sex" work in a performative fashion to constitute the materiality of bodies and, more specifically, to materialize the body's sex, to materialize sexual difference in the service of the consolidation of the heterosexual imperative. (2)

What happens, then, to the specificity of the transgender body is its metaphoricization allowing entry, and absorption, into queer theory. Prosser rightly remarks the problematic "idealization of transgender as a queer transgressive force" and "the consistent decoding of the 'trans' as incessant destabilizing movement between sexual and gender identities" (23): transgender as a "sign of queer sexuality" thus makes its entry into academy (23). The imbrications of transgender and queer theory produces a slippage that effaces the material body—an odd instance given Butler's avowed concern about the materialization of discursive practices. What transgender people live, experience, and articulate about their identities is obscured not so much by the density of academic language, as some would contend, but by the limitations produced by the new discourse, a discourse on sex in its own right and endowed with the power of cultural capital. Within this discourse, the transsexual body is denied not only articulation but even visibility. While cross-dressing, gender trespassing, and drag performances are equally read as signifiers of transgenderism, transsexuality becomes the ultimate sign of gender troubling (i.e., its ultimate stage). As Prosser rightly observes, "like the materiality of the body, the transsexual is the very blind spot of these writings on transsexuality" (14). It is this blind spot that casts doubt as to the celebratory hailing of gender performativity as "troubling" the categories of gender, sex, and sexuality. Not all transgender identities decide to undergo surgical reassignment, and narratives of transsexual and transgender people differentiate profoundly in the way they articulate the sense of the self: "the categories of man and woman" are rearticulated not through biological essentialism, as some would contend, but as stable categories of signification and meaning formation (11). It is the idealization of "becoming man" or "becoming woman" that grounds the notion of identity.

These slippages are not exclusive to Butler's theory. The conflation of the linguistic turn with theories of postmodernity has facilitated the celebration of the performative as a postmodern gesture. Judith Halberstam's comment is perhaps indicative of this trend:

> We are all transsexuals except that the referent of the trans becomes less and less clear (and more and more queer). We are all cross-dressers but where are we crossing from or to what? There is no "other" side, no "opposite" sex, no natural divide to be spanned by surgery, by disguise, by passing. We all pass or we don't.... There are no transsexuals. ("F2M" 153)

In the context of a notion of gender performativity, which is never complete and always already troubled, Halberstam's comment is to the point. Yet it is somewhat baffling that a politics of a queer body, where "queer" is understood not so much as corresponding to homosexuality but as the disturbance of normative sexed and gendered identities, disregards the material consequences of embodiment in everyday life: we may all be transsexuals, but we are not all read as such. Everyday acts acquire a political dimension (i.e., even doing your grocery shopping may endanger your life) and bodies are read within strict grammars by state institutions (i.e., trans people do not cross state borders as non-trans people do). Interestingly, Halberstam's formulation reveals an anxiety about "crossing" that might re-literalize the "natural" body and bridge the gap between biological sex and psychic identification—an anxiety made apparent by the evacuation of the term "transsexual" in her quotation, while the "queering" of identity implicitly assimilates transgenderism to the act of cross-dressing. Paradoxically, it is academic queer theory that seems to raise issues about the "trans" by deploying a "discursive limit," which is not apparent in narratives of embodiment of trans people. Indeed, there is nothing to bridge in terms of personal identity, but only because the "real" is already located where the fiction is, the image (or fantasy of identification) being acknowledged as the source of ego formation.

All identifications, Susan Stryker reminds us, are technologized, but these technologies are different: "Nontranssexual means of embodiment disappear into the fiction of a natural fact, while transsexuality foregrounds the necessity of instrumentalization through its blatant unnaturalness" (595). Stryker's call for "learning to live creatively within technology" and "to begin imagining new modes of subjectivity" deflects the queer re-containment of the "trans" to open up spaces of articulation grounded in the specificity of different locations, which, Stryker rightly observes, may be anywhere but are always located somewhere (596). The emphasis on location is an important one, for the trans subject navigates spaces and conditions that police its existence—yet the trans subject is also and uncompromisingly centred in the body:

> how many years?
> *tearing through these skins:*   *male, female, female, male*
>   *until the body's ceased to matter*
>   the body never does cease to matter
> (Salah, *"where skin breaks," Wanting in Arabic* 37)

Echoing Butler's work on the intricate relationship between materiality and discourse in relation to gender and sex in *Bodies That Matter*, Salah's poem addresses the double inscription of technologies of gender ("male" and "female") as it materializes within the body ("tearing through these skins"). But the lines also playfully disrupt identification ("male, female, female, male") through the slippage of biological sex ("until the body's ceased to matter") and the reminder that the body is, indeed, central to questions of subjectivity, embodiment, agency, and "real" life ("*the body never does cease to matter*"). The materialization of discursive inscription through the body that Butler discusses is thus rearticulated (and re-materialized) by bringing to the fore skin as location of pain, violence, and affective relations to lived life ("tearing through these skins").

Although Stryker also resorts to the language of post-structuralism and postmodernity in her discussion of transsexuality (i.e., the recounting of the imbrications of transsexuality and nuclear technology in the narrative of Christine Jorgensen as a metaphor of the fantasies of technical power over the material world), she is deeply attentive to the materiality of lived conditions and the complex layers of significations and possibilities that are produced at the juncture of structures of power—linguistic, economic, social, and political—individual and collective identifications, and the biological body. By pointing out that "the transsexual body is the one that is literally purchased" (591), she makes visible both questions of technology and commodification. Coherence is a privilege and it definitely costs. That the object status of the sexed body is part of the postmodern condition does not obscure the fact that prostitution, poverty, and social marginalization are more often than not the only possibilities available to transsexuals. It is in this context that the *canonical status* of Butler's theory of performativity becomes even more problematic: through the instrumentalization of transgenderism within a politics of queerness, and the celebration of the transsexual as the ultimate sign of "gender trouble," the specificity of the experience of transsexuals and transgender subjects is negated through different degrees of invisibility. This invisibility, Namaste reminds us, is also contingent on an institutional preoccupation with identity that limits our understanding of social lives with "disastrous results for transsexuals" (19), as well as reinforcing the further marginalization of transsexuality: "I am reminded of this every day in the work I do coordinating a transsexual health project in Québec, when francophones ask me what this 'transgender' thing is all about, and how come on the Internet all the 'transgender' pages are linked to those of lesbians and gays" (21). In the context of Canada, marked by the conditions of official bilingualism and a multi-ethnic society, this work brings to the fore the question of the framing of identity politics, queer theory, and transgenderism within a specific Anglo-American location of which Other spaces, like francophone, multi-ethnic, or immigrant positionalities, though located within the nation, often cannot make much sense.

Namaste's theoretical work articulates a scholarly and critical practice to the specificity and actuality of social identities and individual lives. This includes drawing attention to the conditions of transsexuals and transgender people in Canada, and examining the effects of the legal structures of a colonial state apparatus (e.g., the historical criminalization of transsexual lives until the late 1970s), the institutionalization of knowledge (i.e., the construction of transgenderism and transsexuality through scholarship and teaching practices), cultural representation, and the Anglo-American "cultural bias" that delegitimize transsexual existence. As she notes, these national grammars limit severely transgender existence and even evacuate the discursive possibility of transsexual lives.

THE (TRANS)NATIONAL OF TRANSGENDERISM AND TRANSSEXUALITY

In a recent article published in *New Cinema*, film critic Song Hwee Lim sets out "to interrogate the notion of 'trans-'" and asks "to what extent the prefix 'trans' transcends existing boundaries, whether in relation to the nation or to gender" (39). While Lim problematically reinforces the notion of "trans" as

"troubling" and, indeed, "transcending," this question illuminates the centrality of gender and sex to the discourse of the nation and transnational spaces.
Critics have discussed at length the notion of transnationalism with respect
to activism, identity politics, and belonging in relation to the "queer nation."
Trajectories of affiliation and affinities are established across national borders
to re-situate a notion of belonging along the axis of sexuality, rather than
nationality. The notion of a "queer nation," furthermore, has complicated the
understanding of nation formation in relation to questions of heteronormativ-
ity and the disavowal of homosexuality in the national imaginary—a much-
needed scrutiny that has been particularly fruitful in literary and cultural
studies in relation to cultural representation, genre, and language, as Peter
Dickinson's work, comprising *Here Is Queer: Nationalisms, Sexualities, and the
Literatures of Canada* (1999) and *Screening Gender, Framing Genre: Canadian
Literature into Film* (2007), best shows.

Conversely, transgenderism and transsexuality have hardly been discussed
in relation to the space of the nation-state and transnationalism and, more
importantly, they always constitute a limited chapter in the larger framework
of queerness. Yet trans people occupy a very different position in relation to
the nation and a transnational space. In Canada, until the late 1970s, transsexuals were criminalized and, to date, trans people's citizenship status is constantly put into question through a set of practices, including harassment and
violence, which delegitimize their position of citizen-subjects versus the State.
That trans subjects are also agents of transnational movements and global
flows should not conceal the fact that in many cases this movement is neither
liberatory nor fully intentional, but, rather, produced by the extreme conditions of marginalization and policing to which trans people are often subject
in their countries of birth. The migratory flows of trans people from the global
South, often South America, to the global North, including Canada, looking
for work or, very simply, a free existence and possible communities of affiliation is well documented, but less attention is being given to the way in which
a trans space complicates notions of global migrancy, citizenship, and, indeed,
the imagined community of the nation. Here the diasporic loses its veneer of
respectability and the sexing of labour—for, in the end, sex work plays a dominant role in the seamlessness of the global—complicates the imaginary of the
nation as a liberal space of tolerance and acceptance engrained in the popular
understanding of multiculturalism.

Questions of gender and sex are, therefore, also complicated by cultural
origin, ethnicity, and language: For example, where do we locate a Latin

American Canadian trans culture in relation to a dominant anglophone and, to a lesser degree, francophone Canadianness? Which models, if any, are available? That no attention is being given to these questions in the context of critical and cultural theory in academia also problematizes the role of the institution in shaping a national imaginary that can hardly be referred to as hybrid or multicultural and, especially, that essentializes hybridity and ethnicity as questions of racialization only. At the same time, it also problematizes the relationship between academia and social activism that has arisen amid much controversy in the last decades. Indeed, Namaste's comment on the inability of many trans sex workers in Montreal to make sense of queer politics of identity, of lesbian and gay networks as dominant frameworks of reference in activist work and networks of support, and even of the emerging language of transgenderism, is to the point and draws attention not only to the reverberations of the "two solitudes" model of the imaginary nation, but the inflections of a cultural reality that national grammars attempt to elide or, at least, re-contain. If francophone trans people cannot participate in a dominant Anglo-American discourse, we should also ask how different linguistic-as-cultural identities relate to the space of the nation that the transnational (read ethnic other) increasingly probes. The quotation from Salah's poem at the beginning of the chapter, "Of course I don't speak Arabic," reads subjectivity and belonging as a mining of "genetic memory" that brings together, yet does not conflate, ethnicity, cultural identity, and body narratives (12). But it also invites the reader to raise questions about those immigrants whose trespassing is an everyday act of rearticulation of dominant narratives, double translation of languages and identities, and the carving of a space of invisibility without resulting in erasure: for many transgender people and transsexuals, happiness translates in being anonymous, just "like everybody else," and living within their bodies, truthful to themselves. For most transsexuals and many transgender subjects, the question is not to "trouble" nor intervene into dominant paradigms but, instead, be fully part of the social as recognized individuals. This troubling of "gender trouble" is apparent in Salah's lesbian poetics ("lipstick lesbians" 4) as it interferes with both straight and queer dominant cultures by laying bare the psychic and social investments underlying politics of identity ("who is writing *in* the feminine on whose body" 28), national imaginaries, and political and discursive borders.

It is also significant that discussions and cultural representations of transgenderism and transsexuality in Canada are more visible in the city of Montreal than in anglophone Canada.[6] The specificity of Montreal culture in relation to Québécois nationalism, Canadian nationalism, and linguistic identity, as well as a lived multiculturalism, sheds light on the different levels of otherness produced by the discourse of the nation and on the transnational as the always already within. In this context, it is interesting to consider how filmic adaptations of scripts engaging with issues of gender and sex in different Canadian cities situate differently trans subjectivities and lives in relation to the nation.[7]

In *Screening Gender, Framing Genre*, Dickinson discusses theatrical and filmic representations of queer and trans culture in relation to the national imaginary. The culturally lively and entertaining Toronto gay scene has been marked by a proliferation of drag representations in theatre for a long time— drag scenes that also find a place in subsequent film adaptations such as John Herbert's *Fortune and Men's Eyes* (1971). In Quebec, the figuration of drags in Michel Tremblay's early plays, *La Duchesse de Langeais* (1969) and *Hosanna* (1973), brought to the screen by André Brassard's *Il était une fois dans l'est* (1974), gives visibility to the dreams and illusions of characters that suffer the consequences of sexual as well as national marginalization. Anglophone films seem instead to privilege the absorption of transsexuality within homosexuality. Anne Wheeler's *Better Than Chocolate* (1998) and Brad Fraser's *Leaving Metropolis* (2002), the latter based on his play *Poor Super Man* (1994), are located in Vancouver and Winnipeg respectively. While transsexuals feature here, both films focus on homosexuality as a subversion of heteronormative relationships, whereby the transsexual becomes the image of the other in predictable triangles. Most importantly, while the first film casts the legal controversy between the Vancouver bookstore Little Sister's Book and Art Emporium, located in the predominantly gay Davie village, and Canada Customs over the importation of books with same-sex content (a subject that was also explored in the feature-length documentary film *Little Sister's vs. Big Brother* in 2002), this dynamic remains a subplot and transsexuality is confined to an appendage to the homosexual romance. The film does not pursue the possibilities opened up by questions of borders, state disciplinary practices, community vs. the nation, and the fraught relation of transsexual identity to queerness. Instead, the dominant paradigm of heterosexual romance is straightforwardly replaced by the homosexual romance. Similarly, *Leaving Metropolis* relegates transsexuality to the third space, and the dramatic circumstances of the transsexual character (Shannon) attempting to obtain surgery despite her HIV condition remain marginal to both plot and form. A different strategy is pursued in the Québécois film *Le sexe des étoiles* (1993), by Paule Baillargeon, based on Monique Proulx's 1987 novel. Dickinson rightfully critiques Baillargeon for shifting the centrality of the transsexual character in the novel to the main female character's (Camille) focalization. Yet it should also be noted that this is one of the few Canadian films in which a transsexual character is centre stage and not parasitic to the economy of representation. Given the visibility these films have achieved through awards and nominations at the national and international level and the intrinsic visual power of cinematic representation, the shift of focus of Baillargeon's work, from queerness and gender ambivalence to social relations, is, in my view, an important move.[8] As texts circulating among larger audiences than underground culture, despite the limitations of distribution politics, the textual readings and the cultural interventions they enact depend on the audiences' positioning and the socio-cultural spaces they inhabit (central or marginal to Anglo-American culture), but still establish the importance of refocusing the representation of trans life within the social and the cultural, rather than identity.

Yet these representations fail to bring to light the material instances of trans people living through the effects of national politics. The question of prostitution—for example, its criminalization and centrality to the life experience of many transsexuals—begs attention in relation to the nation and transnationalism. Sex workers are, among transsexuals, the most vulnerable to state governmentality, border policing, and social violence. Often this violence is taken up by transgender activist groups to challenge the dominant gender-sex system. But the "politics of transgender identity" is not always sensitive to the complexities of violence and social attitudes, which are often the result of many variables—racism, xenophobia, homophobia, transphobia, misogyny, poverty, issues of class, cultural background, age of transition, and the many facets that marginalization entails. In a provocative gesture, Namaste notes that this violence is not necessarily directed to trans people *per se* but is the product of social attitudes toward prostitution, which is further exacerbated by cultural constructions of sex workers, trans or not, as dispensable, exploited, disempowered (thus inviting violence), and outsiders to cultural belonging: in the national imaginary there is no place for sex as commodity, nor is there any in the transgender imaginary. The fact that nearly all cases of transsexuals' prostitution are male-to-female brings to the fore the question of "woman" and female sexuality.[9] In her discussion of violence and prostitution, Namaste notes:

This is not an issue of "violence against transgendered people" but an issue of violence against transsexual women and against male-to-female transvestites who are mostly prostitutes.... So the fact that MTFs are the ones who are almost exclusively attacked and killed is something that needs to be pointed out. For every Brandon Teena, there are a thousand TS/TV prostitutes who were raped, stabbed, shot, strangled, beaten to death, burned alive, without ever having had a single book, documentary, or fiction film produced about them. (93)

The reference to the tragic case of Brandon Teena, the young transgendered man who was raped and murdered in Falls City, a small town in Nebraska, and who acquired an international iconic status when his case was brought to screen in the film *Boys Don't Cry*, by Kimberly Peirce, in 1999, shows the imbrications of cultural representation with the notion of transnationalism, whereby the transnational participates in the imagining of what Barbara Harlow calls geographies of struggle, yet elides the social effects of the cultural onto a local space. The case of Brandon Teena was taken up as a sign of "violence against transgendered people," a violence that was specifically against FTM identity, and construed as an icon of transgender-as-transnational activism. Scholarly attention was lavished on this case, as well as its cinematic representation (e.g., Judith Halberstam's extensive discussion in her *In a Queer Time & Place: Transgender Bodies, Subcultural Lives*). Meanwhile, the trans woman, when visible altogether, is confounded with drag ball performances or subsumed by auto-ethnographic cultural practices inviting the explanation of the process of male-to-female transition and, in fact, giving an account of oneself (e.g., "this is who I am," and "this is why I did it"). The question here is not an opposition between transgender man and transsexual woman, but a critical examination of the ways in which the sign of "woman" still operates within national grammars and the specific locations inhabited by transwomen and prostitutes—yet another instance of the imagined and constructed divides between trans and non-trans that Salah's poetics takes to task.

POETICS OF THE BODY, POETICS OF SEX: OF HERE AND THERE

Perhaps these concerns are best brought together—that is, shown in their linkages and relations—in the poetics of Salah's sequence, *Wanting in Arabic*, where the articulation of the trans body makes visible the constitution of subjectivity in language and the relation of the subject-in-process to the structures of the sex-gender system of national and transnational politics. In the poems, different temporalities and spatialities open up spaces to the production of meaningful experience in ways that undermine the structures of erasure and social exclusion that Namaste takes to task in her discussion. Lovemaking, tender friendship, surgery, affective relations in political mobilization, and writing bring to the fore the singularity of the self and the social positionality of the trans subject, yet they also problematize the imagined divide of trans and non-trans people, as the body dwells between the psychic investments of the imaginary-symbolic and the containments of state logic. As the discursive and institutional investments in the body are exposed and subverted (Which bodies belong to the sign of the nation?), memory eschews the troubling terrain of authenticity (of either culture or origins of the self), and re-situates the subject's quest for origins at the junction of the dream of her father's land and tongue—the presentness of her "foreign" past—and the longing for an enduring future:

> Phoenicia ≠ Lebanon
> though they occupy the same place, more or less
> > a) on a map?   do you see
> > b) in my heart?   to the west, the accident
> > c) in this poem, Phoenicia ≠ Lebanon?   that holds you down?

("Phoenicia ≠ Lebanon" 3)

That Phoenicia does not equate Lebanon exposes the irreducibility of sign and referent, culture and territory, the imagined and the real—map, heart, and poem being figurations of both origin and desire. This past that she invokes has definitely existed, but she must have dreamt of it for its claims on the present are forceful yet elusive: the "accident" of geopolitical mapping (the historical contingencies of Phoenicia and Lebanon) evoking the "accident" that binds the body to biological figurations—the body always being mapped onto, in Freud's theory, by the psychic imaginary. The fantastic investments of her childhood ("perhaps that's the origin of my infatuation with high heels" 3) intersect with the realization that desire contaminates the truth of the self ("Memory has an interest / and eros and the unconscious" 10) so that the glamorous Dana International (the Arab Israeli transsexual Sharon Cohen in "Ghazals for Sharon Cohen (Dana International)" 83), and Angela Carter's Tristessa in *The Passion of the New Eve* ("paragon of cinematic / femininity" 69) are as present and real as our fantastic projections on the trans body. And as the body longs for self-articulation ("She awoke to an appetite for narrative" 61), it unravels the false dichotomies of memory and fantasy, body and desire.

Overlaid with psychical and social processes, the body demands different questions and a new language, unsettling received notions of origin, truth, and identity. This is perhaps best evident in "Surgical Diary," a prose poem of diary entries that map transsexual "transition":

Oct. 26, 2000

The question is how I can here try to rewrite this body which is less truth than occasion, which is making a bargain not with a fantasy but with fantasy, all the distortion that entails.

That's a lie, the second to last thing. The fantasy is specific, singular. (Having been a serious marxist boy, and a good feminist, I may have a hard time living it down. Or out.

("Surgical Diary" 66)

The emphasis on transition as open process rather than new essence ("this body which is less truth than occasion" and "That's a lie") is an important move for transsexual politics and cultural rearticulation of national grammars. The tensions and contradictions lying at the heart of our desire of inhabiting and belonging, and the impossibility thereof, suggest productive possibilities in engaging with conditions of social and cultural incongruity (of bodies, ethnicities, and languages). Once again, it is the materiality of transsexual life that is brought to the fore, its "place" and "erasure":

Nov. 3, 2000

Gender Dysphoria (dysphasia)

I used to think dyphoria meant falling,
to fall out of, or even, within,
Not unbearable and so I used to be
Falling out of   not just
Bearing with the difficulty   of mine
Of being a place and its erasure.

("Surgical Diary" 68)

But as place and erasure clearly invoke the conditions of real transsexual life, they also unravel the problematic divide between trans and non-trans people as they gesture toward the incongruous relation of singularity to hegemonic discourses, of desire to social interpellation. Indeed, the poetic voice asks, "If desire is always a ruse, why this time or shape? / Why this cut, here?" ("Surgical Diary" 70).

Salah's transsexual poetics thus unsettles the relationship between nation and foreign, insider and outsider, self and other, trans and non-trans by making visible the ways in which structures of domination are invested in the construction and freezing of social identities, whereby recognition becomes a fundamental process in defining the citizen and citizen-state relations ("It doesn't matter; a body knows / when it should be elsewhere" 10). Poetics of the body, the poems engage in a lyrical meditation on biology, genetics, and corporeal desires (and desire for the corporeal), a meditation that is, foremost, a writing *of* and *with* the body in a way that calls to mind Cixous's notion of woman writing herself. Writing, here, is the key term for this body is material, tangible, and lived embodiment but also text ("if the body, / tears? / tears is a word" 44), and like every text its meanings exceed its materiality, bounded by the power of language ("if i called you 'darling' you would know all words are laden" 27). But there is not a "literal" to which a "figural" is opposed. Salah's poetry unfolds alongside the writing that biology and genetics also are, and their imbrications with identity, subject positions, and relationality: "Y, she, I" (85).

The engagement with the bodily self and desires is apparent in the titles of the four sections that constitute the book: Wanting in Arabic, Language Becoming a Girl, Hysteria of Origins, and Enduring This Future. It is an interweaving of connections that also maps trajectories of meditation without privileging a cause-effect relation or hierarchies of terms. Indeed, the question of *origins* best addresses the trans subject's reclaiming of agency and identity in the body, while this body is being written by the desirous rearticulation of *matter* rather than biological essence. Hysteria of origins, then, brings together the question of the relation of subjectivity to the body for, in the end, it is the body true to oneself that the trans subject writes into being; the interpellation of social discourse and institutions, so that Freud's question, "What does Woman want?" is inflected in the trans and radically pushed to ask, "Who is a Woman?"; the imbrications of language, voice, identity, and the body, which the discourse on hysteria produced by psychoanalysis, and critically reread by feminist theorists, evokes; the question of origin invoked by nationalistic discourses on territory, sovereignty, and national identity, and supported by religious dogmas (the interpretation of "the Word" of sacred texts); the "hysteria" of violence (both state and insurgency) that these produce; and memory as articulation of a different future, indeed the rewriting of origin as non-originary. The interweaving relationship between body, language, and nation thus becomes apparent in the form of the poetry as well as its content, never being confined to one section or another but unfolding and complicating this nexus in productive ways. No hierarchy is being established between different terms and poetic forms (while the lyric mode underlies the whole text, it is postmodern fragmentation, prose poem in the surgery diary, ghazal, invocation, and sequence) and even the possibility of strategic essentialism that a politics of identity may at best embody is displaced by positions, desires, linguistic structures that make the text dynamic. *Poesis* is creative act.

While the notion of hysteria of origins clearly addresses the Palestinian–Israeli conflict and the upsurge of racial violence in the Near East, it also foreshadows the discourse of sovereignty and nationness in the context of Canada's relations to Indigenous populations. Though this avenue is not explicitly foregrounded, the poetic language expressly emphasizes terms and conditions of nation, origin, and sovereignty in ways that, without spelling it out, raise the question of subjectivity, the diasporic, and cultural identity in relation to Canada's First Nations. But it is the exploration of the question of "origin" and "passage" in cultural-as-bodily form that provides perhaps the most interesting aspect of the poem. Indeed, the translation of the diasporic subject (the father of the poetic "i" moving from Lebanon to Canada) is both linguistic and corporeal, the loss of language enmeshed in cultural dislocation and the physical relocation within the narrative of immigrant (exploited) labour:

> so maybe it wasn't my father's plans for us
> that got me so queer
> maybe it was a child's premonition
> of his stroke at 37
> an immigrant's death of stress, a high salt diet, a foreign tongue
> and, let's face it,
> too many years of eighteen hour days
> or perhaps it was smaller
> just the way his mouth got tight about
> his voice strangled [...]

("Phoenicia ≠ Lebanon" 4)

The inscription of memory of the father's tongue and culture enhances, in the writing subject, a queer relation to origins ("perhaps that's the origin of my infatuation with high heels" 3) whereby language both performs and brings into being new possible subjectivities ("my French, my Arabic will mime strangers' tongues / missing my father's tongue" 5).

Indeed, Salah's poetics is attentive not to reduce diaspora, immigration, ethnicity, and transsexuality to self-contained and essentialized worlds. By highlighting the transsexual's social, cultural, and political positionality, the poems critically explore, and show in their articulations, questions of subjectivity and citizenship, bodily transitions, and material relations to the nation-state. The lyric mode of the poetic sequence underlines a concern for the self, and self-expression, which both gestures toward a desire for self-articulation and refuses to be confined to auto-ethnographical dominant practices. But while this concern is there, and is at best visible in the "Surgical Diary" that maps the transition of the transsexual body, it is a relational "i" that the poem writes into the cultural, thus forcing us to rethink the relation of the lyric genre to subjectivity. Here the "i" is a subject-in-process that recognizes the relationality of the self but, foremost, makes visible the ideological structures that close meaning and freeze relations in the interest of power. It is an "i" secure of its ground yet not frozen within essentialist positions that the poem writes into being: an "i" that connects the conditions of the diasporic, the middle passage, and the athwartedness of the foreign to land exploitation, stolen sovereignty, and capitalist exploitation; an "i" whose boundaries are only love for others and the other that is always already the self.

NOTES
Thanks to Trish Salah for her encouragement and precious feedback on an earlier version of this chapter.
1 See Stuart Hall's articulation of cultural identity as "becoming," rather than "being," as a "positioning," rather than an "essence" ("Cultural Identity and Diaspora").
2 Here "knot" evokes Jacques Lacan's formulation of the topological interrelation of the Symbolic, the Imaginary, and the Real.
3 See Nicole Brossard's article "Poetic Politics."
4 The gesture toward Kroetsch's poem "The Sad Phoenician" (1979) also re-situates this exploration in the larger context of Canadian experimental writing and the questioning of "origins" and "national identity" that the experimental long poem of the 1970s investigated. At the same time, it complicates the spatial and temporal axis that the geographical, historical, and figural connection-as-disidentification of Phoenicia and Lebanon entails.
5 Butler also notes this in her article "Critically Queer" (24–25).

6 An explanation could be the special relations that Montreal entertains with the city
   of New York, and the dominance of New York and US culture, including academic
   culture, in the formation of a discourse of queerness, transgenderism, and, only recently,
   transsexuality.

7 I am not addressing here the proliferation of independent documentaries that circulate
   exclusively in underground and social activism circles. At the moment, these are perhaps the most productive avenues of engagement with trans lives.

8 Paule Baillargeon's *Le sexe des étoiles* obtained the Oscar nomination for Best Foreign
   Film in 1994. Fraser's *Leaving Metropolis* (2002) was nominated for the Grand Prix des
   Amériques at the 2002 Montreal World Film Festival. Anne Brad Wheeler's *Better
   Than Chocolate* (1998) won numerous awards at several international festivals.

9 At a recent conference held in May 2008 in Vancouver, BC (conference convenor
   Susan Stryker, Department of Women's Studies at Simon Fraser University, BC), Viv-
   ian Namaste drew attention to the murder of Grayce Baxter, who was killed while working on the street. Her name appears among others on the website for the Transgender
   Day of Remembrance as an example of anti-transgender violence. Yet Baxter passed as
   a "natural" woman and her killer learned she was a transsexual only from the newspaper
   the next day.

Word Warriors
Indigenous Political Consciousness in Prison

Deena Rymhs

Although our struggles on the inside may differ from those of our Brothers and
Sisters in the free world, these prison walls do not alienate the negative forms of
alcoholism, poverty, or prejudice. It is here that we are allowed to recognize our
problems, within these walls we gather strength.

    —Daniel Beatty Pawis, "A Dedication to the Warrior Spirit" (1)

Warrior traditions find new expression in contemporary society as Native people
fight for jobs, rights, or lost lands on many battlefields, including the workplace,
state legislation, courts, and the US Department of the Interior.

    —Gerald McMaster and Clifford E. Trafzer, *Native Universe* (200)

FEW PEOPLE MIGHT LOOK UPON the prison as a site of profound political
change where developments of consequence to Indigenous peoples[1] outside
the prison's walls are taking root. Fewer still might recognize the prison as a
transnational space where prisoners enter into a shared consciousness with
their "brothers" and "sisters" serving time in other countries. Yet, in their
writing and activism from prison, Indigenous prisoners have helped shape the
political blueprint of Indigenous peoples in Canada since the late 1960s. Their
political engagement exceeds the boundaries of this nation: letters from prisoners in Attica, Marion, Leavenworth, and from places as remote as Northern Ireland appear throughout the newsletters published in Canadian prisons.
Indigenous prisoners have used the penal press to raise the intellectual and
political consciousness of other inmates, organizing letter-writing campaigns
for the release of Leonard Peltier, petitioning against the adult sentencing of a
fifteen-year-old Lakota boy, Tony Rios, and supporting Indigenous land claims
in Brazil. Prison Justice Day, 10 August, is now an internationally observed

memorial occasioned by the death of Millhaven prisoner, Eddie Nalon, who bled to death in his segregation cell in 1974. Prisoners in Canada join together with those in the United States, England, France, and Germany to commemorate this day by fasting and refusing to work. As in other moments of history, Indigenous prisoners construct multiple political communities and engage in acts of diplomacy in the spirit of the leaders who have preceded them. Countering the isolating effects of the prison, these communities dissolve the boundary between "inside" and "outside." At the same time, however, Indigenous prisoners see the consciousness they have gained as constituted by the prison, a consciousness born of a place where state-sanctioned violence and colonization persist in our so-called "postcolonial" moment.

At a time when a disproportionate number of Indigenous men spend their time locked up in correctional institutions, examining how these men reconstruct their identities in prison seems particularly urgent; such reconstructions reveal how Indigenous groups transform the prison from a space of colonial suppression to a place of political activism and cultural regeneration. While this chapter focuses on the ways these men empower themselves within the colonially charged space of the prison, to speak about an "Indigenous prison masculinity" can also have troubling implications: Can such a focus disentangle itself from a general public sensibility—magnified by the media—that tends to racialize crime? Reporting six men who escaped from Regina Correctional Centre in August 2008, several newspapers, television news programs, and Internet news sites displayed photographs of the escapees. The almost gratuitous display of these faces—all of Indigenous men—begged the question of the subtext of the news reports. Are such images revelatory or do they merely reinforce stereotypes? Readers responding to CBC's report on its website wavered between the two. Amidst a rush of derisive statements diminishing the value of these men's lives appeared one reader's question: "But hasn't anyone also noticed the similarity of those five faces? I mean, is 'young, male and Indian' the top demographic of Regina Correctional Centre's general population? ... Looking at those faces, I feel there's more to the story" ("Second-Last Regina Jail Escapee Captured in Winnipeg"). This reader, signalling the larger cultural and personal histories that might serve as the backdrop of these photos, unwittingly identifies another "extra-textual" register to this article: what's "more to the story" is told in the photographs of the men. The particular manner in which the media covered this issue plays on a gap between the written and visual; while many of the articles did not explicitly identify the racial profile of the escapees, the use of the photographs did. The inclusion of

these photographs, while calling attention to the demographics of imprisonment, problematically links Indigenous identity to criminality. The five intim-
idating, Indigenous faces staring at the reader make this point unmistakable.
Away from these media depictions, and virtually unknown to these readers,
are the newsletters and magazines published by Indigenous prisoners who present a different view of their crimes and their time in prison.

The current overrepresentation of Indigenous men and women in prison
cannot be disentangled from their colonial histories of institutionally constructed guilt, poverty, physical relocation, and cultural dislocation. While
"diaspora" may seem a peculiar choice of words to describe the experiences
of a people who inhabit the same continent as they did before the arrival of
settler-colonial culture,[2] the term speaks to their histories of deracination as
well as to the number of Indigenous peoples currently locked up in prison.[3]
Diaspora, Leela Gandhi writes, "evokes the specific traumas of human displacement" (131). The use of the prison and other carceral institutions like
the residential school to punish expressions of indigeneity and to remove
individuals from their communities reinforces the prison's place in this historical trauma. The continual transfer of prisoners among correctional institutions today further evokes the sense of fragmentation that diaspora connotes. Yet, one may also look upon the present number of Indigenous prisoners
not strictly as a scattering but as a concentration of cultural influence that
allows for community reformation and empowering resistance. Postcolonial
theory acknowledges the ways that diasporic peoples create new modalities of
identification, a reconfiguration of identity that can run counter to dominant
cultural influences acting upon colonized subjects. "While 'diaspora' is sometimes used interchangeably with 'migration,'" Gandhi writes, "it is generally
invoked as a theoretical device for the interrogation of ethnic identity and
cultural nationalism" (131). The pull away from a Canadian national identity that Indigenous sovereignty movements enact—and which Indigenous
prisoners have articulated in their writing since the emergence of the Red
Power moment in the 1960s—involves the movement toward a different cultural nationalism. This reconceptualization of national identity may recover
distinct tribal histories at the same time as it remains invested in intertribal
alliances, or what is colloquially known as a pan-Indigenous identity.

Some Indigenous prison collectives—the Blackfoot Awareness Group in
Drumheller federal prison, for instance—seek to recover tribally specific tradi-
tions, but these communities locate themselves within the larger alliance of
Native Brotherhood, whose political work they see as overlapping with their

own objectives. The networks that Indigenous prisoners build are also, then, influenced by their immediate context of the prison, where the diverse Indigenous backgrounds of prisoners prompt an intertribal constellation of community. Pointing out a "long-standing tradition of intertribal exchange," Lisa Brooks emphasizes the political networks that were historically important for formulating a discourse of Native rights ("Digging" 253). In recent contexts, the notion of "common ground" continues to shift to include other communities across Indian Country. Recognizing the important political work transacted from borderlands, Craig Womack also remarks that "tribally specific experiences are constantly expanding, even beyond their own borders and out into non-Indian realms"[4] ("Theorizing" 406). The incarcerated Indigenous writers examined in this chapter reveal the cosmopolitan possibilities of intertribalism while they also push beyond an isolationist view of sovereignty that critics of this political position so often emphasize in their rejection of it.

The writing of Indigenous prisoners serves an important function not just for their authors and for those in prison, but for communities outside the prison as well. Citing the work of Black American prisoners in reforming the prison system in the 1960s and 1970s, Auli Ek points out how the Black Muslim prison movement ended segregation not only in prisons but "also contributed to the desegregation efforts in the United States in general" (88). "[C]ombining the personal with the political, the prison autobiographers of the 1960s and 1970s," notes Ek,

> focus on prison masculinity as a transformation process that has had both individual and communal implications. In this process of transformation, the imprisoned individual gains both self respect and respect from the community through socially motivated practices such as educating oneself, becoming more involved in religious or spiritual thought, and raising one's political awareness. (52)

Some of the writing of Indigenous prisoners reveals a similar impetus, constructing a prison masculinity that is situated in political activism. For these writers, regaining their "manhood" and cultural pride are intertwined.

For many Indigenous prisoners, the prison is a place of spiritual recovery. Through the mentoring offered by elders and other individuals in prison, they are re-introduced to Indigenous philosophies and traditions. Sacred circles, sweat lodges, and cultural awareness programs are some of the means by which this personal and cultural recovery takes place. In an editorial in *Arrows to Freedom*, a newsletter published from Drumheller prison, John Umpherville writes:

I went [to the Edmonton Maximum Security Prison] with the white man's beliefs and attitudes, as that was the way I was raised. During my short stay there, I joined the [Native] Brotherhood and [was] introduced to my Native heritage. The brothers at the Max showed me things I never knew existed. They showed me how to become at peace with myself and the Creator. I was introduced to the drum, sweetgrass, sweatlodge, fasting, the ceremonial pipe and the meaning behind these sacred objects [...]. Since that time [...], I have been trying to turn my life around for the better. (2)

Umpherville sees the prison, and specifically the influence of other Indigenous peoples there, as prompting a turning point in his life. This moment of personal transformation is cast in political terms as Umpherville concludes: "The Native people are a strong people again and we should keep up that struggle to stay that way" (2). His individual story of recovery becomes collectively significant, emblematic of a shifting political consciousness and an experientially based conviction in the resilience of Indigenous peoples. Daniel Beatty Pawis similarly writes in *Arrows to Freedom*: "When I began to participate in Elders' workshops, Sweat Lodges, and Pipe Ceremonies, I began to work on something I had struggled with all my life ... my identity. The conflict I experienced in my adolescence as a result of my adoption began to heal" ("Inside the Iron Tipi" 29). The culturally inflected process of healing that Pawis and Umpherville describe differs in some critical ways from the type of rehabilitation promoted in the prison; indeed, the awareness that they have gained is sharply critical of the institutional forces that have brought them there. With its tenor of political resistance, the personal and cultural recovery described by these men carves out a sovereign space for what Indigenous inmates can accomplish from their time in prison.

This transformed awareness involves not only the recovery of cultural identities but also a changed view of freedom. An anonymous work, titled "A Prison Prayer," reads:

> I pray for Freedom
> Show me how to respect it so I do not take it for granted
> Give me strength to grasp it firmly and never again lose it
> . . . .
> Show me a vision of reality that will prepare me for the future
> so I can walk this Sweetgrass Road and leave these cold walls behind me.
> (23–28)

The prison is commonly thought of as a place of introspection and self-discovery. "A Prison Prayer" recasts this self-discovery as a spiritual vision quest. "Freedom," for many of these Indigenous prisoners, does not simply involve physically leaving the prison. Rather, freedom means reconceptualizing their lives and their purpose in prison. As Pawis puts it:

> Prison can be one of two things. It can be the end … or it can be the beginning. For most of us that are associated with the Drumheller Native Brotherhood, prison has become both the end and the beginning. Through our spiritual and cultural rebirth we are given another chance to find and maintain our freedom. Prison can be the end of a chapter in our lives that has brought misery and suffering to ourselves and the people around us. It can be the beginning of new relationships, with the Creator, with our families, and with the communities which we are still a part of regardless of how deep a gouge this isolation has cut into our lives. Prison can be the end of freedom as we knew it, and the beginning of freedom as it is supposed to be. ("The Politics of Freedom" 4)

For Pawis, freedom can exist in prison. In the words of imprisoned political activist, Leonard Peltier: "My body may be locked in here, but my spirit flies with the eagle" (25). Embracing traditional values, these authors suggest, is a political act, a point also made by Taiaiake Alfred, who argues that "[t]he spiritual connections and fundamental respect for each other and for the earth that were our ancestors' way and the foundations of our traditional systems" must be restored as a model for Indigenous governance today (*Peace, Power, Righteousness* xiv).

The struggle that has brought these men to this renewed cultural identity, they insist, is a crucial part of their political and cultural consciousness. Pawis writes: "Due to the access we have had to our Elders and Medicine Men, and Cultural translators, I have been fortunate enough to extract a thing called 'pride' out of a past that is full of shadows and resentments" ("Inside the Iron Tipi" 29). The bitterness and failures of the past, rather than a source of shame, are part of the grammar of recovery that these men construct—a model of recovery that responds to the particular challenges facing Indigenous communities in a present context. "It's unfortunate that we have to experience prison to learn," Pawis continues, "but that's a perspective that can be applied to many things. Some of our nation's most acclaimed addictions counsellors and pipe carriers have been on skidrow, and in prison. Struggle makes a nation strong, and we continue to apply our ancestors' resilience time and time again" ("Inside the Iron Tipi" 30). Again, Pawis moves from the personal to the collective, casting his individual struggles as part of a larger cultural experience. This philosophy of strength, earned through struggle, is integrated into the visual logo of the Blackfoot Confederacy in Drumheller Institution. Their logo consists of "a crooked arrow with two straight lines flanking it. The arrow explains [that though] we have aims and objectives, we tend to stray away and be misled along the way. The straight lines represent the red and spiritual road toward our goals" ("The Blackfoot Awareness Group's Logo" 1). In this sense, Indigenous prisoners are able to achieve something that non-Indigenous prisoners struggle to do—overcome the stigma of imprisonment and see themselves as contributing members of their communities outside the prison. Benjamin Paul, a prisoner at William Head Institution, remarks on this special type of community building: "In one community, we were told that we can walk in their village anytime with our heads held high because of the work we have done helping the youth instead of being ashamed of where we come from" (17). Some Indigenous prisoners find a sense of pride not only in healing themselves, but also in helping to repair the damage done to communities outside the prison.

One of the ways that Indigenous male prisoners regain their sense of value to their cultural communities is by fashioning themselves as "warriors." A particularly charged word after Oka, "warrior" signifies a responsibility to one's cultural communities. This reconfiguration contrasts with the media's image of the "militant Indian," which dominated headlines during the Oka crisis (Valaskakis 44). "There are various concepts of a warrior society," remarks Art Solomon, an Anishinaabe elder who mentored Indigenous men and women in prison (qtd. in Stonechild 3). Solomon explains that, in some Indigenous frameworks, "a warrior society means the men and women of the nation who dedicated themselves to give everything they have to the people" (qtd. in Stonechild 3). "Being a warrior," adds prisoner Benjamin Paul, "is … about helping your people to become strong so that they may face the challenges that come along in life. It's about helping yourself and growing each day" (18). "Warrior" becomes reinvested with new meaning to fit the contemporary realities of Indigenous peoples. Alfred summarizes the strategic recasting of "warrior":

In most people's minds, the words "North American Indian warrior" invoke images of futile angry violence or of noble sacrifice in the face of the white march of triumph over this continent. To Euroamericans, the

descendents [sic] and beneficiaries of conquest, "Indian warriors" are arte-
facts of the past; they are icons of colonization, that version of history in
which the original people of this land have been defiant but defeated [...].
But history has not ended. There are still Onkwehonwe lands, souls, and
minds that have not been conquered. For them, a warrior is what a warrior
has always been: one who protects the people, who stands with dignity and
courage in the face of danger. When lies rule, a warrior creates new truths
for the people to believe. (*Wasáse* 97)

Being a warrior involves a philosophical and correspondingly activist stance.
To claim this role for oneself, Alfred suggests, is a way of countering narratives
of defeat and tragedy.

While Alfred insists that "a warrior is what a warrior has always been,"
he adapts this concept to a specific, historical context. A warrior, as Alfred
mobilizes this term, fights an ongoing war with colonialism. In the past thirty
years particularly, movements like the Mi'kmaq Warrior Society and Mohawk
Warrior Society have gained ascendancy. The Mohawk Warrior Societies that
emerged in the 1970s and 1980s, Alfred points out, bridged traditional teachings with a "contemporary movement ideology" (*Wasáse* 78). This reconception of warrior, then, merges traditional philosophies—many of them spiritually based—with a contemporary model of political activism. The idea of
a "warrior" has also broadened to include both men and women, and thus
expressly differs from "the military masculine" favoured by the media (Valaskakis 39). Yet, as Joyce Green explains, some Indigenous women have been
alienated from and even intimidated by such warrior societies.[5] Alfred, in contrast, sensitively points out that the "male-gendered and soldierly image" of a
warrior "doesn't reflect real Onkwehonwe notions from any of our cultures,
especially that of the ideal we are seeking to understand and apply here, of
men and women involved in a spiritually rooted resurgence of Onkwehonwe
strength" (*Wasáse* 78). He resolutely divests "warrior" of its male-gendered
tradition:

[W]e cannot hold on to a concept of the warrior that is gendered in the way
it once was and that is located in an obsolete view of men's and women's
roles. The battles we are fighting are no longer primarily physical; thus, any
idea of the indigenous warrior framed solely in masculine terms is outdated
and must be ... recast from the solely masculine view of the old traditional
ways to a new concept of the warrior that is freed from colonial gender

constructions and articulated instead with reference to what really counts in our struggles: the qualities and actions of a person, man or woman, in battle. (*Wasáse* 84)

This inclusive redefinition of warrior emerges in Indigenous prisoners' reflections as well. Pawis refers to the many "Brothers and Sisters" in prison who act as "unselfish Warriors" ("A Dedication to the Warrior Spirit" 1). He thus distances warrior from a strictly male association. In their newsletters from prison, Indigenous inmates reveal a similar sensitivity to gender issues; these prison periodicals have served as important venues for political collaboration between male and female Indigenous groups. Letters of support from P4W's Native Sisterhood appear in *Arrows to Freedom*, a newsletter published by Indigenous male prisoners at Drumheller Institution. In 1993, *Arrows to Freedom* raised the concerns expressed by the Native Women's Association of Canada about the continued legal discrimination of Indigenous women under Bill C-31. A 1998 issue of *The Moxie*, published from Bath's federal prison for men, reprints the keynote address from the National Symposium on Aboriginal Women entitled "Real Power, Aboriginal Women—Past, Present, Future." Despite the sex segregation that such institutions impose, one finds in these prison publications inspiring instances of community building in the face of the deleterious impact of colonial legislation on gender relations in Indigenous communities.[6]

In adapting the meaning of warrior to address their present, immediate contexts, and to encompass their personal healing and political activism from prison, Indigenous prisoners invent new "cultural grammars" of their own. Alfred describes a similar process of adaptation: "How do we resurrect the ideals of a warrior in Onkwehonwe societies that are so different from the ancient ones? The need for people who do the things warriors do is still there, but the people who do them, the way they do them, and how they fit within the society all have to be rethought to be brought back to life" (*Wasáse* 83). The battle that Indigenous prisoners see themselves waging becomes a discursive one—a "war of words," as R.D. Jones puts it in a 1970 issue of British Columbia Penitentiary's *Indian Echo*. Drawing on Gerald Vizenor's notion of "word warriors," Dale Turner sees the new warriors of the twenty-first century as mastering the intellectual and political practices of dominant society. While Turner envisages an intellectual elite occupying this role—a "class" of Indigenous peoples, as he puts it, who "hold … intellectual positions of authority" and "mak[e] inroads into the dominant intellectual, legal, and political communities in Canada"

(92–93), Turner's discussion of this concept should not necessarily preclude the type of political work that Indigenous inmates perform from prison. Indigenous prisoners "engage the legal and political discourses of the state" (Turner 72), mediating between these discourses and Indigenous philosophies. Robert A. Williams, working from both Lumbee and American legal traditions, advances an Indigenous political theory similar to those of both Turner and Alfred, one that focuses on Indigenous "legal concepts encoded in treaty discourse, stories [...], ceremonies such as the Pipe Ceremony, objects such as wampum belts, and Indigenous kinship systems and institutions" (S.A. Miller 13). The contemporary relevance that prisoners attach to such concepts as warrior, pipe-carrier, the sacred hoop, and teachings are instances of "indigenous voices … determin[ing] the normative language used for defining the meaning and content" of Indigenous life today (Turner 120).

"Warrior," as it is recast in a modern context, may be said to resonate especially for prisoners. "The new warriors," Alfred formulates, "are committed in the first instance to self-transformation and self-defence against the insidious forms of control that the state and capitalism use to shape lives according to their needs—to fear, to obey, to consume" (Wasáse 29). Indigenous prisoners are perhaps better poised to recognize their betrayal by liberal capitalism and the state's political manipulation of Indigenous peoples. Uniquely positioned to question the promises and concept of justice, Indigenous prisoners often recognize their imprisonment within a broader political context. Describing their lives before their imprisonment—lives that were often characterized by a lack of freedom before they were physically incarcerated—these authors may even recalibrate their readers' notions of justice.

The type of journey that incarcerated Indigenous authors describe themselves as undergoing in prison, moreover, mirrors the teleology of "becoming a warrior." Through a return to traditional practices, they engage in a process of "self-transformation" (Alfred, Wasáse 279) that resembles Alfred's discussion of becoming a warrior. This process, Alfred writes, is

> encouraged through one-to-one mentoring, face-to-face interaction, and small-group dialogue to effect the regeneration of our minds, bodies, and spirits. This is the ancient way of the warrior. All cultures and ancient traditions contain essentially the same teaching on transcendence, which is that regeneration starts with a thorough and proper investigation of one's own life. It is a form of self-challenge, a contest really, between the lies and the truth of the self, where the task is to convince us to take care of

ourselves and to change our lives—to internalize the warrior's journey, the
self-challenge, and the struggle to remake reality on a different and more
truthful footing. (*Wasáse* 279–80)

The process that Alfred outlines above closely parallels the mentoring and
self-examination that Indigenous prisoners describe themselves as undergoing
in prison. This transformation in prison thus resonates with this redefinition
of warrior in a contemporary context.

While Indigenous prisoners empower themselves with traditional knowledge, the prison is also a place where the enduring effects of colonialism
remain markedly evident. The ways in which Indigenous prisoners organize
themselves politically is perhaps not immune to the lasting impact of colonially imposed structures. Even though one finds instances of Indigenous men
in prison addressing gender discrimination in their writing—and thus recognizing how decolonization is linked to rethinking gender practices—their
political formations remain in some ways bound by models of governance that
are the by-products of colonialism. Native Brotherhoods, which emerged in
Canadian prisons as early as the 1950s, typically elect a chief and council.
Native Brotherhood acts as a political body, representing the concerns of
Indigenous inmates to the warden and liaising with political groups outside
the prison. Pawis describes Native Brotherhood's political model as mirror-
ing that of the band council on a reserve: "Elected delegates of the Brotherhood deal with the Administration at each Pen which can be compared to
the dealings of Native Bands dealing with Government agencies at a Federal
and Provincial level" ("Brotherhood" 8). The political models that Native
Brotherhoods follow, then, might be said to conform to a received colonial
framework, a manifestation of the "intellectual landscapes," as Turner calls it,
"that have been forced on Aboriginal peoples" (88).

At the same time, however, this deference to received political structures
does not necessarily equate to political submission or to an inability to reimagine new strategies of cultural preservation within such frameworks. An
Alcoholics Anonymous group in Drumheller prison and the Métis Addiction Council Alcohol Treatment Program in Okimaw Ohci Penitentiary
are examples of cultural influence extending two ways rather than one. The
Métis Addiction Council Alcohol Treatment Program combines Indigenous
spiritual teachings with addiction counselling. Similarly, the Alcoholics
Anonymous program in Drumheller prison, renamed "Free Spirit," incorporates Indigenous spiritual philosophies as well as traditional practices like

smudging. An "'Indianized' A.A. Group" (Daychief 7), Free Spirit is a culturally inflected recovery program registered with Alcoholics Anonymous' head office. This "Indianization" is especially interesting given the Christian derivation of Alcoholics Anonymous and its twelve-step program. Many HIV workshops in prison are following the same direction, attending to Indigenous spirituality alongside their mandate of educating and counselling Indigenous prisoners. Approaching healing from a cultural perspective, this merging of approaches shows how Indigenous prisoners, positioned between different cultural systems, reinvent new strategies for preserving traditional knowledge within existing frameworks.

Prison periodicals have served as important venues for Indigenous prisoners to address not only their prison conditions but also issues of wider political importance. When the White Paper was introduced in 1969, many Indigenous prison newsletters ran articles opposing the legislation. A 1969 issue of *Indian*, published from William Head Institution, features an editorial by Kenzie Basil about the "New Indian Policy." The editorial outlines the liberal basis of the policy, pointing out the insistent inequities and lack of representation of Indigenous peoples in government that belie such aspirations of equality. "They ... say we use the reservation as a 'crutch' to go back to when we fail to adjust to city life," writes Basil. "We do not wish to forget our culture," he responds, "nor do we desire to entirely accept another. We are attempting to educate our young people and, through education, afford them the choice, the choice of taking the best from each culture in order that the end result will be a richer, fuller, more meaningful life for them" (n.p.). In 1971, at the peak of opposition to the White Paper, *Indian Echo* ran a feature on unsettled land rights in British Columbia. The use of prison newsletters to educate Indigenous inmates on matters affecting their communities outside the prison continued in the following decades. A single 1993 issue of *Arrows to Freedom* contains articles on James Bay, Justice McEachern's ruling on the Gitksan and Wet'suwet'en, the Oldman Dam construction, and an interview with Milton Born with a Tooth, the leader of the Peigan Lonefighters Society protesting the Oldman Dam construction who was imprisoned for almost five years. These prison publications attest to Indigenous prisoners' engagement in political developments affecting communities outside the prison.

Political groups outside the prison are increasingly recognizing the value of the prisoners' political input as well. In 1991, a panel struck by the Assembly of First Nations visited Stony Mountain Prison to consult with Indigenous prisoners about proposed constitutional reform, reforms that were later repackaged as the Charlottetown Accord. Stony Mountain Prison's *Native Brotherhood Newsletter* reprinted an article run by *The Globe and Mail* on the consultations. Talks moved from the proposed constitutional changes to larger issues of concern, including language, the environment, and self-government. The direction that the discussions took indicates Indigenous prisoners' desire to have a hand in shaping the political agenda. Horace Massan acknowledged the significance of this consultation: "[T]his is history. Every constitution we know was developed without the input of that society's rejected citizens. We are the rejected" (qtd. in D. Roberts 10). Whether "rejected citizens" applies to Indigenous people or to the prisoners specifically remains poignantly ambiguous here. The implied point is the similarity between Indigenous peoples inside and outside the prison.

Mending the various divisions that separate Indigenous groups inside and outside the prison, and urging Indigenous prisoners to band together to promote their shared political concerns, Indigenous prisoners engage in what one might call a form of intertribal diplomacy. The pan-Indigenous identity reinforced in prison by sacred circles, pipe ceremonies, and sweats is more than a generalized and arbitrary construction: it is a strategic way of encouraging Indigenous prisoners to identify collectively. A 1981 issue of *Tribal Ways*, published from Collins Bay Institution, addresses the need to end hostility between status and non-status Indians. Drumheller Institution's *Native Brotherhood Newsletter* echoes these concerns, remarking:

> If a community like ours were to actualize the definitions that have been given to us by white society: (IE. STATUS, NONSTATUS, METIS, INUIT)—there would be a disruption in progress because of the division that this categorical placement calls for. Why do we allow someone who is neither of the four mentioned peoples tell us who we are? (Pawis, "Brotherhood" 9)

These statements counter the divisive language of colonial legislation while they also recognize the political empowerment of Indigenous peoples working in a coordinated manner. An article titled "Why Settle the BC Land Question" in a 1971 issue of *Indian Echo* similarly emphasizes the importance of Nishga Tribal Council acting "in concert with the Union of BC Chiefs" instead of alone (Dennis 2). A year earlier, *Indian Echo* wrote about empowering political collaboration among West Coast Indigenous groups:

> In former days the Shuswap Indian people ... were in a state of almost con-
> tinual warfare with the Chilcothin Indian people from the North. Today,
> how-ever [sic], they no longer are at war with one another, but united
> along with other British Columbia Indian people, to fight a different kind
> of war. A war of words with the government. (Jones 8)

As the battles that Indigenous peoples fight change, so too do the methods of
warfare. An invitation from the Six Nations Council of Chiefs to the Grand
Council of North American Indian People to discuss the *First Nations Char-
tered Lands Act*, published in a 1993 issue of *Arrows to Freedom*, represents
a similar attempt at rethinking political strategies and promoting political
collaboration. The publication of this invitation within a prison newsletter
represents a further gesture of inclusion and a widening political community.
Since the 1960s, Indigenous prisoners have recognized the importance of such
collaboration. The Indian Education Club, established in 1966 at William
Head Institution and modelled after a group earlier formed in British Columbia Penitentiary, states its three mandates: "1) to seek ways to curtail and
reform the large numbers of Indians who go to jail.... 2) to promote a better understanding and relationship between Indians and non-Indians. 3) to
encourage unity amongst Indians" (Antoine 2).

The alliances that Indigenous prisoners seek in their writing extend to
non-Indigenous communities as well. R.D. Jones writes in a 1970 issue of
Indian Echo: "[O]nly by understanding one another shall our goals become
reality and the discriminative attitude between whites and Reds cease to be
the barrier" (2). These gestures are more than an attempt to transcend barriers
of discrimination: they implicitly advance Indigenous sovereignty. "We must
be united," continues Jones, "to do all we can to secure the future peace of
two great nations" (2). The type of collaboration envisaged here is that of two
nations. In such ways, prisoners engage with the "intellectual landscapes that
have been forced on Aboriginal peoples—for example, the language of rights,
sovereignty, and nationalism" (Turner 88) and attempt to position themselves
within this discourse in empowering ways.

The stance of these texts is thus "post-national" in the intertribal identities they advocate, in the notion of sovereignty they put forth, and in the
international communities with which they engage. These movements across
inter-, intra-, and extra-latitudes resemble a cosmopolitanism "partly rooted
in local cultures, particularly positioned in global networks" (Anderson 78).
Rather than seeing the histories of Indigenous groups solely in terms of their

relationship to Euro-Canadian settler cultures, these currents of identification direct attention to the local-to-local interactions of groups on the periphery. Indigenous prisoners have long acknowledged the need to work within multiple communities. In their writing can be seen the desire to mend divisions along lines of gender and tribal identification, to dissolve the boundary of those inside and outside the prison, and to attend to the needs of Indigenous communities nationally as well as globally. These prison publications belong to a larger history of the Indigenous small press, which includes newsletters like *The National Indian*, *Nesika*, *Akwasasne Notes*, *Indian World*, *TAWOW*, and the *Kainai News*, which, as Jeanette Armstrong observes, critically shaped Indigenous politics, history, and literary expression ("Four Decades"). Prison newsletters provide a window into the vital role Indigenous prisoners play in continuing the intellectual, political, philosophical, and activist tradition begun with Red Power and in returning to a tradition of historical political writing, as Sean Teuton observes. In the model of activism and political collaboration that Red Power provided, these publications show how "histories come together in the experiences of different Indigenous nations 'on the ground'" (Lawrence, "Rewriting" 26).

In a place that could not be more redolent of colonial history, Indigenous prisoners engage in a significant process of cultural renewal. The prison is a particularly charged place from which to perform a localized postcolonial analysis of the relationship between Indigenous nations and the state. Remarkably, Indigenous prisoners harness the force of their experiences to fortify a political consciousness that is unafraid to admit individual past failures and the strength gained from those failures. In doing so, they re-inflect the notion of "corrections" and reframe rehabilitation in Indigenous terms. By engaging in personal and political acts of self-construction alongside an existing philosophical tradition of prison writing, they also reinscribe that literary tradition and the type of conversion associated with it. In his distillation of contemporary strategies for transcending colonial identities and for effecting meaningful change, Alfred emphasizes a reflexive process that starts with the basic question: "Are we living culturally as Onkwehonwe?" (*Wasáse* 81). In the pared-down existence of prison, many Indigenous prisoners are living as Onkwehonwe.

NOTES

1 I use term "Indigenous" rather than "Aboriginal" or "First Nations" because I see the former as more inclusive and less steeped in Canadian legislative discourse. "Indigenous" also suggests a wider global community, a cosmopolitanism that is fitting for the transnational connections that Indigenous peoples in Canada have often identified between themselves and Indigenous constituencies in other geopolitical contexts.

2 This particular understanding of diaspora—as a dispersal and uprooting of a people who, in turn, become collectively defined by their dislocation—forms the basis of Lee Maracle's rejection of the concept for describing Indigenous peoples. Strategically inverting conventional uses of "diaspora," she instead applies the term to settler communities in Canada. In doing so, she implicitly asserts Indigenous peoples' rootedness and intimate connection to their lands.

3 In drawing on the concept of "diaspora," I am also mindful of Arif Dirlik's caution against using this term "uncritically without due attention to differences of place" ("Race Talk" 1373). "Diaspora," argues Dirlik, "lends itself to cultural and racial reification in endowing populations that are the products of different historical trajectories with identity on the basis of descent from a common 'nation,' itself a recent historical product of complex population interactions" (1373). While persuasive, Dirlik's argument might prompt further discussion of how the notion of "nationhood"—rather than necessarily operating as part of a colonial genealogy—differs in Indigenous cultural contexts. Moreover, the construction of a "pan-Indigenous" identity historically has been an important and empowering move for Indigenous communities in Canada and the United States. David L. Eng's identification of what he calls "queer diasporas," which suggest identifications that exist "outside the boundaries of territorial sovereignty," harnesses the power of this conceptual category to describe alternative political communities (1483).

4 For a compelling example of the cross-pollination that Womack describes, see Hugh Brody's film, *The Meaning of Life*. Filmed in Kwikwexwelhp prison in the Fraser Valley of British Columbia, this documentary explores a collaborative partnership between the prison's administration and the neighbouring Chehalis First Nation. The minimum-security prison offers programs for Indigenous and non-Indigenous prisoners based on Indigenous spiritual and cultural philosophies.

5 In 1993, during a conflict between the Manitoba government and the Rosseau River band council over gaming jurisdiction, women on the reserve expressed concern over their safety. Some women reported that they had been threatened by the warrior society, who had seized the role of the tribal police after the band council had ordered the police off the reserve. For further discussion, see Green.

6 As Julia Emberley argues, Euro-Canadian government policies—beginning with the *Indian Act*, and continuing with the introduction of institutions like residential schools—worked to dissolve traditional kinship structures in Indigenous communities. The patriarchal bias of the *Indian Act*, which entrenched patrilineal descent and promoted male political leadership in Indigenous communities, created gender inequities between men and women. Martha Flaherty, president of Pauktuutit Inuit Women's Association, summarizes the discrimination that Indigenous women experience: "women have suffered doubly for we lost status in our own society and were subjected to the patriarchal institutions born in the south" (qtd. in Emberley, *Defamiliarizing* 67).

Works Cited

"Aboriginal Rights." *Tar Sands Watch: Polaris Institute's Energy Program.* <http://www
.tarsandswatch.org/aboriginal-rights>.

Abraham, Nicolas. "Notes on the Phantom: A Complement to Freud's Metapsychol-
ogy." *The Shell and the Kernel* by Nicolas Abraham and Maria Torok. Ed. and intro.
by Nicholas T. Rand. Chicago: U of Chicago P, 1994. 171–76.

Acoose, Janice. "A Vanishing Indian? Or Acoose: Woman Standing above Ground?"
(Ad)dressing Our Words: Aboriginal Perspectives on Aboriginal Literatures. Ed. Armand
Ruffo. Penticton: Theytus, 2001. 37–56.

Ahmad, Aijaz. *In Theory: Classes, Nations, Literatures.* New York: Verso, 1992.

Alfred, Taiaiake. *Peace, Power, Righteousness: An Indigenous Manifesto.* Don Mills:
Oxford UP, 1999.

———. Personal interview with Sam McKegney, April 2007.

———. *Wasáse: Indigenous Pathways of Action and Freedom.* Peterborough: Broadview,
2005.

Algoo-Baksh, Stella. *Austin C. Clarke: A Biography.* Toronto: ECW, 1994.

Allen, Paula Gunn. *The Sacred Hoop: Recovering the Feminine in American Indian Traditions.* Boston: Beacon, 1986.

Anderson, Alan. "Diaspora and Exile: A Canadian and Comparative Perspective."
International Journal of Canadian Studies 18 (Fall 1998): 13–30.

Anderson, Amanda. *The Way We Argue Now: A Study in the Cultures of Theory.* Princeton: Princeton UP, 2006.

Anderson, Benedict. *Imagined Communities.* London and New York: Verso, 1983.

Andrews, Jennifer. "Irony, Métis Style: Reading the Poetry of Marilyn Dumont and
Gregory Scofield." *Canadian Poetry* 50 (2002): 6–31.

Antoine, C.J. "Annual Report of the Indian Education Club of William Head Institution." *Indian* (April 1969): 2–3.

Appiah, Kwame Anthony. *In My Father's House: Africa in the Philosophy of Culture.*
Oxford: Oxford UP, 1993.

Arendt, Hannah. *Between Past and Future: Eight Exercises in Political Thought.* 1968. New York: Penguin Books, 2006.

Armstrong, Jeannette. "Four Decades: An Anthology of Canadian Native Poetry from 1960 to 2000." *Native Poetry in Canada: A Contemporary Anthology.* Ed. Jeannette Armstrong and Lally Grauer. Peterborough: Broadview, 2001. xv–xx.

———. "Land Speaking." *Speaking for the Generations: Native Writers on Writing.* Tucson: U of Arizona P, 1998. 175–94.

———. *Slash.* Penticton: Theytus Books, 1985.

———. *Whispering in Shadows.* Penticton: Theytus Books, 2000.

Ashcroft, Bill, Gareth Griffiths, and Helen Tiffin. *The Empire Writes Back: Theory and Practice in Post-colonial Literatures.* New York: Routledge, 1989.

———. "Introduction to Part Sixteen. Diaspora." *The Post-colonial Studies Reader.* 2nd ed. Ed. Bill Ashcroft, Gareth Griffiths, and Helen Tiffin. London and New York: Routledge, 2006. 425–27.

———. *Key Concepts in Post-colonial Studies.* London and New York: Routledge, 1998.

———. *The Post-colonial Studies Reader.* 2nd ed. Ed. Bill Ashcroft, Gareth Griffiths, and Helen Tiffin. London and New York: Routledge, 2006. 425–27.

Avery, Donald. *"Dangerous Foreigners": European Immigrant Workers and Labour Radicalism in Canada, 1896–1932.* Toronto: McClelland & Stewart, 1979.

Badami, Anita Rau. *Tamarind Mem.* Toronto: Penguin, 1996.

Bakan, Abigail B., and Daiva Stasiulus. "Negotiating Citizenship: The Case of Foreign Domestic Workers in Canada." *Feminist Review* 57 (Autumn 1997): 121–39.

Baldwin, Shauna Singh. *English Lessons and Other Stories.* 1996. New Delhi: HarperCollins, 1999.

———. *The Tiger Claw.* Toronto: Vintage Canada, 2005.

———. *What the Body Remembers.* Toronto: Vintage Canada, 2000.

———. *We Are Not in Pakistan.* Fredericton: Goose Lane, 2007.

Balzer, Geraldine. "'Bring[ing] Them Back from the Inside Out': Coming Home through Story in Richard Wagamese's *Keeper'n Me.*" *Essays in Canadian Writing* 83 (Fall 2004): 222–39.

Bannerji, Himani. *The Dark Side of the Nation: Essays on Multiculturalism, Nationalism, and Gender.* Toronto: Canadian Scholars', 2000.

———. *Thinking Through: Essays on Feminism, Marxism, and Anti-racism.* Toronto: Canadian Scholars' and Women's, 1995.

Base de Datos de Libros Publicados en España. Gobierno de España. Ministerio de Cultura. <http://www.mcu.es/libro/CE/AgenciaISBN/BBDDLibros/Sobre.html>.

Basil, Kenzie. "Editorial." *Indian* (September 1969): n.p.

Bates, Judy Fong. *China Dog and Other Tales from a Chinese Laundry.* Toronto: Sister Vision, 1997.

———. *Midnight at the Dragon Café.* Toronto: McClelland & Stewart, 2004.

Baucom, Ian. "Spectres of the Atlantic." *South Atlantic Quarterly* 100.1 (2001): 61–82.

Beach, Edward Allen. *The Potencies of God(s).* Albany: State U of New York P, 1994.

Beauregard, Guy. "Unsettled, unsettling." Rev. of Kerri Sakamoto's *The Electrical Field. Canadian Literature* 163 (1999): 191–93.

Belmore, Rebecca. "Vigil." Talking Stick Festival, Full Circle, First Nations Perform-ances. Firehall Theatre, Vancouver, BC, 2002. <http://www.rebeccabelmore.com/video/Vigil.html>.

Benjamin, Walter. "On the Concept of History." *Selected Writings (1938–1940)*. Ed. Howard Eiland and Michael W. Jennings. Trans. Edmund Jephcott et al. Vol. 4. Cambridge: Belknap, 2003. 389–400.

Berger, John. *A Seventh Man*. Photo. Jean Mohr. Harmondsworth: Penguin, 1975.

Bertelsmann AG. "Structure." <http://www.bertelsmann.com/bertelsmann_corp/wms41/bm/index.php?ci=1&language=2>.

Bhabha, Homi. *The Location of Culture*. New York and London: Routledge, 1994.

Bhandar, Davina. "Resistance, Detainment, Asylum: The Onto-Political Limits of Bor-der Crossing in North America." *War, Citizenship, Territory*. Ed. Deborah Cowen and Emily Gilbert. New York and London: Routledge, 2008. 281–302.

Birney, Earle. "The Universality of Abraham Klein." *Spreading Time*. Montreal: Vehicule, 1980.

"The Blackfoot Awareness Group's Logo." *Nitsitapi Newsletter* 2.1 (1994): 1.

Blaeser, Kimberly. "Native Literature: Seeking a Critical Center." *Looking at the Words of Our People: First Nations Analysis of Literature*. Ed. Jeannette Armstrong. Pentic-ton: Theytus, 1993. 53–61.

Bogel, Fredric V. "The Difference Satire Makes: Reading Swift's Poems." *Theorizing Sat-ire*. Ed. Brian A. Connery and Kirk Combe. New York: St. Martin's, 1995. 43–53.

Bourdieu, Pierre. *The Field of Cultural Production: Essays on Art and Literature*. Ed. Ran-dal Johnson. New York: Columbia UP, 1993.

Boyarin, Daniel, and Jonathan Boyarin. "Diaspora: Generation and the Ground of Jew-ish Identity." *Critical Inquiry* 19 (Summer 1993): 693–725.

———. *Powers of Diaspora*. Minneapolis: U of Minnesota P, 2002.

Boym, Svetlana. *The Future of Nostalgia*. New York: Basic Books, 2001.

Brah, Avtar. *Cartographies of Diaspora*. London: Routledge, 1996.

Brand, Dionne. *Bread Out of Stone*. Toronto: Vintage, 1998.

———. *Land to Light On*. Toronto: McClelland & Stewart, 1997.

———. "Notes for Writing thru Race." *Bread Out of Stone*. Toronto: Coach House, 1994. 173–80.

———. *What We All Long For*. Toronto: Vintage, 2005.

Braziel, Jana Evans, and Anita Mannur. "Nation, Migration, Globalization: Points of Contention in Diaspora Studies." *Theorizing Diaspora*. Ed. Jana Evans Braziel and Anita Mannur. Malden: Blackwell, 2003. 1–22.

Brennan, Timothy. *Wars of Position: Cultural Politics of the Left and Right*. New York: Columbia UP, 2006.

Brody, Hugh, dir. *The Meaning of Life*. Isuma Distribution International, 2008. Film.

Brooks, Lisa. "Afterword: At the Gathering Place." Weaver et al. 225–52.

———. *The Common Pot: The Recovery of Native Space in the Northeast*. Minneapolis: U of Minnesota P, 2008.

———. "Digging at the Roots: Locating an Ethical, Native Criticism." Womack et al. 234–64.

Brossard, Nicole. "Poetic Politics." *Fluid Arguments*. Toronto: Mercury, 2005. 26–36.

Brouillette, Sarah. "South Asian Literature and Global Publishing." *Wasafiri* 22.3 (2007): 34–38.

Brown, Lloyd W. *Eldorado and Paradise: Canada and the Caribbean in Austin Clarke's Fiction*. London: U of Western Ontario, 1989.

Brydon, Diana. "Introduction: Reading Postcoloniality, Reading Canada." *Essays on Canadian Writing* 56 (Fall 1995): 1–19.

———. "It's Time for a New Set of Questions." *Essays on Canadian Writing* 71 (2000): 14–25.

———. "Metamorphoses of a Discipline." *Trans.Can.Lit.: Resituating the Study of Canadian Literature*. Ed. Smaro Kamboureli and Roy Miki. Waterloo: Wilfrid Laurier UP, 2007. 1–16.

———. "Postcolonialism Now: Autonomy, Cosmopolitanism, and Diaspora." *University of Toronto Quarterly* 73.2 (Spring 2004): 691–706.

Burman, Jenny, ed. *Diasporic Pasts and Futures: Transnational Cultural Studies in Canada*. Special issue of *Topia* 17 (Spring 2007).

Butler, Judith. *Bodies That Matter: On the Discursive Limits of "Sex."* New York: Routledge, 1993.

———. "Critically Queer." *glq: A Journal of Lesbian and Gay Studies* 1 (1993): 17–32.

——— *Gender Trouble: Feminism and the Subversion of Identity*. New York: Routledge, 1990.

———. "Violence, Mourning, Politics." *Precarious Life*. London and New York: Verso, 2004. 19–49.

Campbell, Maria. *Halfbreed*. Toronto: McClelland & Stewart, 1973.

Canada. "An Act Respecting the Electoral Franchise." *Acts of the Parliament of the Dominion of Canada*. Parliament 5, Session 3. Ottawa: B. Chamberlin, 1885. 19–53.

———. *Official Report of the Debates of the House of Commons of the Dominion of Canada*. Vol. 18. Parliament 5, Session 3. Ottawa: MacLean, Roger, 1885.

———. "Relocation of Aboriginal Communities." *Looking Forward, Looking Back. Report of the Royal Commission of Aboriginal Peoples*. Vol. 1. Ottawa: Minister of Supply and Services, 1996. 411–543.

Canada Council for the Arts/Conseil des Arts du Canada. Grant Programs/Writing and Publishing/International Translation Grants. <http://www.canadacouncil.ca/grants/writing/wr127227348212968750.htm>.

Canadian Heritage/Patrimoine canadiene. "Cultural Affairs: Books." <http://www.pch.gc.ca/progs/ac-ca/pol/livre-book/index_e.cfm>.

Caputo, John D. *The Prayers and Tears of Jacques Derrida: Religion without Religion*. Bloomington: Indiana UP, 1997.

Chakrabarty, Dipesh. *Provincializing Europe*. Princeton: Princeton UP, 2000.

Chamberlin, J. Edward. *If This Is Your Land, Where Are Your Stories? Finding Common Ground*. Toronto: Alfred A. Knopf Canada, 2003.

Chambers, Cynthia, Dwayne Donald, and Erica Hasebe-Ludt. "Metissage." December 2002.<http://www.ccfi.educ.ubc.ca/publication/insights/v07n02/Métissage/Métiscript.html>.

Chan, Anthony B. *Gold Mountain: The Chinese in the New World.* Vancouver: New Star Books, 1983.

Chao, Lien. *Tiger Girl (Hu Nu): A Creative Memoir.* Toronto: TSAR, 2001.

Chao, Lien, and Jim Wong-Chu, eds. *Strike the Wok: An Anthology of Contemporary Chinese Canadian Fiction.* Toronto: TSAR, 2003.

Chariandy, David. "Postcolonial Diasporas." *Postcolonial Text* 2.1 (2006). <http://postcolonial.org/index.php/pct/article/view/440/159>. 39 pars.

———. *Soucouyant.* Vancouver: Arsenal Pulp, 2007.

Chariandy, David, and Sophie McCall, eds. *Citizenship and Cultural Belonging.* Special issue of *West Coast Line* 59.3 (2008).

Chatterjee, Partha. "Whose Imagined Community?" *Mapping the Nation.* Ed. Gopal Balakrishnan. London and New York: Verso and *New Left Review*, 1996. 214–25.

Cheah, Pheng. "Given Culture: Rethinking Cosmopolitical Freedom in Transnationalism." *Cosmopolitics.* Ed. Pheng Cheah and Bruce Robbins. Minneapolis: U of Minnesota P, 1998. 290–328.

———. "Obscure Gifts: On Jacques Derrida." *differences* 16.3 (2005): 41–51.

Cheng, Anne Anlin. *The Melancholy of Race.* New York: Oxford UP, 2001.

Cho, Charlie. "Asian-History Anniversaries Begin to Coalesce." *Georgia Straight* 21 September 2006. <http://www.straight.com/asian-history-anniversaries-begin-to-coalesce>.

Cho, Lily. "Diaporic Citzenship," *Trans.Can.Lit.* Ed. Smaro Kamboureli and Roy Miki. Waterloo: Wilfrid Laurier UP, 2007. 93–110.

———. "'How Taste Remembers Life': Diasporic Memory and Community in Fred Wah's *Diamond Grill.*" *Culture, Identity, Commodity: Diasporic Chinese Literatures in English.* Ed. Tseen Khoo and Kam Louie. Hong Kong: Hong Kong UP, 2005. 81–106.

———. "Rereading Chinese Head Tax Racism: Redress, Stereotype, and Antiracist Critical Practice." *Essays on Canadian Writing* 75 (Winter 2001): 62–86.

———. "The Turn to Diaspora." *Topia* 17 (2006): 11–29.

Chong, Denise. *The Concubine's Children: Portrait of a Family Divided.* Toronto: Viking, 1994.

Clarke, Austin. *The Bigger Light.* Toronto: Little, Brown, 1975.

———. *The Meeting Point.* Toronto: Macmillan, 1967.

———. *Nine Men Who Laughed.* Markham: Penguin Books Canada, 1986.

———. *Storm of Fortune.* Toronto: Little, Brown, 1971.

———. "The West Indian in Canada." 1962. Box 20, F.5, Austin Clarke Papers. McMaster U, Hamilton.

———. "West Indian Domestics: Canada's Loneliest Immigrants." 1962. Box 20, F.5, Austin Clarke Papers. McMaster U, Hamilton.

———. *When He Was Free and Young and He Used to Wear Silks.* Toronto: Anansi, 1971.

Clifford, James. "Diasporas." *Cultural Anthropology* 9.3 (1994): 302–38.

———. "Diasporas." *Routes: Travel and Translation in the Late Twentieth Century.* Cambridge: Harvard UP, 1997. 244–77.

Cohen, Robin. *Global Diasporas*. 2nd ed. London and New York: Routledge, 2008.

Coleman, Daniel. "Austin Clarke." *Encyclopedia of Literature in Canada*. Ed. W.H. New. Toronto: U of Toronto P, 2002. 208.

———. *Masculine Migrations*. Toronto: U of Toronto P, 1998.

———. *White Civility*. Toronto: U of Toronto P, 2006.

"Commemoration." *Oxford English Dictionary*. 2nd ed. 1989. <http://dictionary.oed .com/cgi/entry/50044860?single=1&query_type=word&queryword=commemorat ion&first=1&max_to_show=10>.

"Court Hears from Victims' Families." *Globe and Mail* 11 December 2007. <http://www .theglobeandmail.com/servlet/story/RTGAM.20071211.wpi/>.

Cox, James. *Muting White Noise: Native American and European American Novel Traditions*. Norman: U of Oklahoma P, 2006.

Cresswell, Tim. "Introduction. Theorizing Place." *Mobilizing Place, Placing Mobility. Theories of Representation in a Globalized World*. Ed. Ginette Verstraete and Tim Cresswell. New York: Rodopi, 2002. 11–31.

Cruikshank, Julie. *Social Life of Stories: Narrative and Knowledge in the Yukon Territory*. Lincoln and London: U of Nebraska P, 1998.

Cuder-Domínguez, Pilar. "Portraits of the Artist in Dionne Brand's *What We All Long for* (2005) and Madeleine Thien's *Certainty* (2006)." <http://myuminfo.umanitoba .ca/Documents/i2099/CuderPvv.pdf>.

Culhane, Dara. *The Pleasure of the Crown: Anthropology, Law, and First Nations*. Burnaby: Talon Books, 1998.

Dahab, Elizabeth, ed. *Voices in the Desert: An Anthology of Arabic-Canadian Women Writers*. Toronto: Guernica, 2002.

Davey, Frank. "Uneasy Companions: Canadian, Cultural, and Postcolonial Studies in Canada." Unpublished lecture delivered at the 31st Annual Conference of the Spanish Association for English and American Studies AEDEAN. A Coruña: Universidade da Coruña, 14–17 November 2007.

Davis, Rocio G. *Transcultural Reinventions: Asian American and Asian Canadian Short-Story Cycles*. Toronto: TSAR, 2001.

Daychief, Vic. "Free Spirit A.A." *Arrows to Freedom* (Summer 1993): 7.

de Botton, Alain. *The Art of Travel*. London: Penguin, 2002.

Deleuze, Gilles, and Félix Guattari. *Capitalisme et Schizophrénie. Mille Plateaux*. Paris: Les Éditions de minuit, 1980.

Denning, Michael. *The Cultural Front*. London: Verso, 1997.

Dennis, Kenneth V. "Why Settle the BC Land Question?" *Indian Echo* (January 1971): 1–4.

Derrida, Jacques. *Given Time: I. Counterfeit Money*. Trans. Peggy Kamuf. Chicago: U of Chicago P, 1992.

Dickinson, Peter. *Here Is Queer: Nationalisms, Sexualities, and the Literatures of Canada*. Toronto: U of Toronto P, 1999.

———. *Screening Gender, Framing Genre: Canadian Literature into Film*. Toronto: U of Toronto P, 2007.

Dirlik, Arif. *Postmodernity's Histories*. Lanham: Rowman & Littlefield, 2000.

———. "Race Talk, Race, and Contemporary Racism." *PMLA* 123.5 (2008): 1363–79.

Doubleday Publishing Group. "Our Imprints." <http://doubleday.com/imprints/>.

Driskill, Qwo-Li. "'Call Me Brother': Two-Spiritedness, the Erotic, and Mixedblood Identity as Sites of Sovereignty and Resistance in Gregory Scofield's Poetry." *Speak to Me Words: Essays on Contemporary Indian Poetry*. Ed. Dean Rader and Janice Gould. Tucson: U of Arizona P, 2003. 222–34.

Dudek, Louis. "A.M Klein." *A.M. Klein*. Toronto: Ryerson P, 1970. 66–74.

Dunlop, Rishma, and Priscilla Uppal, eds. *Red Silk: An Anthology of South Asian Canadian Women Poets*. Toronto: Mansfield, 2004.

Ek, Auli. *Race and Masculinity in Contemporary American Prison Narratives*. New York: Routledge, 2005.

Elden, Stuart. "The State of Territory under Globalization." Margaroni and Yiannopoulous 47–66.

Elgersma, Sandra. "Temporary Foreign Workers." *Library of Parliament, Parliamentary Information, and Research Service*. 7 September 2007. Web. 19 June 2008. <http://www.parl.gc.ca/Content/LOP/ResearchPublications/prb0711-e.htm>.

Eliot, T.S. "Tradition and the Individual Talent." *The Norton Anthology of Theory and Criticism*. Ed. Vincent B. Leitch. New York: Norton, 2001. 1092–98.

Emberley, Julia. *Defamiliarizing the Aboriginal: Cultural Practices and Decolonization in Canada*. 2007. Toronto: U of Toronto P, 2009.

———. "Economies of Dissimulation: The Western Bourgeois Woman and the Limits of Libidinal Power." *Topia* 13 (Spring 2005): 55–72.

Eng, David. "The End(s) of Race." *PMLA* 123.5 (2008): 1479–93.

Eng, David L., and David Kazanjian. "Introduction: Mourning Remains." *Loss*. Ed. David L. Eng and David Kazanjian. Berkeley and Los Angeles: U of California P, 2003. 1–25.

Fagan, Kristina. "Tewatatha:wi: Aboriginal Nationalism in Taiaiake Alfred's *Peace, Power, Righteousness: An Indigenous Manifesto*." *American Indian Quarterly* 28.1 and 2 (2004): 12–29.

Fagan, Kristina, and Sam McKegney. "Circling the Question of Nationalism in Native Canadian Literature and Its Study." *Review* 41.1 (May 2008): 31–42.

Fanon, Frantz. *Black Skin, White Masks*. New York: Grove, 1967.

———. *Les damnés de la terre*. Paris: François Maspero éditeur, 1961.

Fee, Margery. "Writing Orality: Interpreting Literature in English by Aboriginal Writers in North America, Australia, and New Zealand." *Journal of Intercultural Studies* 18.1 (1997): 23–39.

Felman, Shoshana, and Dori Laub. *Testimony: Crisis of Witnessing in Literature, Psychoanalysis, and History*. New York: Routledge, 1992.

Feltes, Norman N. *Modes of Production of Victorian Novels*. Chicago and London: U of Chicago P, 1986.

Fingard, Judith. "The Winter's Tale: The Seasonal Contours of Pre-industrial Poverty in British North America, 1815–1860." *Canadian Working Class History*. Ed. Laurel Sefton MacDowell and Ian Radforth. Toronto: Canadian Scholars', 1992. 81–105.

Flotow, Luise von. "Revealing the 'Soul of Which Nation?': Translated Literature as
    Cultural Diplomacy." In *Translation—Reflections, Refractions, Transformations*. Ed.
    Paul St.-Pierre and Prafulla C. Kar. Amsterdam: John Benjamins, 2007. 187–200.

Folson, Rose Baaba, ed. *Calculated Kindness: Global Restructuring, Immigration, and
    Settlement in Canada*. Halifax: Fernwood, 2004.

Foster, Cecil. "A Long Sojourn." Interview with Donna Nurse. *Books in Canada* 24.6
    (September 1995): 18–21.

———. *A Place Called Heaven*. Toronto: HarperCollins, 1996.

———. *Slammin' Tar*. Toronto: Random House, 1998.

Foucault, Michel. "Of Other Spaces." Trans. Jay Miskowiec. *Diacritics* (Spring 1986):
    22–27.

Fournier, Suzanne, and Ernie Crey. *Stolen from Our Embrace: The Abduction of First
    Nations Children and the Restoration of Aboriginal Communities*. Vancouver: Douglas
    & McIntyre, 1997.

Frank, Anne. *Diary of a Young Girl: The Definitive Edition*. Ed. Otto Frank. New York:
    Doubleday, 1995.

Freud, Sigmund. "Mourning and Melancholia." *Collected Papers*. Trans. Joan Rivière.
    Vol. 4. New York: Basic Books, 1959. 152–70.

———. "The Uncanny." *Writings on Art and Literature*. Ed. James Strachey. Stanford:
    Stanford UP, 1997. 192–233.

Gagnon, Monika Kin. *Other Conundrums: Race, Culture, and Canadian Art*. Vancouver:
    Arsenal, 2000.

Gagnon, Monika Kin, and Richard Fung, eds. *13 Conversations about Art and Cultural
    Race Politics*. Montreal: Artextes Editions, 2002.

Gandhi, Leela. *Postcolonial Theory: A Critical Introduction*. New York: Columbia UP,
    1998.

Ganguly, Keya. *States of Exception: Everyday Life and Postcolonial Identity*. Minneapolis:
    U of Minnesota P, 2001.

Ghatage, Shree. *Awake When All the World Is Asleep*. Toronto: Anansi, 1997.

———. *Brahma's Dream*. Toronto: Doubleday, 2004.

Gilroy, Paul. *Against Race: Imagining Political Culture beyond the Color Line*. Cambridge:
    Harvard UP, 2000.

———. *The Black Atlantic*. Cambridge: Harvard UP, 1993.

Glissant, Édouard. *Poetics of Relation*. Trans. Betsy Wing. Ann Arbor: U of Michigan
    P, 1997.

Godard, Barbara. *Canadian Literature at the Crossroads of Language and Culture*. Edmon-
    ton: NeWest, 2008.

———. "Notes from the Cultural Field: Canadian Literature from Identity to Hybrid-
    ity." *Essays on Canadian Writing* 72 (2000): 209–47.

Goellnicht, Donald. "Asian Kanadian, Eh?" *Canadian Literature* 199 (2008): 71–99.

Goffman, Erving. *The Presentation of Self in Everyday Life*. Garden City: Doubleday,
    1959.

Gopinath, Gayatri. *Impossible Desires: Queer Diasporas and South Asian Public Cultures*.
    Durham and London: Duke UP, 2005.

————. "Nostalgia, Desire, Diaspora: South Asian Sexualities in Motion." *Theorizing Diaspora*. Ed. Jana Evans Braziel and Anita Mannur. Malden: Blackwell Publishing, 2003. 261–90.

Goto, Hiromi. *Hopeful Monsters*. Vancouver: Arsenal Pulp, 2004.

————. *The Kappa Child*. Calgary: Red Deer, 2001.

Green, Joyce. "Constitutionalizing the Patriarchy: Aboriginal Women and Aboriginal Government." *Expressions of Canadian Native Studies*. Ed. Ron LaLiberte et al. Saskatoon: U Extension P, 2000. 328–53.

Grewal, Inderpal, and Caren Kaplan. *Scattered Hegemonies: Postmodernity and Transnational Feminist Practices*. Minneapolis: U of Minnesota P, 1994.

Gunew, Sneja. *Haunted Nations: The Colonial Dimensions of Multiculturalisms*. London: Routledge, 2004.

Gupta, Nila. *The Sherpa and Other Fictions*. Toronto: Sumach, 2008.

Habib, Jasmin. *Routes of Belonging*. Toronto: U of Toronto P, 2004.

Halberstam, Judith. "F2M: The Making of Female Masculinity." *The Lesbian Postmodern*. Ed. Laura Doan. New York: Columbia UP, 1994. 210–28.

————. *In a Queer Time & Place: Transgender Bodies, Subcultural Lives*. New York: New York UP, 2005.

Hage, Ghassan. *Against Paranoid Nationalism: Searching for Hope in a Shrinking Society*. London: Merlin, 2003.

Hall, Stuart. "Cultural Identity and Diaspora." *Identity: Community, Culture, Difference*. Ed. Jonathan Rutherford. London: Lawrence and Wishart, 1990. 222–37.

Hanley, Wayne. *The Status of Migrant Farm Workers in Canada, 2008–2009*. Rexdale: UFCW Canada and the Agricultural Workers Alliance, 2009.

Hardt, Michael, and Antonio Negri. *Empire*. Cambridge: Harvard UP, 2000.

Harney, Robert. "Men without Women: Italian Migrants in Canada, 1885–1930." *A Nation of Immigrants: Women, Workers, and Communities in Canadian History, 1840s–1960s*. Ed. Franca Iacovetta with Paula Draper and Robert Ventresca. Toronto: U of Toronto P, 1998. 206–30.

Harris, Cole. *Making Native Space: Colonialism, Resistance, and Reserves in British Columbia*. Vancouver: UBC P, 2002.

Harris, Wilson. "History, Fable, and Myth in the Caribbean and Guianas." *Selected Essays of Wilson Harris*. Ed. A.J.M. Bundy. London: Routledge, 1999. 152–66.

Harting, Heike. "The Poetics of Vulnerability: Diaspora, Race, and Global Citizenship in A.M. Klein's *The Second Scroll* and Dionne Brand's *Thirsty*." *Studies in Canadian Literature* 32.2 (2007): 177–99.

Heaven Knows Mr. Allison. Dir. John Huston. Perfs. Deborah Kerr and Robert Mitchum. DVD. Twentieth-Century Fox, 1957; dist. Fox Home Entertainment, 2003.

Highway, Tomson. *The Rez Sisters*. Saskatoon: Fifth House, 1988.

Hirsch, Marianne. *Family Frames*. Cambridge and London: Harvard UP, 1997.

————. "The Generation of Postmemory." *Poetics Today* 29.1 (Spring 2008): 103–28.

————. "Surviving Images: Holocaust Photographs and the Work of Postmemory." *The Yale Journal of Criticism* 14.1 (2001): 5–37.

Hobson, Geary. *The Remembered Earth: An Anthology of Contemporary Native American Literature*. Albuquerque: Red Earth, 1979.

Hoerder, Dirk. *Labor Migration in the Atlantic Economies: The European and North American Working Classes during the Period of Industrialization*. Westport: Greenwood, 1985.

Hopkinson, Nalo. *Skin Folk*. New York: Warner Aspect, 2001.

Hountondji, Paulin J. *African Philosophy: Myth and Reality*. Trans. Henri Evans. 1983. Bloomington and Indianapolis: Indiana UP, 1996.

Hoy, Helen. *How Should I Read These? Native Women's Writing in Canada*. Toronto: U of Toronto P, 2001.

Huggan, Graham. *The Post-colonial Exotic: Marketing the Margins*. London and New York: Routledge, 2001.

Hutcheon, Linda. "Circling the Downspout of Empire." *Ariel* 20.4 (1989): 149–75.

Islands. Dir. Richard Fung. Videocassette. Fungus Productions, 2002.

Jacobs, Beverley, and Andrea J. Williams. "Legacy of Residential Schools: Missing and Murdered Aboriginal Women." *From Truth to Reconciliation: Transforming the Legacy of Residential Schools*. Ed. Marlene Brant Castellano, Linda Archibald, and Mike DeGagné. Ottawa: Aboriginal Healing Foundation, 2008. 119–40.

Jiwani, Yasmin. "The Exotic, the Erotic, and the Dangerous: South Asian Women in Popular Film." *Canadian Woman Studies/Les cahiers de la femme* 13.1 (1992): 42–46.

Jiwani, Yasmin, and Mary Lynn Young. "Missing and Murdered Women: Reproducing Marginality in News Discourse." *Canadian Journal of Communication* 31 (2006): 895–917.

Joe, Rita, with the assistance of Lynn Henry. *Song of Rita Joe*. Charlottetown: Ragweed, 1996.

Jonas, Joyce. *Anancy in the Great House*. New York: Greenwood, 1990.

Jones, R.D. "A War of Words." *Indian Echo* (March 1970): 8.

Justice, Daniel Heath, panelist. "Canadian Indian Literary Nationalism? Examining Literary Nationalist Approaches in Canadian Indigenous Contexts." A roundtable organized by the Canadian Association of Commonwealth Literature and Language Studies (CACLALS). Congress 2008, University of British Columbia, 1 June 2008.

———. *Dreyd: The Way of Thorn and Thunder, Book Two*. Wiarton: Kegedonce, 2007.

———. "'Go away, Water!': Kinship Criticism and the Decolonization Imperative." Womack et al. 147–68.

———. *Kynship: The Way of Thorn and Thunder, Book One*. Wiarton: Kegedonce, 2005.

———. "The Necessity of Nationhood: Affirming the Sovereignty of Indigenous National Literatures." *Moveable Margins*. Ed. Chelva Kanaganayakam. Toronto: TSAR, 2005. 143–59.

———. *Our Fire Survives the Storm: A Cherokee Literary History*. Minneapolis: U of Minnesota P, 2006.

———. *Wyrwood: The Way of Thorn and Thunder, Book Two*. Wiarton: Kegedonce, 2006.

Kalb, Don. "After Hybridity." *Focaal* 47 (2006): v–vii.

Kamboureli, Smaro. "Preface." *Trans.Can.Lit.: Resituating the Study of Canadian Literature*. Ed. Smaro Kamboureli and Roy Miki. Waterloo: Wilfrid Laurier UP, 2007. vii–xv.

———. *Scandalous Bodies: Diasporic Literature in English Canada*. Don Mills: Oxford UP, 2000.

Kamboureli, Smaro, and Fred Wah. "Shrink Wrapped: The National Packaging of Race Writing." *National Literatures in English and the Global Market*. Ed. Belén Martín-Lucas and Ana Bringas López. *The Atlantic Literary Review* 2.4 (2001): 132–40.

Kaplan, Caren. *Questions of Travel*. Durham: Duke UP, 1996.

Kim, Christine. "Troubling the Mosaic: Larissa Lai's *When Fox Is a Thousand*, Shani Mootoo's *Cereus Blooms at Night*, and Representations of Social Differences." *Asian Canadian Writing beyond Autoethnography*. Ed. Eleanor Ty and Christl Verduyn. Waterloo: Wilfrid Laurier UP, 2008. 153–77.

King, Thomas. "Godzilla vs. Post-colonial." *World Literature Written in English* 30.2 (1990): 10–16.

King, W.L. Mackenzie. *Report by W.L. Mackenzie King, C.M.G., Deputy Minister of Labour, Commissioner Appointed to Investigate into the Losses Sustained by the Chinese Population of Vancouver, BC, on the Occasion of the Riots in That City in September, 1907*. Ottawa: S.E. Dawson, 1908.

———. *Report by W.L. Mackenzie King, C.M.G., Deputy Minister of Labour, Commissioner Appointed to Investigate into the Losses Sustained by the Japanese Population of Vancouver, BC, on the Occasion of the Riots in That City in September, 1907*. Ottawa: S.E. Dawson, 1908.

Kirman, Paula E. "Cultural Selves: An Interview with Richard Wagamese." *Paragraph: The Canadian Fiction Review* 20.1 (1998): 2–5.

Klein, A.M. *Hath Not a Jew ...* New York: Behrman: 1940.

———. *The Rocking Chair and Other Poems*. Toronto: Ryerson, 1948.

Kogawa, Joy. *Obasan*. 1981. Toronto: Penguin Canada, 2003.

Kristeva, Julia. *Nations without Nationalism*. Trans. Leon S. Roudiez. New York: Columbia UP, 1993.

Kulchyski, Peter. *Like the Sound of a Drum: Aboriginal Cultural Politics in Denendeh and Nunavut*. Winnipeg: U of Manitoba P, 2005.

Kwa, Lydia. *This Place Called Absence*. Winnipeg: Turnstone, 2000.

LaCapra, Dominick. *Representing the Holocaust: History, Theory, Trauma*. Ithaca and London: Cornell UP, 1994.

———. *Writing History, Writing Trauma*. Ithaca: Cornell UP, 1996.

Ladha, Yasmin. *Lion's Granddaughter and Other Stories*. Edmonton: NeWest, 1992.

———. *Women Dancing on Rooftops. Bring Your Belly Close*. Toronto: Coach House, 1997.

Lai, Larissa. "Brand Canada: Oppositional Politics, Global Flows, and a People to Come." *Reading(s) from a Distance: European Perspectives on Canadian Women's Writing*. Ed. Charlotte von Sturgess and Martin Kuester. Augsburg: Wissner-Verlag, 2008. 23–32.

————. "Community Action, Global Spillage: Writing the Race of Capital." *West Coast Line* 59.3 (Fall 2008): 116–28.

————. "Corrupted Lineage: Narrative in the Gaps of History." *In-Equations: can asia pacific*. Ed. Glen Lowry and Sook C. Kong. *West Coast Line* 34.3 (2001): 40–53.

————. "Political Animals and the Body of History." *Canadian Literature* 163 (1999): 145–54.

————. *Salt Fish Girl*. Toronto: Thomas Allen, 2002.

————. "Strategizing the Body of History. Anxious Writing, Absent Subjects, and Marketing the Nation." *Asian Canadian Writing beyond Autoethnography*. Ed. Eleanor Ty and Christl Verduyn. Waterloo: Wilfrid Laurier UP, 2008. 87–114.

————. *When Fox Is a Thousand*. Vancouver: Press Gang, 1995.

LaRocque, Emma. "The Métis in English Canadian Literature." *Canadian Journal of Native Studies* 3.1: 85–94.

————. "Native Identity and the Métis: Otehpayimsuak Peoples." *A Passion for Identity: Canadian Studies for the 21st Century*. Ed. David Taras and Beverly Rasprich. Scarborough: Nelson Thomson Learning, 2001. 381–99.

————. "Teaching Aboriginal Literature: The Discourse of Margins and Mainstreams." *Creating Community: A Roundtable on Canadian Aboriginal Literature*. Ed. Renate Eigenbrod and Jo-Ann Episkenew. Penticton: Theytus, 2002. 209–34.

Laugrand, Frédéric, and Jarich Oosten, eds. *Introduction*. Iqaluit: Nunavut Arctic College, 1999. Interviewing Inuit Elders 1.

Laugrand, Frédéric, Jarich Oosten, and Wim Rasing, eds. *Perspectives on Traditional Law*. Iqaluit: Nunavut Arctic College, 2000. Interviewing Inuit Elders 2.

Lawrence, Bonita. *"Real" Indians and Others: Mixed-Blood Urban Native Peoples and Indigenous Nationhood*. Vancouver: UBC P, 2004.

————. "Rewriting Histories of the Land: Colonization and Indigenous Resistance in Eastern Canada." *Race, Space, and the Law: Unmapping a White Settler Society*. Ed. Sherene H. Razack. Toronto: Between the Lines, 2002. 21–48.

Lee, Erika. "Hemispheric Orientalism and the 1907 Pacific Coast Race Riots." *Amerasia Journal* 33.2 (2007): 19–47.

Lee, Nancy. *Dead Girls*. Toronto: McClelland & Stewart, 2002.

Lee, SKY. *Bellydancer Stories*. Vancouver: Press Gang, 1994.

————. *Disappearing Moon Cafe*. Vancouver: Douglas & McIntyre, 1990.

Li, Xiaoping. *Voices Rising: Asian Canadian Cultural Activism*. Vancouver and Toronto: UBC P, 2007.

Lim, Song Hwee. "Is the Trans- in Transnational the Trans- in Transgender?" *New Cinema: Journal of Contemporary Film* 5.1 (2007): 39–52.

Mackey, Eva. *The House of Difference: Cultural Politics and National Identity in Canada*. London and New York: Routledge, 1999.

Maclear, Kyo. *Beclouded Visions*. Albany: State U of New York P, 1999.

————. *The Letter Opener*. Toronto: HarperCollins Publishers, 2007.

————. "Race to the Page: Positioning as a Writer of 'Mixed Race.'" *Resources for Feminist Research* 24.1–2 (1995): 14–22.

Malkki, Liisa. "National Geographic: The Rooting of Peoples and the Territorializa-
tion of National Identity among Scholars and Refugees." *Cultural Anthropology* 7.1
(1992): 24–44.

Mara, Rachna. *Of Customs and Excise*. Toronto: Second Story, 1991.

———. *Entre o costume e a ruptura*. Trans. María Reimóndez. Vigo: Xerais, 1998.

Maracle, Lee. *I Am Woman: A Native Perspective on Sociology and Feminism*. 2nd ed.
Vancouver: Press Gang, 1996.

———. "Oratory on Oratory." *Trans.Can.Lit: Resituating the Study of Canadian Literature*. Ed. Smaro Kamboureli and Roy Miki. Waterloo: Wilfrid Laurier UP, 2007.
55–70.

———. "Ramparts Hanging in the Air." *Telling It: Women and Language across Cultures*. Ed. Telling It Book Collective. Vancouver: Press Gang, 1990. 161–75.

Maracle, Sylvia. "The Eagle Has Landed: Native Women, Leadership, and Community
Development." *Strong Women's Stories: Native Vision and Community Survival*. Ed.
Kim Anderson and Bonita Lawrence. Toronto: Sumach, 2003. 70–80.

Margaroni, Maria, and Effie Yiannopoulou, eds. *Metaphoricity and the Politics of Mobility*.
Amsterdam: Rodopi, 2006.

Marlatt, Daphne. "In the Feminine." *In the Feminine: Women and Words Conference
Proceedings*. Ed. Daphne Marlatt, Barbara Pulling, Victoria Freeman, and Betsy
Warland. Edmonton: Longspoon, 1983. 11–17.

Martín-Lucas, Belén. "Indo Canadian Women's Fiction in English: Feminist Anti-
racist Politics and Poetics Resist Indo-Chic." *Transnational Poetics: Asian Canadian
Women's Fiction of the 1990s*. Pilar Cuder-Domínguez, Belén Martín-Lucas, and
Sonia Villegas-López. Toronto: TSAR, 2011. 3–43.

———. "Metaphors of the (M)Otherland: The Rhetoric and Grammar of National-
ism." *Leur na-rration: narration au féminin de la nation canadienne/Her Na-rra-tion,
Women's Narratives of the Canadian Nation*. Ed. Françoise Le Jeune and Charlotte
Sturgess. Nantes: Les Éditions du CRINI-Université de Nantes, 2009. 105–15.

Martínez-Zalce, Graciela. "¿Es visible la cultura canadiense." *Hoja por Hoja. Suplemento
de Libros* 137 (October 2008). <http://www.hojaporhoja.com.mx/articulo3.php?
identificador=6839&reportaje=1&numero=135>.

———. "Exporting Canadian Literature for Mexican Readers: The Vagaries of Translation in the Age of Globalization." *Topia* 5 (Spring 2001): 61–74. <https://pi.library
.yorku.ca/ojs/index.php/topia/article/viewFile/106/98>.

Massey, Doreen. *Space, Place, and Gender*. Cambridge: Polity, 1994.

Massumi, Brian. "Navigating Movements." *Hope: New Philosophies for Change*. Ed. and
interviewer Mary Zournazi. New York: Routledge, 2003. 210–42.

Matas, Robert. "Pickton Shows No Emotion to Guilty Verdict." *Globe and Mail*
10 December 2007: A1+.

Matthews, John. "Abraham Klein and the Problem of Synthesis." *A.M. Klein*. Toronto:
Ryerson P, 1970.

Mathur, Ashok. "Transubracination: How Writers of Colour Became CanLit." *Trans.
Can.Lit.: Resituating the Study of Canadian Literature*. Ed. Smaro Kamboureli and
Roy Miki. Waterloo: Wilfrid Laurier UP, 2007. 141–51.

Maxwell, Rachael. "The Place of Arts and Culture in Canadian Foreign Policy." Canadian Conference of the Arts/Conférence canadienne des arts. <http://www.ccarts.ca/fr/events/documents/PDS-BackgrounddocumentENGFINALgs27.09.07.pdf>.

Mayr, Suzette. *Moon Honey*. Edmonton: NeWest, 1995.

———. *Venous Hum*. Vancouver: Arsenal Pulp, 2005.

McAllister, Kirsten E. "Narrating Japanese Canadians In and Out of the Canadian Nation: A Critique of Realist Forums of Representation." *Canadian Journal of Communication* 24.1 (Winter 1999): 79–103.

McClelland & Stewart. "McClelland.com: About Us." <http://www.mcclelland.com/about/index.html>.

McFarlane, Scott Toguri. "The Haunt of Race: Canada's *Multiculturalism Act*, the Politics of Incorporation, and Writing thru Race." *Fuse Magazine* 18.3 (1995): 18–31.

McGifford, Diane, and Judith Kearns, eds. *Shakti's Words: An Anthology of South Asian Canadian Women's Poetry*. Toronto: TSAR, 1993.

McKegney, Sam. *Magic Weapons: Aboriginal Writers Remaking Community after Residential School*. Winnipeg: U of Manitoba P, 2007.

McLeod, Neal. "Coming Home through Stories." *(Ad)dressing Our Words*. Ed. Armand Garnet Ruffo. Penticton: Theytus Books, 2001. 17–36.

McMaster, Gerald, and Clifford E. Trafzer. *Native Universe: Voices of Indian America*. Washington, DC: National Museum of the American Indian, 2004.

McNeil, Kent. *Defining Aboriginal Title in the 90s: Has the Supreme Court Finally Got It Right?* Toronto: York U, Robarts Centre for Canadian Studies, 1998.

Mehta, Deepa, dir. *Bollywood/Hollywood*. Bollywood/Hollywood Productions Inc., 2002.

Mehta, Gita. *Karma Cola. Marketing the Mystic East*. New York: Vintage, 1994.

Mickleburgh, Rod. "Guilty Verdicts Make for a Bittersweet Day." *The Globe and Mail* 10 December 2007: A16.

Miki, Roy. *Broken Entries*. Toronto: Mercury, 1998.

———. "Can Asian Adian? Reading the Scenes of 'Asian Canadian.'" *West Coast Line* 34.3 (2001): 56–77.

———. "Globalization, (Canadian) Culture, and Critical Pedagogy: A Primer." *Home-Work: Postcolonialism, Pedagogy, and Canadian Literature*. Ed. Cynthia Sugars. Ottawa: U of Ottawa P, 2004. 87–100.

——— *Redress: Inside the Japanese Canadian Call for Justice*. Vancouver: Raincoast Books, 2004.

Miller, Eric. "Tasting the Dirt Again." Rev. of *Dream Wheels. Books in Canada* 36.1 (January/February 2007): 5–6.

Miller, Susan A. "Native America Writes Back: The Origin of the Indigenous Paradigm in Historiography." *Wicazo Sa Review* 23.2 (2008): 9–28.

Momaday, N. Scott. "The Man Made of Words." *Literature of the American Indians*. New York: New American Library, 1975. 96–110.

Mootoo, Shani. *Cereus Blooms at Night*. 1996. Toronto: McClelland & Stewart, 1998.

Moses, Daniel David, and Terry Goldie, eds. *An Anthology of Canadian Native Literature in English*. 3rd ed. Don Mills: Oxford UP, 2005.

Moss, Laura, ed. *Is Canada Postcolonial? Unsettling Canadian Literature*. Waterloo: Wilfrid Laurier UP, 2003.

Moure, Erín. *Little Theatres (teatriños) ou/or aturuxos calados*. Toronto: Anansi, 2005.

———. *Teatriños ou Aturuxos Calados*. Trans. María Reimóndez. Vigo: Galaxia, 2007.

Mukherjee, Arun. *Postcolonialism: My Living*. Toronto: TSAR, 1998.

Namaste, Viviane. *Sex Change, Social Change: Reflections on Identity, Institutions, and Imperialism*. Toronto: Women's, 2005.

Niessen, Sandra, Ann Marie Leshkowich, and Carla Jones. *Re-orienting Fashion: The Globalization of Asian Dress*. New York: Berg, 2003.

Nungak, Zebedee. "Contemplating an Inuit Presence in Literature." *Windspeaker* 22.1 (2004): 21, 26.

Omi, Michael, and Howard Winant. *Racial Formation in the United States*. New York: Routledge, 1986.

"100 Years of Change: from Race Riots to TransPacific Canada." *Anniversaries of Change*. 2007. <http://www.anniversaries07.ca/vision.php>.

Osteen, Mark, ed. *The Question of the Gift: Essays across Disciplines*. New York: Routledge, 2002.

Parameswaran, Uma. *The Forever Banyan Tree*. Winnipeg: Larkuma, 2007.

———. *Mangoes on the Maple Tree*. Fredericton: Broken Jaw, 2002.

Paul, Benjamin. "In Search of My Warrior." *Out of Bounds* (Fall 2005): 16–18.

Pawis, Daniel Beatty. "Brotherhood ... Realizing Our Purpose." *Drumheller Native Brotherhood Newsletter* (Summer 1984): 8–9.

———. "A Dedication to the Warrior Spirit." *Arrows to Freedom* (Summer 1996): 1.

———. "Inside the Iron Tipi." *Arrows to Freedom* (Summer 1996): 28–30.

"A Peaceful Place to Mourn." *Globe and Mail* 19 January 2008. <http://www.theglobeandmail.com/servlet/story/RTGAM.20081901.wpi/>.

Peltier, Leonard. *Prison Writings: My Life Is My Sun Dance*. New York: St. Martin's, 1999.

Le petit Robert: dictionnaire de la langue française. Paris: Dictionnaires Le Robert, 1996.

Petrone, Penny, ed. *First People, First Voices*. Toronto: U of Toronto P, 1983.

Philip, M. Nourbese. *Frontiers: Essays and Writings on Racism and Culture*. Toronto: Mercury, 1992.

"The Pickton Letters: In His Own Words." *Vancouver Sun* 10 December 2007. CanWest MediaWorks Publications, Inc. <http://www.canada.com/>.

"The Politics of Freedom." *Arrows to Freedom* (Summer 1996): 3–4.

Pollock, Zailig. *A.M. Klein, Complete Poems*. Ed. Zailig Pollock. Toronto: U of Toronto P, 1990.

Popham, E.A. "A.M. Klein, the Impulse to Define." *Canadian Literature* 79 (1978): 5–17.

Price, John. "'Orienting' the Empire: Mackenzie King and the Aftermath of the 1907 Race Riots." *BC Studies* 156/157 (Winter 2007/Spring 2008): 53–81.

"A Prison Prayer." *Arrows to Freedom* (Summer 1996): 1.

Prosser, Jay. *Second Skins: The Body Narratives of Transsexuality*. New York: Columbia UP, 1998.

Pulitano, Elvira. *Toward a Native American Critical Theory*. Lincoln: U of Nebraska P, 2003.

Rahman, Shazia. "Marketing the Mem: The Packaging and Selling of a First Novel." *Toronto Review of Contemporary Writing Abroad* 18.1 (Fall 1999): 86–99.

Random House Canada "RandomHouse.ca: About Us." <http://www.randomhouse.ca/about/index.html>.

Random House Inc. "Our Publishers." <http://www.randomhouse.biz/ourpublishers/>.

Ray, Amit. *Negotiating the Modern: Orientalism and Indianness in the Anglophone World*. New York and London: Routledge, 2007.

"A Reaffirmation." *Powell Street Review* 1.1 (1972): 2–3.

"Real Power, Aboriginal Women—Past, Present, and Future." *The Moxie* 1.2 (1998): n.p.

Renan, Ernst. "What Is a Nation?" *Nation and Narration*. Ed. Homi K. Bhabha. Trans. Martin Thom. New York: Routledge, 1990. 8–22.

Rimstead, Roxanne. "Working-Class Intruders: Female Domestics in *Kamouraska* and *Alias Grace*." *Canadian Literature* 175 (Winter 2002): 44–65.

Roberts, David. "Native Convicts Share Fears, Dreams at 'Parallel Constitutional Hearings.'" *Globe and Mail* 30 January 1992: A6. Rpt. in *The Native Brotherhood Newsletter* (Fall 1992): 9–10.

Roberts, Susan, Anna Secor, and Matthew Sparke. "Neoliberal Geopolitics." *Antipode* 35.5 (2003): 886–97.

Roy, Patricia E. *A White Man's Province: British Columbia Politicians and Chinese and Japanese Immigrants, 1858–1914*. Vancouver: UBC P, 1989.

Rushdie, Salman. *Imaginary Homelands*. New York: Penguin Books, 1991.

Ryerson Library. "Asian Heritage in Canada: Authors." <http://www.ryerson.ca/library/events/asian_heritage/authors.html>.

Safran, William. "Diasporas in Modern Societies: Myths of Homeland and Return." *Diaspora* 1.1 (Spring 1991): 83–99.

Said, Edward. *Culture and Imperialism*. New York: Vintage, 1993.

———. *Orientalism*. New York: Vintage, 1978.

Salah, Trish. *Wanting in Arabic*. Toronto: TSAR, 2002.

Salter, Denis. "The Idea of a National Theatre." *Canadian Canons*. Ed. Robert Lecker. Toronto: U of Toronto P, 1991. 71–90.

Satzewich, Vic. *Racism and the Incorporation of Foreign Labour: Farm Labour Migration to Canada Since 1945*. New York: Routledge, 1991.

Scofield, Gregory. *The Gathering: Stones from the Medicine Wheel*. Vancouver: Polestar, 1993.

———. *I Knew Two Métis Women*. Saskatoon: Gabriel Dumont Institute, 2010.

———. *Native Canadiana: Songs from the Urban Rez*. Vancouver: Polestar, 1996.

———. *Singing Home the Bones*. Vancouver: Raincoast, 2005.

———. *Thunder through My Veins: Memories of a Métis Childhood*. Toronto: Harper-Flamingo, 1999.

Scudeler, June. Personal communication. 13 May 2009.

————. "'The Song I Am Singing': Gregory Scofield's Interweavings of Métis, Gay, and Jewish Selfhoods." *Studies in Canadian Literature* 31.1 (2006): 129–45.

"Second-Last Regina Jail Escapee Captured in Winnipeg." *CBC Online*. 17 September 2008. <http://www.cbc.ca/canada/saskatchewan/story/2008/09/17/wolfe-captured.html#social comments>.

Sedgwick, Eve Kosofsky. *Between Men: English Literature and Male Homosocial Desire*. New York: Columbia UP, 1985.

————. *Epistemology of the Closet*. Berkeley: U of California P, 1990.

————. "Paranoid Reading and Reparative Reading, or, You're So Paranoid, You Probably Think This Essay Is about You." *Touching Feeling: Affect, Pedagogy, Performativity*. Durham: Duke UP, 2003. 123–51.

————. "Queer Performativity: Henry James's The Art of the Novel." *glq: A Journal of Lesbian and Gay Studies* 1.1 (1993): 1–16.

Selvadurai, Shyam, ed. *Story Wallah!: A Celebration of South Asian Fiction*. Toronto: Thomas Allen, 2004.

Sharma, Nandita. *Home Economics: Nationalism and the Making of "Migrant Workers" in Canada*. Toronto: U of Toronto P, 2006.

Sherrill, Rowland A. *Road-Book America: Contemporary Culture and the New Picaresque*. Chicago: U of Illinois P, 2000.

Shikatani, Gerry, and David Aylward, eds. *Paper Doors: An Anthology of Japanese-Canadian Poetry*. Toronto: Coach House, 1981.

Silvera, Makeda. *Silenced*. Toronto: Sister Vision, 1983.

Simpson, Mark. *Trafficking Subjects: The Politics of Mobility in Nineteenth-Century America*. Minneapolis: U of Minnesota P, 2005.

"Slideshow: The Trouble with DNA." *The Globe and Mail*. 4 December 2007. <http://theglobeandmail.com/picktontrial/>.

Smith, Andrew. "Migrancy, Hybridity, and Postcolonial Literary Studies." *The Cambridge Companion to Postcolonial Literary Studies*. Ed. Neil Lazarus. Cambridge: Cambridge UP, 2004. 241–61.

Spivak, Gayatri Chakravorty. "Can the Subaltern Speak?" *Marxism and the Interpretation of Culture*. Ed. Cary Nelson and Lawrence Grossberg. Basingstoke: Macmillan Education, 1988. 271–313.

————. "Responsibility." *Other Asias*. Malden: Blackwell Publishing, 2007. 58–96.

Steinbeck, John. *Cannery Row*. New York: Viking, 1945.

Steinberg. M.W. "Poet of a Living Past." *A.M. Klein*. Ed. Tom Marshall. Toronto: Ryerson P, 1970. 99–118.

Stewart, Susan. *On Longing: Narratives of the Miniature, the Gigantic, the Souvenir, the Collection*. Durham and London: Duke UP, 1993.

Stigter, Shelley. "The Dialectics and Dialogics of Code-Switching in the Poetry of Gregory Scofield and Louise Halfe." *American Indian Quarterly* 30.1 and 2 (2006): 49–60.

Stone, Anne, and Amber Dean. "Representations of Murdered and Missing Women: Introduction." *West Coast Line* 41.1 (2007): 14–24.

Stonechild, K.L. "Editorial." *Arrows to Freedom* (Summer 1993): 3.

Strong-Boag, Veronica. "The Citizenship Debates." *Contesting Canadian Citizenship: Historical Readings*. Ed. Robert Adamoski et al. Peterborough: Broadview, 2002. 69–94.

Struthers, James. *No Fault of Their Own: Unemployment and the Canadian Welfare State, 1914–1941*. Toronto: U of Toronto P, 1983.

Stryker, Susan. "Transsexuality: The Postmodern Body and/as Technology." In *The Cybercultures Reader*. Ed. David Bell and Barbara M. Kennedy. New York: Routledge, 2000. 588–97.

Su, John. *Ethnics and Nostalgia in the Contemporary Novel*. Cambridge and New York: Cambridge UP, 2005.

Sugars, Cynthia. "Postcolonial Pedagogy and the Impossibility of Teaching: Outside in the (Canadian Literature) Classroom." *Home-Work: Postcolonialism, Pedagogy, and Canadian Literature*. Ed. Cynthia Sugars. Ottawa: U of Ottawa P, 2004. 1–33.

Sugimoto, Howard H. *Japanese Immigration, the Vancouver Riots, and Canadian Diplomacy*. New York: Arno, 1978.

Sutherland, John. "Canadian Comment." *A.M. Klein*. Toronto: Ryerson, 1970. 59–65.

Teuton, Sean. "The Callout: Writing American Indian Politics." Womack et al. 105–25.

Teuton, Sean Kicummah. *Red Land, Red Power: Grounding Knowledge in the American Indian Novel*. Durham: Duke UP, 2008.

Thien, Madeleine. *Certainty*. Toronto: McClelland & Stewart, 2006.

Thom, Jo-Ann. "The Effect of Readers' Responses on the Development of Aboriginal Literature in Canada: A Study of Maria Campbell's *Halfbreed*, Beatrice Culleton's *In Search of April Raintree*, and Richard Wagamese's *Keeper'n Me*. In Search of April Raintree: Critical Edition. Ed. Cheryl Suzack. Winnipeg: Portage & Main, 1999. 295–306.

Tölölyan, Khachig. "Rethinking Diaspora(s): Stateless Power in the Transnational Moment." *Diaspora* 5.1 (1996): 3–36.

Toor, Saadia 2000: "Indo-Chic: The Cultural Politics of Consumption in Post-liberalization India." *SOAS Literary Review* 2. <http://www.soas.ac.uk/soaslit/issue2/TOOR.PDF>.

Trehearne, Brian. *The Montreal Forties: Modernist Poetry in Transition*. Toronto: U of Toronto P, 1999.

Turner, Dale. *This Is Not a Peace Pipe: Towards a Critical Indigenous Philosophy*. Toronto: U of Toronto P, 2006.

Ty, Eleanor, and Christl Verduyn, eds. *Asian Canadian Writing beyond Autoethnography*. Waterloo: Wilfrid Laurier UP, 2008.

Umpherville, John. "Editorial." *Arrows to Freedom* (Spring 1993): 2.

Valaskakis, Gail Guthrie. *Indian Country: Essays on Contemporary Native Culture*. Waterloo: Wilfrid Laurier UP, 2005.

Vallières, Pierre. *Négres blancs d'Amérique : autobiographie précoce d'un "terroriste" québécois*. 1968. 2nd rev. ed. Montreal: Parti Pris, 1969.

The Vancouver Sun <www.canada.com/vancouversun/gallery/PicktonChapter1>.

Verdery, Katherine. "'Whiter 'Nation' and 'Nationalism'?" *Mapping the Nation*. Ed. Gopal Balakrishnan. London and New York: Verso and *New Left Review*, 1996. 226–34.

"Victim Impact Statement of Marnie Frey's Father Rick." *The Vancouver Sun* 19 June 2009.<http://www2.canada.com/vancouversun/news/story.html?id=59dcea7f-b98f -4fad-92c5-33cc7924444>.

Vidler, Anthony. *The Architectural Uncanny*. London: MIT, 1999.

Wagamese, Richard. "Cross-racial Tragedy." *Literary Review of Canada* 16.9 (November 2008): 19.

———. *Dream Wheels*. Toronto: Doubleday Canada, 2006.

———. *For Joshua: An Ojibway Father Teaches His Son*. Toronto: Doubleday Canada, 2002.

———. *Keeper'n Me*. Toronto: Doubleday Canada, 1994.

———. *A Quality of Light*. Toronto: Doubleday Canada, 1997.

———. *Ragged Company*. Toronto: Doubleday Canada, 2008.

Wah, Fred. "A Poetics of Ethnicity." *Faking It: Poetics and Hybridity*. Edmonton: NeWest, 2000. 51–66.

Walcott, Rinaldo. *Black Like Who?* 2nd rev. ed. Toronto: Arsenal Pulp, 2003.

Ward, W. Peter. *White Canada Forever: Popular Attitudes and Public Policy toward Orientals in British Columbia*. 1972. Montreal and Kingston: McGill-Queen's UP, 2002.

Warriar, Nalini. *Blues from the Malabar Coast: Stories*. Toronto: TSAR, 2002.

Warrior, Robert. "Native Critics in the World: Edward Said and Nationalism." Weaver et al. 179–223.

———. *The People and the Word: Reading Native Nonfiction*. Minneapolis: U of Minnesota P, 2005.

———. *Tribal Secrets: Recovering American Indian Intellectual Traditions*. Minneapolis: U of Minnesota P, 1995.

Wasyliw, Jac-Lynn. *Imagining Adoption: Filiation and Affiliation in the Works of Richard Wagamese*. MA thesis. U of Manitoba, 2007.

Weaver, Jace. *That the People Might Live: Native American Literatures and Native American Community*. New York: Oxford UP, 1997.

———. "Splitting the Earth: First Utterances and Pluralist Separatism." Weaver et al. 1–89.

Weaver, Jace, Craig S. Womack, and Robert Warrior. *American Indian Literary Nationalism*. Albuquerque: U of New Mexico P, 2006.

———. "Preface." Weaver et al. xv–xxii.

Whitlock, Gillian. *Soft Weapons: Autobiography in Transit*. Chicago and London: Chicago UP, 2006.

Williams, Raymond. *The Country and the City*. London: Chatto & Windus, 1973.

Williams, Robert A. *Linking Arms Together: American Indian Treaty Visions of Law and Peace, 1600–1800*. New York: Oxford UP, 1997.

Willmott, Glenn. "Modernism and Aboriginal Modernity: The Appropriation of Products of West Coast Native Heritage as National Goods." *Essays on Canadian Writing* 83 (2004): 75–139.

Wilson, Kathi, and Evelyn J. Peters. "'You Can Make a Place for It': Remapping Urban First Nations Spaces of Identity." *Environment and Planning D: Society and Space* 23 (2005): 395–413.

Womack, Craig S. *Art as Performance, Story as Criticism: Reflections on Native Literary Aesthetics*. Norman: U of Oklahoma P, 2009.

———. *Drowning in Fire*. Tucson: U of Arizona P, 2001.

———. "Howling at the Moon: The Queer but True Story of My Life as a Hank Williams Song." *As We Are Now: Mixblood Essays on Race and Identity*. Ed. William S. Penn. Berkeley and Los Angeles: U of California P, 1997. 28–49.

———. "The Integrity of American Indian Claims (or, How I Learned to Stop Worrying and Love My Hybridity)." Weaver et al. 91–177.

———. *Red on Red: Native American Literary Separatism*. Minneapolis: U of Minnesota P, 1999.

———. "A Single Decade: Book-Length Native Literary Criticism between 1986 and 1997." Womack et al. 3–104.

———. "Theorizing American Indian Experience." Womack et al. 353–410.

Womack, Craig S., Daniel Heath Justice, and Christopher B. Teuton, eds. *Reasoning Together: The Native Critics Collective*. Norman: U of Oklahoma P, 2008.

Yoshiaki, Yoshimi. Trans. Susanne O'Brien. *Comfort Women: Sexual Slavery in the Japanese Military during World War II*. New York: Columbia UP, 2000.

Young, Robert. "The Cultural Politics of Hybridity." Ashcroft, Griffiths, and Tiffin 158–62.

Contributors

MELINA BAUM SINGER is a doctoral candidate in the Department of English at the University of Western Ontario. Her research explores the transnational and diasporic literatures in English Canada. She has co-edited, with Lily Cho, two special issues of *Open Letter*, "Poetics and Public Culture" and "Dialogues on Poetics and Public Culture," and has a recent article, "Is Richler Canadian Content?: Jewishness, Race, and Diaspora," in *Canadian Literature* 27 (2010).

ALESSANDRA CAPPERDONI teaches modern and contemporary literature in the Department of English at Simon Fraser University. She specializes in Canadian and anglophone literatures, feminist poetics, critical theory, and postcolonial and European studies. Her articles have appeared in *Translating from the Margins / Traduire des marges*, *Translation Effects: The Making of Modern Canadian Culture*, *Inspiring Collaborations: Canadian Literature, Culture, and Theory*, and the journals *TTR: Traduction, traductologie, rédaction*, *Open Letter*, and *West Coast Line*. She is currently working on a book manuscript titled *Shifting Geographies: Poetics of Citizenship in the Age of Global Modernity*.

LILY CHO is associate professor of English at York University in Toronto. Her recent publications include "Future Perfect Loss: Richard Fung's *Sea in the Blood*," *Screen* 49.4 (2008); "Asian Canadian Futures: Indenture Routes and Diasporic Passages," *Canadian Literature* 199 (2009); and *Eating Chinese: Culture on the Menu in Small Town Canada* (University of Toronto Press, 2010).

RENATE EIGENBROD is associate professor and head of the Department of Native Studies at the University of Manitoba, specializing in Aboriginal literatures. Besides the publication of her monograph, entitled *Travelling*

Knowledge: Positioning the Im/Migrant Reader of Aboriginal Literatures in Canada, she has co-edited several volumes of scholarly articles, most recently a special literature issue of *The Canadian Journal of Native Studies* and the volume *Across Cultures/Across Borders*, published by Broadview Press.

JULIA EMBERLEY is professor of English at the University of Western Ontario. Her recent book is *Defamiliarizing the Aboriginal: Cultural Practices and Decolonization in Canada*. Recently, she has published articles in *English Studies in Canada*, *Topia*, *The Journal of Visual Culture*, *Humanities Research*, and *Fashion Theory*.

KRISTINA FAGAN teaches Aboriginal literature and storytelling in the Department of English at the University of Saskatchewan. She co-edited Henry Pennier's autobiography, *Call Me Hank: A Sto:lo Man's Reflections on Living, Logging, and Growing Old*, which was launched with a traditional Sto:lo feast and book-burning (so that the dead can read the book). She is a member of the Labrador Métis Nation, and her current project is a study of Labrador Métis narrative and identity.

DANIEL HEATH JUSTICE is an enrolled Canadian citizen of the Cherokee Nation and the author of *Our Fire Survives the Storm: A Cherokee Literary History* (University of Minnesota Press), *The Way of Thorn and Thunder* (published as a trilogy by Kegedonce, and a single-volume omnibus edition by the University of New Mexico Press), and numerous articles on Indigenous literary criticism, history, and cultural studies. He is the co-editor of the forthcoming *Oxford Handbook of Indigenous North American Literatures* and associate professor of Aboriginal literatures and Aboriginal studies at the University of Toronto.

CHRISTINE KIM is assistant professor of English at Simon Fraser University. Her teaching and research focus on Asian North American literature and theory, contemporary Canadian literature, and diasporic writing. Her journal publications include *Open Letter*, *Studies in Canadian Literature*, *Mosaic*, and *Interventions* (forthcoming). She is currently working on a book-length project titled *Racialized Publics*.

CHRISTOPHER LEE is assistant professor of English at the University of British Columbia. His articles have appeared in *Amerasia Journal*, *Canadian Literature*, *Modern Fiction Studies*, *Journal of Asian American Studies*, *Router*, and *differences*. His book *The Semblance of Identity: Aesthetic Mediation in Asian American Literature* will be published by Stanford University Press in 2012. His current research focuses on trans-Pacific literary formalism during the Cold War and formations of "Asia" across settler colonial societies.

KEAVY MARTIN lives in Treaty 6 territory, where she is assistant professor of Indigenous literatures at the University of Alberta. Her articles have appeared in journals such as the *American Indian Culture and Research Journal, English Studies in Canada*, and *Canadian Literature*, and she is currently completing a book-length project on Inuit literature in Canada. In the summer, she teaches with the University of Manitoba's annual program in Pangnirtung, Nunavut.

BELÉN MARTÍN-LUCAS teaches postcolonial literatures in English and diasporic film and literatures at the University of Vigo, Spain. Her research focuses on the politics of resistance in contemporary postcolonial feminist fiction, looking at the diverse strategies employed in literary works, such as tropes and genres.

JODY MASON is assistant professor in the Department of English at Carleton University in Ottawa. Her book, which analyzes discourses of unemployment in twentieth-century Canadian literatures, is forthcoming in 2012 with the University of Toronto Press. Mason has published work on the relations among class, diasporic formations, and the politics of mobility in *Canadian Literature, Studies in Canadian Literature, Papers of the Bibliographical Society of Canada*, and *University of Toronto Quarterly*.

SOPHIE McCALL teaches contemporary Canadian and Indigenous literatures in the English department at Simon Fraser University. Her book, *First Person Plural: Aboriginal Storytelling and the Ethics of Collaborative Authorship* (2011), explores the complexity of the issue of "voice" by examining double-voiced, cross-cultural, composite productions among Aboriginal and non-Aboriginal collaborators. She has published articles in *Essays on Canadian Writing, Canadian Review of American Studies, Resources for Feminist Research, Canadian Literature*, and *C.L.R. James Journal*.

SAM McKEGNEY is a settler scholar of Indigenous literatures. He grew up in Anishinaabe territory on the Saugeen Peninsula along the shores of Lake Huron, and currently resides with his partner and their two daughters in lands of shared stewardship between the Haudenosaunee and Algonquin nations, where he is an associate professor of Indigenous and Canadian literatures at Queen's University. He has written a book entitled *Magic Weapons: Aboriginal Writers Remaking Community after Residential School* and articles on such topics as environmental kinship, masculinity theory, prison writing, Indigenous governance, and Canadian hockey mythologies.

DEANNA REDER (Cree/Métis) received her PhD from the Department of English at the University of British Columbia in 2007 and is currently assistant professor in English and First Nations studies at Simon Fraser University. She co-edited an anthology with Linda Morra (Bishops University) titled *Troubling Tricksters: Revisiting Critical Conversations* (2010) and is currently working on a monograph on Cree and Métis autobiography in Canada. Her article, "Writing Autobiographically: A Neglected Indigenous Intellectual Tradition," is included in *Across Cultures/Across Borders: Canadian Aboriginal and Native American Literatures* (2009).

DEENA RYMHS is associate professor of English and women's and gender studies at the University of British Columbia. She is the author of *From the Iron House: Imprisonment in First Nations Writing* (Wilfrid Laurier University Press, 2008), and her work on imprisoned authors has appeared in *Life Writing, Biography*, and the *Journal of Gender Studies*. She is currently writing another book on spaces of violence in Indigenous literature.

NIIGAANWEWIDAM JAMES SINCLAIR (Anishinaabe) is originally from St. Peter's (Little Peguis) Indian Settlement and is an assistant professor in the departments of English and Native Studies at the University of Manitoba. In 2009, he co-edited (with Renate Eigenbrod) a double issue of *The Canadian Journal of Native Studies* (29.1 and 2), focusing on "Responsible, Ethical, and Indigenous-Centred Literary Criticisms of Indigenous Literatures" and was a featured author in *The Exile Book of Native Canadian Fiction and Drama*, edited by Daniel David Moses (2011). He currently has two books under contract, the first (co-edited with Warren Cariou) is an anthology of Manitoba Aboriginal writing over the past three centuries titled *Manitowapow* (Portage & Main Press) and the second (co-edited with Jill Doerfler and Heidi Kiiwetinepinesiik Stark) is a collection of critical and creative works on Anishinaabe story titled *Centering Anishinaabeg Studies* (Michigan State University Press).

Index

9/11, 8, 105

Aboriginal rights, 8, 17n6, 31, 39n8; Tar Sands Watch, 39n8
Acoose, Janice, 24, 28–29, 41n20, 54, 62n4
affect, 15, 66–68, 74, 82–99, 102–6, 116, 181, 186–88, 223; racial, 173–77
Alfred, Taiaiake, 40n11, 54, 62n4, 234
American Indian Literary Nationalism, 26, 29, 39n6, 44, 51, 63n13. *See also* Indigenous literary nationalism
Anderson, Alan, 153–54
Anderson, Benedict, 2, 48, 242
"Anniversaries of Change," 13, 121, 131, 132n5
anti-Asian riots (Vancouver 1907), 1, 8, 119–20, 132n1, 178
apology, 8, 130, 178, 186, 188n4
Appiah, Kwame Anthony, 17n5, 83
Arar, Maher, 178
Arendt, Hannah, 132
Armstrong, Jeannette, 41n20, 45, 62n1, 137, 243
Arrows to Freedom, 236–42
assimilation, 5, 104, 109, 113, 126, 136, 142–45, 183–84
Atleo, Richard, 56
autobiography, 90; of Gregory Scofield, 23, 57

Badami, Anita Rau, 12, 87–92, 95n8, 96n21
Baldwin, Shauna Singh, 89–91, 96n21; *English Lessons*, 86, 96n19, *The Tiger Claw*, 91; *What the Body Remembers*, 12
Bannerji, Himani, 2, 4–5, 93; *The Dark Side of the Nation*, 4; *Thinking Through*, 17n5
Baucom, Ian, 192–97, 204
Beauregard, Guy, 92–93
Belmore, Rebecca, 81–82; *The Named and the Unnamed*, 82n3. *See also* memorials
belonging, 5–10, 23–26, 38, 40n11, 107–15, 135, 140, 144, 146, 175, 224; cultural, 76, 207–8, 221; ethnic-national, 23, 101–2, 128, 186, 205, 218. *See also* home
Benjamin, Walter, 131–32, 178; "On the Concept of History," 123; "Theses on the Philosophy of History," 178
Berger, John, 153
Bhabha, Homi, 48, 115, 156, 207
Bill C-31, 26, 39n7, 237
bio-capital, 66–73
Birney, Earle, 111
Bourdieu, Pierre, 85, 91, 132n7
Boyarin, Daniel, and Jonathan Boyarin, 99–102, 108–11, 180
Boym, Svetlana, 202–3, 205n2
Brah, Avtar, 115
Brand, Dionne, 17n3, 93, 94n2, 104, 114; *Bread Out of Stone*, 187; *Land to Light On*,